THE ETHICS OF STAYING

SOUTH ASIA IN MOTION

MUBBASHIR A. RIZVI

THE ETHICS
OF STAYING

*Social Movements and Land Rights Politics
in Pakistan*

STANFORD UNIVERSITY PRESS

STANFORD, CALIFORNIA

Stanford University Press
Stanford, California

Printed in the United States of America on acid-free, archival-quality paper

Library of Congress Cataloging-in-Publication Data

Names: Rizvi, Mubbashir A. (Mubbashir Abbas), author.
Title: The ethics of staying : social movements and land rights politics in Pakistan / Mubbashir A. Rizvi.
Description: Stanford, California : Stanford University Press, 2019. | Series: South Asia in motion | Includes bibliographical references and index.
Identifiers: LCCN 2018033656 (print) | LCCN 2018037789 (ebook) | ISBN 9781503608771 (electronic) | ISBN 9781503608092 (cloth : alk. paper) | ISBN 9781503608764 (pbk. : alk. paper)
Subjects: LCSH: Peasants—Political activity—Pakistan—Punjab. | Land tenure—Pakistan—Punjab. | Land reform—Pakistan—Punjab. | Social movements—Pakistan—Punjab. | Civil-military relations—Pakistan—Punjab.
Classification: LCC HD1537.P18 (ebook) | LCC HD1537.P18 R59 2019 (print) | DDC 333.3/154914—dc23
LC record available at https://lccn.loc.gov/2018033656

Typeset by Newgen in 11/14 Adobe Caslon Pro
Cover design by Angela Moody
Cover photo: Checkpoint in tenants' fields. Author photo.

CONTENTS

"Do you know that you are sitting in a room full of terrorists?"

Hanif's unexpected remark caught me by surprise as I reached into my backpack to retrieve a pen and a notepad. The room full of men and elderly women burst into laughter as people debated who was the most dangerous terrorist in the room. Was it the elder Munir, or Maryam Bibi, or her daughter-in-law? Hanif was mocking the anti-terror criminal cases (ATC section 7) registered against him and thousands of peasant farmers for resisting the Pakistani military's policy to monetize land relations on state-owned military farms. I was attending a gathering of a local chapter of the Punjab Tenants Association (Anjuman Mazarin Punjab; AMP) to discuss an upcoming meeting with state officials and military officers. The AMP has been resisting the Pakistan military's unilateral plans for farmlands for the past twenty years.

Hanif's joke lifted the gloomy mood on that emotional afternoon in April 2008. There was nervous energy in the air as tenant leaders discussed the upcoming meeting with the military officers; the AMP was coming under pressure after a protracted détente that lasted four years, and military authorities were installing new checkpoints, fences, and gates at the southeastern perimeter of their village. Hanif struck a chord with the gathering by calling out the absurdity of the state's attempt to brand tenant farmers as terrorists, while also acknowledging the troubling feeling that this might be the start of a new campaign of intimidation. Hanif's joke was prescient; a series of extrajudicial measures and anti-terror codes, such as the 2014 Pakistan Protection Act and the National Action Plan, have been used to criminalize and arrest the AMP leadership.

The AMP was formed in the summer of 2000 to resist the Pakistan military's unilateral policy to monetize land relations on the vast state-owned military farms (approximately seventy thousand acres) throughout

Punjab. The army sought to replace the century-old practice of rent-in-kind sharecropping with a cash-based land lease program. This obscure change in land tenure policy led to the largest rural peasant mobilization in postcolonial Punjab. The announcement came after years of whirling rumors about the military's legal rights over these farms, and there was great speculation about the future of these farms. The tenants' doubt was intensified by military investigation into the dramatic decline in farm revenue from 40.79 million rupees in 1995–1996 to 15.87 million rupees in 1999–2000 (Akhter and Karriaper 2009). The audit of these obscure military farming estates gained a new urgency because its findings were made shortly after the military coup in 1999, when General Pervez Musharraf dismissed Nawaz Sharif's elected parliamentary government over charges of corruption. At that time, General Musharraf was able to cast his regime as different from past military regimes by invoking the discourse of open market reforms, transparent governance, and technocratic rule tempered with moderation (Liberalism) to ensure a proper transition to democracy. General Musharraf traded in his military uniform for business suits as he fashioned himself as the "CEO" of Pakistan, a military leader fit to take Pakistan into the neoliberal age.

Farid Daula, the widely respected elder leader of the AMP, recalled the suspense and the rumors surrounding President Musharraf's intentions when the military was reviewing the military farms operations. "I heard that the jarnails [common Urdu pronunciation of "general"] were about to sell the land to Lever Brothers Company" (interview by the author, June 3, 2004, Okara Military Farms). Other tenants disagreed vehemently, Farid recalled; some tenants even speculated that General Musharraf wanted to establish his reputation and gain popular support in Punjab by redistributing the land to tenant farmers. Unbeknownst to anyone at the time, this obscure meeting in the park grounds of Okara in June 2000 would spark the rise of the largest peasant mobilization in Punjab since 1947.

General Qamar Zaman Chatha, the military officer in charge of investigating the decline in military farms revenue, surprised the tenants at the large gathering of tenant farmers in Okara City with his findings. He announced that the military farm operations were rife with corruption and that the farm management had been stealing harvest revenue from sharecroppers and selling the produce in the market while blaming the tenant farmers for huge losses. According to my interlocutors, this was the first time any official had recognized what the peasant farmers had been complaining about all along, and it reflected the new style of "transparent" governance and straight talk championed by General Musharraf.

After stating his initial findings, General Chatha announced the implementation of a new land tenure system that would replace the existing system of *battai* (sharecropping, rent in kind) with a new, cash-based system of land tenure. The new tenure system was designed to "end the culture of corruption" (*baimani*) and poverty in these farms. He announced that the new land tenure system was the first step in the impending programs of development involving "model villages," clinics, and schools. This was a unilateral decision made by the military, and the new lease system was scheduled to start at the end of the month.

The reform program got a mixed response from the farmers. Better-off farmers like Farid Daula (a prominent elder and a well-to-do farmer from the village Chak 45/3 R)[1] were at first supportive of the plan. As he put it, "We were happy [to hear about the end of sharecropping] because there has been so much oppression [*zulm*] here, and we were finally going to be free of this servitude [*ghulami*]" (interview by the author, June 4, 2004).[2] The existing *battai* tenure system was widely disliked. According to this system, the tenant farmers had to surrender half of their harvest to village administrators, who were supposed to provide inputs such as seeds, fertilizers, pesticides, and water. This sharecropping system left the tenant farmers susceptible to rent-seeking by farm managers. According to the AMP, the farm managers (chaks-in-charge) routinely inflated crop estimates, stole from the farmers' harvests, and intimidated the peasants with fines. However, other less-well-to-do farmers like Ghulam Rasool were concerned about the full implications of a cash-based land tenure system. They feared that they would be subject to eviction if they failed to pay cash rents on time. The old *battai* system, even if it proved to be exploitive, guaranteed usufruct (permanent land use rights) to tenant farmers and occupancy rights to their houses in the village, as outlined in the 1887 Punjab Tenancy Act.[3] The sudden change in land relations in the military farms generated great distress among tenant farmers who had tilled this land for a century under sharecropping.

As Younus, an AMP activist put it, "The new cash lease system did not guarantee our land rights. We learned that as soon as we accept this contract system, they will start to throw us out of these lands. . . . We found this out through our sources. . . . We established contacts in the revenue office to get this information, with a little help from Quaid-e Azam [euphemism for money bribe] . . . and they [the revenue officials] told us not to sign the contract because the army wants to move us out to sell plots" (interview by the author, May 3, 2007). The tenants' correspondence also confirmed rumors and family stories passed down through generations that challenged the military's legal claim to the land. The earliest military farm villages had been established by a Catholic Jesuit order in 1913. They had been transferred in 1913 to the Punjab government, which leased them to the British Indian Army in a twenty-five-year lease that expired in 1938. The last payment for these farms was received in 1942. Moreover, the tenants learned that there were no records showing the existence of these farms as agricultural estates; rather, they were classified as oat and hay feed farms for the military's livestock and horse farms. There were no records for the billions of tons of wheat, sugarcane, corn, and cotton that had been extracted from these tenant families since the farms' inception in 1913. The military farms reported revenues only for dairy and fodder. It was as if these farms did not exist. The tenants, however, had receipts for sugar and wheat going back two to four generations.

The tenants mobilized and came together to resist the imposition of cash contract farming. They started a campaign of civil disobedience by refusing to pay any rent in kind or cash and by evicting the farm management from their villages. The Okara district administration called in the police to restore order. When the police were unable to quell the protest, they started a campaign of repression by calling in the paramilitary Rangers force to the nineteen villages in Okara where farmers were mobilizing. In a matter of months, the AMP protests spread into nine other districts of Punjab.[4]

The total land in these ten districts—approximately sixty-eight thousand acres—was leased in the early twentieth century by the Punjab government to the various government departments, including the Ministry of Defense, the Punjab Seed Corporation (in Pirowal, Khanewal), the Maize and Cotton Research Departments (in Sahiwal), the Rice Research Department (in Kala Shah Kaku and Faisalabad) and the Livestock Department (in Sargodha and Sahiwal).

The state suppression of the AMP reached its peak between 2002 and 2004, especially during crucial sowing and harvest seasons (April–June, September–November). Eight tenant farmers were killed when the military and paramilitary launched attacks on villages; many more died as a result of a prolonged curfew, which prevented many villagers and, most crucially, women in labor from getting to hospitals for months. However, the government denied any culpability in the killings, and it blamed the tenant farmers for the violence; for instance, the military's public relations department tried displace the issue by blaming the death of sixty-one-year-old Ameer Ali on two nonexistent ethnic clans (Sindhis and Macchis) in the village. This strange attribution was the state's attempt to create the impression that a distinctly "other" ethnic group of peasant farmers lived in these villages.

The arrest of AMP activists and leaders resulted in dramatic scenes of resistance in Punjab's villages and cities. Men and women, Muslim and Christian tenants, traveled to Lahore (the provincial capital of Punjab) and Islamabad (the national capital) to protest by holding hunger strikes in front of private cable news channels in Islamabad and confronting political officials. As Hanif, one of my interlocutors, put it, "We've sacrificed ourselves and the well-being of our children for this army, we worked for grains and seeds, we considered them to be our protectors, but look at what they are doing to us. They [Pakistan Army] treat us like enemies, the way [Indians] treat Kashmiris. They want the land, not the people." The news about the siege on military farms reached human rights organizations, civil society groups, and the wider public. The tenants' plight created public sympathy as parallel strikes against cash contracts spread to other state-owned farms throughout Punjab. The military was forced to back down after its attempts to portray the AMP as a criminal threat failed.

However, Pakistan's ever-shifting political scenario swung dramatically against the AMP in 2008 as a result of a growing Taliban insurgency in Pakistan's borderlands and attacks in metropolitan centers. I was reaching the end of my fieldwork at the time, and most of it had been characterized by an informal understanding between the tenant farmers and the military, whereby the tenant farmers occupied the land without public protests and the military kept a close watch over the movement and village harvests without demanding rent in kind or cash. The Taliban attacks were a catalyst for a new wave of state repression against all forms of civilian protest. In Okara, the state authorities began installing new checkpoints, border fences, and gates at the southeastern perimeter of some of the villages adjacent to Okara cantonment. Hanif's prescient warning about the use of the counterterror policies against the AMP was realized in the form of the extrajudicial anti-terror stricture in 2014, after the Pakistan Protection Act, a series of measures, detention, and arrest laws that criminalized all kinds of dissent, including that of the AMP leadership and a local journalist, charging offenders with terrorism as defined by the National Action Plan. Thus, when Hanif spoke at the gathering about the absurdity of the state's attempt to brand peasant farmers as terrorists for refusing the sign cash leases, he articulated what was on the minds of many in attendance. The political space for dissent was shrinking rapidly, as the Pakistani state has shifted from development to security as the primary justification to enforce the changes in land relations.[5] The tenants' ability to resist and disobey the state authorities has disappeared almost entirely. Today, a large portion of the AMP leadership is incarcerated. However, the tenant farmers are still occupying their farmlands without paying any rent in kind or cash.

ACKNOWLEDGMENTS

Writing an academic book is a difficult task, especially when the ground is shifting beneath one's feet, as is the case with social movements and politics in Pakistan. This book was made possible by the loving support of my family, friends, colleagues, teachers, and mentors. I start by thanking my acquaintances, friends, and teachers in Okara Military Farms and Punjab Seed Farms (Pirowal) and members of the Anjuman Mazarin Punjab (AMP) who entrusted me with their stories, welcomed me into their homes, patiently answered my questions, and taught me so much about resistance, resilience, and the ethics of staying in place. I regret that I cannot publicly acknowledge the people who were central to my research and my thinking about the meaning of land rights, political subjectivity, and the struggle to maintain basic subsistence. However, I can mention a few names: The late Busra Bibi was a pillar of strength for women and men in her village during times of hardships in Okara Military Farms. I salute the bravery of the late Sarwar Mujahid, a freelance reporter who risked his safety and his family's economic future by writing about the protests he witnessed in Okara for the Urdu daily *Nawai Waqt*. Sarwar's son Hasnain Raza continues the legacy of speaking truth to power.

The AMP started off as a protest against cash contracts, but it became a movement because of the efforts of its young leaders, like Younus Iqbal, whose tireless energy and dedication helped spread the word about the movement to other villages and cities. Mehr Abdul Sattar won the trust of thousands of tenant sharecroppers throughout Punjab as he led the AMP through the tumultuous decade from Musharraf's dictatorship to democratic setup. Sattar and Iqbal were at odds at times, but both of them were dedicated to the movement. Both leaders are incarcerated in maximum-security prisons, as this book goes to print, for refusing to compromise with the state. The AMP has persevered and lived through the hardships of Musharraf's dictatorship and two elected governments that reneged on their promises to tenant farmers, and it will continue to survive in one form or another. I hope this book will help document an important part of this ongoing story, as well as the larger story of the people's struggle for basic dignity and democracy in Pakistan.

In Lahore, I was lucky to befriend a group of scholars and activists, including Sadaf Aziz, Fatimah Khan, and Asad Farooq, who were generous with their time, ideas, and contacts. I thank Asad for connecting me with other land struggles going on in Pakistan. A big thank-you goes to Asha Amirali for putting me in touch with the AMP. I have met very few people who are as dedicated to social change as Aasim Sajjad Akhtar, who spent his weeks traveling on buses to different meetings and protests when not teaching and mentoring students. I thank Asma Mundrawala, Raheem ul Haq, Sarah Suhail, Gwendolyn Kullick, Bani Abidi, and Huma Mulji for their friendship during fieldwork. I also thank Mrs. Tasneem Munir for showing me such warm hospitality and for hosting me from time to time. I owe a big thank-you to Iqbal Riza for allowing me and my family to stay in his house in Lahore.

I was fortunate to have a brilliant and caring adviser, Kamran Ali, at the University of Texas at Austin. Kamran has set an impossible standard for mentorship, critical inquiry, and generosity. I have turned to Kamran's books and articles from time to time to learn from his generous thought and supple analysis. I will be learning from his example for many years to come. Kathleen Stewart inspired me, like she has inspired so many others, with her ability to evoke and animate the world by bringing out the uncanny in the ordinary routines of life in contemporary America. I thank Charles Hale for provoking a discipline-wide conversation on social movements and political activism in cultural anthropology. Charlie's questions about the role of social movement in the production of knowledge played an important role in my research. Kaushik Ghosh is a mentor and a friend; there are few anthropologists who can match Kaushik's ability to carefully listen to indigenous leaders and treat rural activists as complex theorists, interpreters, and commentators of the modern state or capitalism. I thank David Gilmartin for his mentorship and for stoking my curiosity about the long-term implications of canal irrigation works in Punjab. In Austin, I drew inspiration from a brilliant community of friends and colleagues: Azfar Moin, Serap Ruken Sengul, Hisyar Ozsoy, Salih Can Ozcan, Mathangi Krishnamurthy, Raja Swamyraj, Mohan Ambikaipaker, Briana Mohan, Teresa Velasquez, Nicholas Copeland, Diya Mehra, Shaka McGlotten, Mark Westmoreland, Christopher Loperena, Tessa Farmer, Hafeez Jamali, Noman Baig, Abdul Haq Chang, Kiran Ahmed, Scott Webel, Omer Ozcan, Celeste Henry, Saikat Maitra, Nathan Tabor, Ken MacLeish, Alisa Perkins, and Lynn Selby.

At Georgetown University, I have found great colleagues and community with Denise Brennan, Lauri King, Amrita Ibrahim, Sylvia Onder, Joanne Rapapport, Susan Terrio, Gwendolyn Mikkel, Andrew Bickford, Ernesto Vasquez del Aguila, Shiloh Krupar, Kate Chandler, Ananya Chakravarty, Terrence Johnson, Nathan Hensley, and J. R. Osborn. I also thank my students, who inspire me with their enthusiasm and fresh perspectives.

Music is my antidepressant; I would be negligent if I didn't give a shout-out to Bob Marley, Munshi Raziuddin and Farid Ayaz, the Sabri Brothers, John Coltrane, They Might Be Giants, Hari Prasad Chaurasia, Fela Kuti, Lupe Fiasco, Mos Def, Yousuf Lateef, and the Magnetic Fields for creating music that lifted my spirits and fed my soul.

My journey to anthropology and to UT Austin would not have been possible if not for my friend Junaid Rana, who told me about this discipline in which one could read, hang out, and learn to see the world from different perspectives. I thank Biju Mathews, Raza Mir, Linta Verghese, Richard Blint, and Anjali Kamat for their enduring friendship. Brooklyn College and the City University of New York opened my eyes to the cosmopolitan possibilities of New York City that are not to be found anywhere else. I thank a brilliant group of friends—Farhad Asghar, Teresa Ventura, William Kopp, Bryan Addison, Habiba Ibrahim, Peter King, Zohra Saeed, and Lubna Chaudhary—who believed in me and encouraged me to follow my intellectual interests. I also thank Paisley Currah for his seminars in political theory, his mentorship, and his encouragement to finish college even when there were other pressures. A big thank-you goes to Moustafa Bayoumi, whose course on postcolonial literature allowed me to see the poetry behind the theory. I thank Peter Bratsis for introducing me to the Frankfurt School and giving me such impossible essays by Henri Lefebvre to puzzle over.

I am forever in debt to the sacrifices made by my parents, who left a very hard-won middle-class existence in Karachi to start all over in America in their mid-thirties for me, my sister, and my brother. My mother, Narjis Rizvi, passed away much too early, and her loss weighs heavy on me and everyone who knew her. She was a source of strength and inspiration to me and to so many others. I cannot imagine the difficulties that she must have faced as a doctoral student, a working woman, and a young mother who commuted on crowded buses to Karachi University while also taking care of three kids in a milieu where it was unusual. My mother's resolve, her love for education, and her example help me whenever I feel overwhelmed and intimidated. I thank her for supporting my decision to forgo a stable professional track to pursue a risky path in academia. My father has influenced me in more ways than he can imagine. His commitment to social justice, his kindness, and his sense of duty and moral obligations have played a major role in shaping my outlook on life. I cherish my close relationship and friendship with my sister, Nusrat Zaidi, and brother, Asad Rizvi. A big thank-you goes to Nusrat and Ahmed and my nephews and niece, Zain, Zara, and Saif, for the joy they bring to our family. I also thank Asad and Mona for traveling long distances to stay in touch; it's a treat for us to see them and Leila. I thank the extended Rizvi family, which is now spread out all over the world, from Azamgarh to Zurich, and the Abidi family: Ishrat Abidi, Manzar Abidi, Wasif, Asif, Sadaf, Ali, and Abid, and the Zaidi family. I deeply regret sacrificing precious time with my uncles Mohammad Atta and Hasan Atta, who both passed away much too early in life. Much love goes to Gatiara Rizvi and Rehana Rizvi.

I am forever grateful to Birjis and Kausar Hasan Khan for welcoming me into their family and treating me like a son. I especially thank the Hasan Khan and Ansari family: Irum, Aminey, Zahid, Ayela, and Iman. I thank Aminey and Irum for making those long trips from the UK to Austin and Zahid for his warm hospitality. It has been a pleasure to watch Ayela and Iman grow into sophisticated and discerning adults.

My children, Noor and Ali, have brought me more joy and perspective on life than anyone else. I hope that their generation learns to live with difference and creates a better world than the one we are giving them. I don't think I could've gotten anywhere in life without Alia. I don't have the words to express my gratitude for the love, patience, and sacrifices she has shown me. I thank her for bearing so many years of uncertainty and so many years of conversations about anthropology and history. I don't think that I can ever pay her back, but I will keep trying.

THE ETHICS OF STAYING

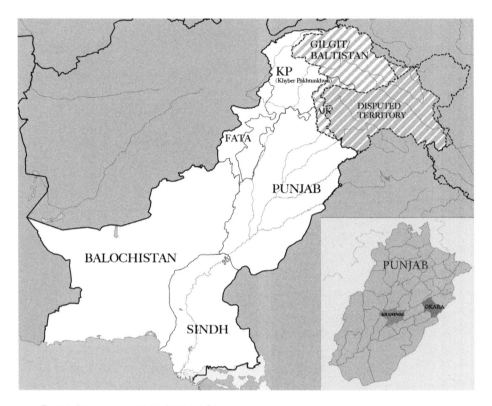

Punjab district map with highlighted Okara.

INTRODUCTION
Masters, Not Friends

THIS BOOK brings into dialogue two major topics in anthropology and South Asian studies that are rarely studied together in contemporary contexts: subaltern social movements and military-state-society relations. In doing so, it opens up the question of political subjectivity and land relations to provide a novel approach to both. The central focus of this book is on the rise of the peasant land rights organization the Anjuman Mazarin Punjab (the Punjab Tenants Association; AMP), which is made up of a cross section of rural peasantry, including Muslim and Christian tenant farmers, landless farm laborers, and middle peasant families who receive remittance incomes from family members working in the Persian Gulf. The unexpected rise and success of the AMP raises several paradoxical questions about state and society relations in Pakistan: Why is an army that could easily overthrow a parliamentary elected government unable to suppress its own tenant sharecroppers? On what basis are the army's tenant sharecroppers willing to risk their lives in order to occupy the land that they do not legally own? Following from this, what conception of rights do the tenants invoke to make claims to this land? To address these questions, this book analyzes the rise of the AMP to understand the lineages of land rights and political subjectivity in Central Punjab, which is commonly viewed as the pro-military heartland of Pakistan.

AMP tenant farmers gathered for a meeting. Source: Author photo.

The Ethics of Staying makes three major arguments that explain how
the AMP was able to disarm the Pakistan military's control over this
contested farmland by making a moral argument for land rights tied to
the material history of infrastructural development. The AMP forged a
network of support with urban activists and nongovernmental organizations (NGOs) to organize a contemporary social movement defying
military rule. First, I argue that the political agency of tenant farmers is
shaped by the spatial politics of this region. The disputed military farms
are located in a region that is associated with prosperity and proximity to
state power. This region of Central Punjab underwent dramatic transformation through canal colonization at the turn of the twentieth century
and transfer of population during partition. A key element of the AMP's
land rights struggle has been shaped by the cultural politics of canal colonization under British colonial rule at the time. By analyzing the politics
of infrastructure, the meaning of land rights in contemporary Pakistan is
illuminated in a new way.[1]

With "politics of infrastructure" I refer to the growing literature on the social-cultural impact of modern technologies of communication, transportation, and utilities on integrating spaces by incorporating and differentiating disparate populations within the modern state. In the case of Punjab, the politics of infrastructure lie in the forms of reciprocity established during the massive irrigation and land settlement. The present-day conflict in Okara Military Farms is contextualized by examining the history of state and peasant relations as they were established by canal colonization, irrigation, and land settlement of the Indus Plain. The canal colony project in Punjab and, more broadly, the project of modernization were accommodated, translated, and embedded through symbolic and material exchange. Tenants' claims to land rights are tied to a politics of recognition that emerges out of the multilayered history of irrigation, territorial formation, and sharecropping in Central Punjab.

The infrastructural modernity of this region of Punjab and the folkloric image of the tenant farmers upended the military's initial justification to forcibly impose cash contracts for "improvement." The rise of the AMP is a *critical event* in the sense that sociologists and anthropologists describe events that rupture the preexisting political understandings about a people and place by offering new insights into overlooked histories, new forms of inquiry into power, and new possibilities to imagine different political horizons. The material and cultural significance of this contested land can be further examined by pairing the literature on infrastructure studies with social movements. This approach broadens the emerging study of infrastructures by combining insights from science and technology studies and subaltern studies to examine the legacy of canal colonization in the articulation of land rights in postcolonial Pakistan.

Infrastructures, unlike social movements, remain invisible during the course of their operation as they meld into the background and become a part of the landscape and routine of administration. As Susan Leigh Star (1999, 382) puts it, the breakdown of systems can become the basis for a more detailed understanding of the relations and procedures rendered invisible by the smooth flow of infrastructure. Roads, trains, and canals form the background of a networked sociality. The simple change in land relations in the military farms had far-reaching consequences and meaning for tenant farmers who understand the changes in land relations as a threat to their livelihood and continued existence as peasant farmers. Hence, the ordinary conceit about the collaborative state-society relations in Punjab was challenged overnight by the *mazarin* (tenants) who made claims to land rights based on a hundred-year history of suffering, laboring, and settling this land. The AMP saw the military's moves to change the terms of their contract as social death, which they repeated in the refrain of "Malki ya maut" (ownership or death) during protests, rallies, and public gatherings from the start of the AMP in the summer of 2000. Looking through an infrastructural lens at the social movement shows a more complex account of political agency, which incorporates the role of material history, technology, and administrative practices in shaping the conditions of possibility for the efficacy and visibility of particular mobilizations and their ability to extract concessions.

Building on this history of colonial technology and governance, my *second* intervention is an analysis of the diverse and creative ways in which the AMP has articulated the language of rights to offset the imposition of the cash contract farm lease system. The tenants demand land rights in relational and ethical terms by invoking customs and obligations based on the hardship of sharecropping and memory of suffering on the land. The AMP differs from many contemporary land rights movements in that its claim is not based on notions of origin or indigeneity. Nor is it based on the model of Movimento Sem Terra in Brazil, which has championed the moral right of landless peasant occupation of unused land from absentee landlords (Wolford 2010). The AMP makes land rights claims based on the ethics of subsistence, as in the right to food, clothing, and shelter that has been the cornerstone of popular politics in South Asia. The AMP was able to challenge the army's narrative of development by foregrounding a local history of claim by invoking moral claims to livelihood. Recent scholarship on postcolonial government highlights the dialogical relationship between reciprocity and rights, client-patronage relations and postcolonial governmentality, in which the practice of claim making is generative of new understandings and subjects of rights (Moore 2005; Subramanian 2010; Bjorkman 2015). Cultural anthropologists and historians have adopted Michel Foucault's theories of governmentality and biopolitics to challenge the received ideas of citizenship and political rights by analyzing how these concepts are generated in specific historical contexts, and for specific communities (see Pels 1997; Radcliffe 2001; Hansen and Stepputat 2001).[2] Throughout this book I show how the different-positioned tenant farmers in Punjab, including AMP leaders, laborers, sweepers, and landless laborers, have been affected by the land settlement, revenue extraction, and governmental policies.

The *third* contribution is a grounded analysis of the relationship between the AMP and its translocal partners, specifically NGOs, left-leaning parties, and urban activists. As a grassroots mobilization, the AMP sought and welcomed coalitional links with urban activists and NGOs to gain visibility and spread the narrative of their struggle. The AMP's success is rooted in local claims to land, but it was also routed through NGOs and urban activists who were able to make tenants' demands legible through the transnational discourse of a rights-based framework for advocacy that gained new saliency in the post–Cold War era. However, the AMP's growing connections with civil society also changed the dynamics within the movement. The partnership forged between the AMP and NGOs like Action Aid, Shirkat Gah, and Applied Social Research (ASR) helped the tenant farmers gain national and international press coverage. But the loose, horizontal, almost acephalous nature of the AMP mobilization was altered as NGOs sought out leaders and spokespersons for the movement. The prospect of NGO funds and projects resulted in a growing controversy about the role of money in the movement, and accusations of corruption appeared along traditional lines of religious and/or *biradari* (patrilineal descent) difference. I analyze the pitfalls and possibilities of grassroots mobilization in contemporary frameworks.

A final concern of this book is to show how the rhetoric of the "war on terror," which has come to dominate Western perceptions about Pakistan, enables the Pakistani state to use brutal military tactics to suppress popular social movements by labeling them as terrorists. The Pakistan state uses counterterror laws as a cover to arrest tenant farmers on Okara Military Farms and, more generally, political activists, ethnic nationalists, journalists, and civil society activists (Human Rights Watch 2004, 2016).

Thus, the state justifies extrajudicial policies as a necessary move to ensure security and development (Rizvi 2018).

Currently, the AMP stands at the crossroads as it weathers a new wave of repression. The fallout from the war on terror created the conditions of possibility for a new state of exception, a new shock doctrine, whereby the Pakistani state was empowered to suspend basic rights of assembly and public protests in the name of security and to arrest activists who were deemed a threat to law and order. The passage of laws like the Pakistan Protection Act and National Action Plan gave extrajudicial and exceptional authority to nonelected institutions like the military and district bureaucrats to target and rein in social movements like the AMP that had made provisional gains and recognition by occupying the disputed farms since 2003. The AMP's role in the restoration of parliamentary democracy by initiating a chain of grassroots protests in Punjab was quickly forgotten by Pakistan Peoples Party and the Pakistan Muslim League–Nawaz, who reneged on their promises to the tenant farmers by sanctioning severe state repression of the AMP. Thus, the case of the AMP also sheds light on the broader aspects of political agency and rule in South Asia, which cannot be fitted easily into democratic politics or military authoritarianism.

The title of this chapter plays on *Friends Not Masters*, the title of the autobiography of Pakistan's first military dictator, General Ayub Khan. In this 1967 work he directly addresses American policy makers, asking them to treat Pakistan as a partner state rather than a client. The book was written at the peak of the Cold War, and it sought to salvage US-Pakistan relations at a time of growing uncertainty. Ayub sought to craft a new narrative by invoking himself as a reliable strongman in Asia and by painting Pakistan as modern Muslim state.[3] Reading against the grain, Ayub's book can also been seen as case study of how Cold War American support for the postcolonial dictatorships skewed the balance of power in favor of the military and military strongmen who grew to dominate and overshadow the elected and civilian officials in the new nation-states (Gardezi and Rashid 1983). The strong links between the undemocratic institutions and imperial pacts have come to preoccupy the postcolonial regime in Pakistan, which sees them as vital components of national security over and above public works and human development. Ayub Khan's government, which seemed so well entrenched in power that it could abrogate constitutions, shift the national capital from Karachi to Islamabad, dissolve the provincial units, and dictate the terms of elections as it saw fit, lost power in the late 1960s with a groundswell of student protests in East and West Pakistan that organized against the model of military rule.

RETERRITORIALIZING PAKISTAN

Pakistan has been continuously struggling over defining a political identity for itself and its citizens since its inception in 1947. The debate over the meaning of Pakistan can set off conflicts over the roles of religion, ethnic identity, linguistic rights, and sectarian differences. These contested meanings of Pakistan speak to what the historian Manu Goswami calls the problem of "methodological nationalism" as "entailing the common practice of presupposing, rather than examining, the global trends within and against which specific national and regional sub-national struggles begin" (Goswami 2009, 4). The failure to understand the spatial dimensions of the Pakistani nation-state has resulted in the narrow framework of viewing Muslim nationalism as a parochial development in British India (read: communal development). This approach fails to analyze the infrastructural and administrative effects of colonial policies, such as permanent land settlement, public works projects, and the territoriality of nationalist politics in the formation of political subjectivities around national, communal/sectarian, and regional identities.[4]

Pakistan's official state narrative evades particular regional, and ethnic identities in favor of Muslim universalism, even though the everyday life of Pakistanis is circumscribed by local ethnic, religious, and linguistic identities. Naveeda Khan (2012) provocatively calls this contradiction between Muslim universalism and regional and sectarian particularism as a politics of "Muslim becoming," or the idea of Pakistan as an aspirational national project rather than an existing one. This contradiction is least visible in Punjab, where the Pakistani state's nationalist project is most hegemonic. Pakistani nationalism became hegemonic in Punjab in the aftermath of genocidal violence that ripped apart the regional solidarities that shaped a distinct ecumenical Punjabi identity over centuries of co-existence. My approach to the political subjectivity of the AMP takes inspiration from Antonio Gramsci's writings on the Southern question (see Gramsci 2005). Gramsci takes a historical and cultural approach to studying the numerous ways in which political subjects can be conceived and political projects undertaken in a particular place and time. As Edward Said has observed, Gramsci's attention to specific details of Southern Italy gives "paramount focus to the territorial, spatial, geographical foundations of social life" (Said 1995, 26).

The AMP struggle highlights the spatial history of power and the different meanings that are attached to Pakistan as a moral community, a political project, and place of belonging in Central Punjab. This moral ecology, or what recent scholarship has termed the "cultural politics of place," is forged through the history of land relations, customary notions of sovereignty, and development based on the politics of recognition (Ghosh 2006, 503; Foucault 2007, 106).

Central Punjab (home to eighteen commercial farms that form the core membership of the AMP) is admired and feared for its dominant status in the national life of Pakistan. It is known for a dynamic rural economy based on small land holdings and intensive commercial agriculture made possible by a reliable supply of water and a good road-rail infrastructure that connects most villages to market towns. Some cities in this region have enjoyed rapid growth rates as heavy industries relocated there since the 1970s (Ali 2013).[5] Punjabi elites, along with Muhajirs (Urdu-speaking immigrants who moved from India to Pakistan), traditionally subscribe to the tenets of Muslim nationalism and the cultural legacy of the Urdu language.[6] The hegemony of Pakistan's nationalism in Punjab is linked to several factors, which include the bloody legacy of partition that forced some fifteen million people to seek sanctuary with their respective coreligionists across a hastily drawn national border. Prior to partition, this region was the site of some of the most ambitious projects of irrigation, town planning, and colonial administration that strengthened the links between rural communities and the colonial paternalist state and heaviest levels of military recruitment in the British Empire (Gilmartin 2015). Thus, Punjab has been at the center of military and bureaucratic recruitment since the mid-nineteenth century.

Pakistan's underprivileged regions—rural Sindh and Balochistan, southwestern Punjab, East Pakistan (up until 1971)—routinely single out Punjab (or the Punjabi establishment) as the prime beneficiary of centralized authoritarian rule, so much so that the Muhajir community from North India, which is widely perceived as the vanguard of Pakistani nationalism, has moved away from state nationalism to ethnic-nationalist Muhajir politics since the 1980s owing to a sense of marginalization from the Punjab-dominated state administration at the center (Alavi 1989).[7] The ethnic-nationalist regional parties like the Muttahida Qaumi Movement, representing Muhajirs, the Awami National Party Pakhtuns, and the Sindh National Front (Jeay Sindh Qaumi Mahaz), see Punjab as the dominant center of power that benefits from a network of farms, factories, and landholdings that consume the biggest share of national resources (Verkaaik 2004).[8] The Pakistani state (or, more specifically, its executive military and bureaucratic branches in Islamabad) dismisses the critique of uneven development and Punjab's dominance as anti-national propaganda or feudal paranoia that gets in the way of national development.

The rise of the AMP ruptured the monolithic image of Punjab and brought attention to the subaltern class politics in rural Punjab. The AMP's slogans, such as "Ownership or death" and "Whoever sows the land shall reap the harvest," highlighted a class politics of land rights that cuts across rural and regional divides. These sentiments are captured by Zafar Ali, one of the AMP's leaders, who said the following when I asked him what drives the tenants to mobilize: "For us, Pakistan was never created; we are still living the same way as our ancestors did under the British. We never achieved any independence. We have been living under slavery [*ghulami*] instead. . . . Are we outsiders? They [the military, the courts, the bureaucracy] treat us this way? After all, we are Pakistanis too" (interview by the author, April 12, 2007). Zafar's ambivalent feelings about Pakistan are marked by estrangement and desire. His statement questions the very existence of Pakistan, while at the same time he expresses a wish for such recognition (or perhaps desire for such an idea of Pakistan based on inclusion, better economic social justice, or land rights). Here the idea of nation (Pakistanis) is posed against the state (Pakistan).

Furthermore, my interlocutors in the AMP movement admitted that their close attachments to Pakistani military became frailer as the state shifted away from what they once considered a paternalist institution (*ma-bap*—or benevolent protector, as some put it) to a compromised state that is a facilitator for international corporations like Nestlé (which is a new major player as a buyer of milk and bottled water in the region) and American policies. Murad, a dedicated village-level leader in the AMP who spent three months in jail in 2004 for participating in the tenants' movement, expressed his growing disillusionment with Pakistan as a nation and state in a conversation when he engaged me about my research.

Murad inquired about my research and reacted strongly when I stated that I was interested in the changing relationship between the tenant farmers and the Pakistani state. He replied, "I think there is no such thing as Pakistan. There are no Muslims; everyone is Muslim in name only. No *Musalmani* way. I always see these rich people—they always say don't give anything to the poor or help the poor people. A Muslim is one who is sensitive [*ehsas*] to everyone else's pain." I replied by stating that on average, Pakistanis show higher rates of philanthropy. Murad countered that he was talking about the government and gave the following example: "In olden days kings would think about the poor, that these people are poor—don't bother them; help them. These police officers—what do they do? I was just in the jail, and all the jail officers used to ask the prisoners who didn't get any visitors, 'Why didn't someone [relatives] come to visit you and give us some money? If they give us some, then you can make your life easy for yourselves and get out of here.' What do we call this government?" (interview by the author, April 15, 2007, Okara Military Farms).

Murad's remarks were echoed by the AMP leaders and ordinary tenant farmers who voiced growing concern about the unsustainable cost of living, the decreasing returns from agriculture, and the "jarnails" greed for the land. The tenants' comments illustrate something different from what Benedict Anderson defines as an "imaginary community living in empty homogenous time" (Anderson 1991, 26). Instead, here we see diverse ideas of nation, community, and even temporality signified by "Pakistan." Zafar's and Murad's comments highlight a subaltern critique of land monetization that cuts across different regimes of power. The tenants make claims on this land by invoking a century-old history of suffering, and toiling under sharecropping rules that impoverished them yet guaranteed minimum subsistence.

The tenants' ability to carry out militant protests against state authorities was made possible by a cultural politics of place, in which the visibility of these farms, the tenants' subjectivity, and their historically close association prevented the state from convincingly branding the tenant farmers as a seditious or terrorist group at the start of the movement. The tenants' status as peasant sharecroppers and not owners also placed them in vulnerable position vis-à-vis the state. The rise of the AMP highlights the sociospatial politics of power that illustrate how the postcolonial state constitutes itself as it constitutes its population. The preexisting norms about land are indispensable tools for understanding how the tenants' political agency is tied to sovereignty and governmentality based on land relations. This genealogical method allows me to pry apart the homology of nation-state to understand the historic conjuncture of land rights and political subjectivity in Central Punjab versus other regions of Pakistan and more broadly in South Asia, where land relations are embedded in different configurations of power. As I show in Chapter 3, the historical proximity between these *abadkar* (tenant settlers) and the state in Punjab upends the military's unilateral plans to change land relations in the military farms. The military struggles to justify its use of overwhelming force against this population.

The schematic formulation of the "subaltern" or "peasant" as an idealized non-Westernized subject has resulted in a univocal—or what Eric Wolf might have called the "billiard ball"—model of subalternity, where the "subaltern(s)" take on "the qualities of internally homogeneous and externally distinctive bounded objects" (Wolf 1982, 4). Wolf critiqued the role of historians and anthropologists in creating a binary "model of the world as a global pool hall in which the entities spin off each other like so many hard and round billiard balls" (5). For instance, a "billiard ball" model of subalternity works through oppositional binaries of margin versus center, hegemony versus domination, custom versus contract, tradition versus modernity, and religion versus secularism, in which the imperial colonial stick is always hitting the colonized in its direction. This form of theorization veers away from Antonio Gramsci's and Ranajit Guha's original formulation of subalternity as a range of hybrid, contradictory, regional, messy, fragmentary, and mimetic exchanges that cut across the lines of consent and compulsion (Crehan 2002).

The early subaltern studies school of Indian historiography attributed a great degree of autonomy to the subaltern who lived outside of the hegemonic structures and/or disciplinary institutions of colonial rule, whereas the early nationalist elite occupied a liminal gray zone between tradition and modernity, which were both framed by the power/knowledge effects of Orientalism (van der Veer and Lehmann 1999).[9] However, these configurations of center, middle, and periphery work through concentrated models of power that exclude the interweaving connections between different forms of labor, capital, and territory. The rural countryside in South Asia has been connected to global trade and disciplinary mechanisms of land revenue fiscalism for as long as there have been colonial cities (Marx and Engels 1967, 135). The rural is integrated into the modern state formation through the imposition of a private property regime, forestry policies, and primitive forms of accumulation starting from the first Permanent Settlement of Bengal in 1793.

In a close reading of racialized dispossession in Zimbabwe, Donald Moore contrasts the ontological framing of subalternity as a consciousness, with Gramsci's original formulation as a contingent and crosscutting historical condition (Moore 1998, 352). Subaltern existence is not defined by its marginality (which presupposes center and periphery boundaries) but rather its conjunctural condition, a threshold or a meeting point of multiple histories, spatialities, temporalities, and subjectivities.[10] Subalternity is internally differentiated with its own received notions of rights and sovereignty; it is the outer limits of modern governmental power, the locus where state power becomes capillary, where other moral and material attributes of life enter politics and alter it (Foucault 2003, 27). The subaltern and the nationalist elite are co-constitutive of the biopolitical process of modern state formation that asserts control over security, population, and territory under the homogenizing and differentiating rubric of sovereign rule (Agamben 1998). Thus, in this book I challenge the ontological premise of subalternity by giving a historical, regional, and anthropological description of the ways in which the rural geography of Central Punjab, including its physical features, were coproduced by governmental technologies of irrigation and land settlement.

Land is the silent hyphen that connects nations to state, as the geographer Matthew Sparke (2005, 170) has noted. A systematic historical and geographic discussion of territory is missing in theories of nationalism and globalization, which often draw on the evolutionary models of territoriality to justify their sovereign power. These ideational tropes of rural South Asia often leave out the preexisting global connections that defined agrarian and pastoral relations in different regions of South Asia (Gidwani 2004). Donald Moore's (2005) political ethnography on racial dispossession in Zimbabwe, Ajantha Subramanian's (2010) ethnography of Fisher communities in South India, and Tania Li's (2014) ethnographic mapping of frontier spaces of capital have all explored this question of territoriality through the lens of governmentality. These scholars focus on the entanglement between emerging forces of capitalism and prior histories, beliefs, and environments in generating new understandings of space, rights, and market and the collective "governmentalization" of society.

The anthropological scholarship on sovereignty and governmentality has greatly extended Phillip Abrams's call to scholars to challenge the "misplaced concreteness" and "isolated representation" of the state to examine its historical sociocultural production and its "politically organized subjection" (Corrigan and Sayer 1985, 3; see also Abrams 1988).[11] I provide historical and ethnographic accounts of the ways in which the Pakistani state is experienced, acted on, and imagined in everyday life in the semirural locality of the Okara district. As I show in Chapters 3 and 4, the application of land allotment policies varied greatly through the two centuries of colonial era, which continues to affect the mode of governance between the state and specific population groups in contemporary times. There is nothing natural about Punjab being the conservative heartland, Sindh being identified as feudal, or Balochistan being identified with tribalism. These cultural slots have a history tied to the existing relationship between sovereignty and rights, which has to be analyzed rather than be taken as a given.

Antonio Gramsci's and Michel Foucault's respective formulations of power have undermined the monolithic notion of the state as an entity that is "outside" or "above" society. Instead, their theories enable me to analyze the ways in which the state becomes visible during specific struggles over natural resources, like the farmland at Okara Military Farms. Looking at the state through the prism of the disputed military farms shows how relations between subjects, community, and nation are not consecutive, as they are conceived in theories of nationalism. State formation when localized and limited to historical contexts give us an idea of how "'projects of change' have emerged over specific struggles over resources, entitlement and political control in the making of localities" (Stepputat 2001, 286). For Foucault, the state is not a "thing" in itself but an accumulated effect of a wider range of disciplinary practices, and dispersed powers of classification, regulation, and punishment (Foucault 1977, 2003, 2007).

Postcolonial theory has focused on the representational and ideological frame of British colonialism in South Asia and relatively less so on the infrastructural legacies of colonial rule and their material entanglements in the production of territory and subjects in South Asia. There is comparatively little theoretical reflection given to the equivalence drawn between qualitatively different types of land relations in South Asia with Liberal ideas of private property. Henri Lefebvre (1991) refers to this transformation as the production of space that changes the use value of land into an abstract exchange value, through the standardization of the property regime.[12] This form of simplification is similar to James Scott's (1998) reading of revenue modernization schemes, but Lefebvre argues that the local is never fully emptied out of its particular distinction. As the geographer Majed Akhter (2015) has argued, the homogenizing effects of infrastructure projects are interrupted and differentiated by the encounter with environmental variables and clashes with preexisting political, economic, and historical contexts. In the next section, I describe some of the historical and regional modalities that have shaped land relations and the lineage of sovereignty in Pakistan.

HISTORICIZING SOVEREIGNTY

The transition from precolonial sovereignty as embodied by the Mughal kingship (and its successor states) to the East India Company's rule represents an epochal shift in the constitution of governance in South Asia and the transition of global trade from the Indian Ocean and Silk Road to the North Atlantic world system. Between 1757 and 1849 (the annexation of Punjab), the East India Company spread its territorial authority from its eastern and southern ports of entry in Bengal and Madras to the northwestern regions of the subcontinent that constitute Pakistan today. The ebb and flow of mercantile trade hardened into the territorial administration of land, monopoly control trade, and population during the century leading to Punjab's annexation. The process of territorialization and subject formation varied greatly in different regions of South Asia that came under British colonial rule over the course of two centuries.[13] I offer a brief survey of precolonial sovereignty to highlight the significance of spatial politics in shaping differential lineage of land rights as they are articulated by social movements like the AMP.

Precolonial territorial polities of the Mughals and successor native sovereign rulers were not invested with the idea of linking territory with a particular notion of "the people" or in regulating the movement of populations; rather, these polities were grounded in different understandings of sovereignty, which was based on the idea of the moral community as vested in the sacred authority of kingship, associated with the Mughal court and the successor states and embodied in its patronage and protection of shrines of saints, monuments, temples, and symbolism that conveyed its transcendental authority (Moin 2012). As Atul Mishra succinctly argues:

> Pre-colonial polities were not organized along strictly defined borders—a neat separation of the "inside" from the "outside," delineating the state's legal personae from aliens. They did not exhibit the hard edges of modern states. Moral sovereignty of communities preceded territorial exclusiveness. (Mishra 2007)

The political geography of precolonial South Asia was character-ized by flexible and decentralized polities that could accommodate the heterotopia of overlapping religious, linguistic, and regional differences. These polities were not egalitarian, yet they did not seek to control the population and territory as extensively and exclusively as the East India Company, the British colonial state. The precolonial revenue administra-tion did not view land as a private alienable resource, but rather saw land relations in the moral terms of revenue built into a customary system of rights based on patronage and obligations. The Mughal revenue sys-tem made extensive use of paper documentation and bureaucracy, but the revenue collection was collaborative and less centralized in its execu-tive decision making (Chatterjee 1993; Bellenoit 2017). For instance, the revenue assessment could be subject to negotiation because of changes in monsoon rains, or local testimony was used to check written records, or preexisting debt and default were negotiated with an eye to preserv-ing the moral order (*tahzeeb*). In addition to farming, there was wide ac-ceptance of itinerant and less-hierarchical nomadic livelihoods involving livestock, craft manufacturing, seasonal labor, and trade that made South Asia conducive to long-distance trade for centuries. The extensive net-work of merchants and pilgrims and the itinerant spiritual wanderings of Qalandars, fakirs, and yogis all characterized a landscape of extensive movement (Markovits, Pouchepadass, and Subrahmanyam 2006; Bhat-tacharya 2006). This form of nomadic circulation of ideas and goods was criminalized by the 1871 Criminal Tribes Act.

The East India Company heralded a new sovereign form that was unlike any that had existed before in South Asia. As a British joint stock company, its primary goal was to ensure regular dividends for its inves-tors and maintain monopoly over Bengal's export commodities, which included textiles, indigo, saltpeter, and lucrative spices. The East India Company's move to territorial rule was largely driven by the prospects of greater surplus generated from land revenue to pay for its expansion on the subcontinent and throughout the world. To ensure these profits, the East India Company maximized its revenue demands by instituting an inflexible private property regime. The company came to depend on this revenue stream to pay for its expanding war debts. The British crown used its share of company revenue to fund its warfare across the globe, thus creating a tradition of military fiscalism as the primary end of tax revenue (Travers 2007).

The British adapted Mughal administrative records and nomenclature (from record manuals like Abul Fazl's detailed document recording the administration of Mughal emperor Ain-e Akbari [(1591) 1894]) to institute a private property regime and claim sovereign power of taxation. Thus, as Bernard Cohn (1996) has argued in a series of essays, the British colonial government consolidated its rule over Indian society by exerting its authority to enumerate and codify Indians to demand a greater share of land revenue. Hayden Bellenoit, a historian of the colonial administration, has noted the revenue demands by the East India Company went up somewhere between 143 percent to 325 percent over span of a decade between 1808 and 1818 (Bellenoit 2017, 97). The Permanent Settlement of Bengal initiated the private property regime in South Asia by conferring exclusive land ownership rights to its elite allies, the zamindars, who were charged with collecting revenue from the peasantry at very high rates.

A simple stroke of the pen transformed the fortunes of millions of cultivators; some became landlords and overlords, while most peasants saw their customary rights to land, grazing, seasonal foraging, and water compromised (Smith 1985; Gilmartin 2015). The new system of private property disembedded economic relations from customary rights by stripping away the shared distribution of risks, liabilities, and surplus from land and replacing them with exclusive rights to land conferred to a new class of private landowners, the zamindars, whose property rights were protected and regulated by the state via a permanent standing army (Bagchi 1982; Smith 1985; Gilmartin 2015). Having established itself as the guarantor of "property," the colonial state falsely assumed sovereign claim over "public" land by labeling uncultivated lands as waste, thus taking over forests and scrublands inhabited by pastoralists, foragers, and seasonal farming communities (Locke 2003; Gidwani 2008).[14] East India Company's jurists and scholars like Henry Sumner Maine justified its rapid colonization as a necessary means to rationalize land relations by shifting from "status to contract" (1861, 170).[15]

The land settlement reports, revenue records, and cartographic maps created their own morphology of districts and villages in the Indus Plain, where only scant homesteads existed prior to irrigation projects. District-level manuals were written for civil service administrators in such a way as to turn incidents and accidents of history into teleology, and these manuals of custom classified different groups of natives into categories, whether they fit or not (Craib 2004). The success of the East India Company became increasingly linked to its ability to extract revenue by reaching deeper into the essence of the village republic, the elementary unit of Indian sociality, and to transform the agrarian economy by effecting change at the village level while retaining customary institutions to preserve order.[16]

By the late nineteenth century, South Asia was visualized as a distinct entity, the cartographic "geo-body" of India, that could be governed by paper (Winichakul 1994). Slowly the idea of an abstract and timeless "village republic" came to stand for "authentic" India that corresponded with the Orientalist obsession with civilizational origin.[17] The philological projects of translation and commentary on ancient texts were invoked to produce a uniform type of civilizational history confirming British redemption of a great ancient tradition that was burdened by despotic (read: Muslim) rule.

The Orientalist scholarship was mined to come up with a system of land relations that was open to marketing fiscal commercialization but largely governed through customary dictates and obligations determined via religious and ethnic differences that were further differentiated by caste. The notion of the eternal village republic became all the more significant after control over British India passed from the East India Company to the British crown in 1857. Outside India, the concept of the village republic has had a profound impact on Western notions of Asian and Indian society, as theorized by Maine (1861), who influenced twentieth-century political scientists, anthropologists, and economists. As Karuna Mantena (2010) has argued, the ahistorical notion of village republics offered an unchanging, functionalist understanding of Asian peasant life. The official policy of preservation and nonintervention actually put in place institutions, practices, and economic relations that were taken as representative of rural India, which in fact had evolved in line or in collaboration with the military fiscalism of the East India Company.

The question of property was central in structuring the relationship between the colonial state and the public. English bureaucrats and economists like Baden-Powell expressed great confusion about the complex range of land relations in India throughout the nineteenth century (Gilmartin 2015). However, the company enforced a rule for property to establish an administrative footing to extract maximum land revenue. It recognized that British notions of private property did not correspond to land relations in India, where land use rights were not necessarily tied to individual ownership. The zamindari tenure system of Bengal was heavily criticized by the East India Company for failing to secure sufficient funds for the company military rule even as it accelerated bankruptcies, famines, and economic misery in Bengal, Bihar, and the Eastern Upper Provinces (later renamed Uttar Pradesh) countryside.[18] However, the zamindari system had a lasting impact in Bengal in shaping the sociocultural and political dynamics of state-society relations and the urban-rural divide in Bengal, where the predominantly Muslim peasantry in eastern Bengal did not fully embrace the nationalist rhetoric of two major Indian nationalist parties (the Indian National Congress, or Congress Party, and the Muslim League), because both were heavily represented by landed gentry, urban salariat, or *bhadrolok* (salariat).[19]

Punjab, in contrast to Bengal, was not colonized by the British for another hundred years. The assessment of land revenue proved to be difficult in Central Punjab (the site of the disputed military farms), because it was a pastoral frontier, the North-West Frontier. As a frontier space, Punjab came to be seen as a site of experimentation and boundary making. Precolonial Central Punjab and Sindh were characterized by extensive nomadic trade with scant agriculture in the riverine areas. Much of the sedentary population in this region lived along ancient cities that ring around the five rivers, but the vast plains were sparsely inhabited. The precolonial regional states collected a grazing tax, known as *tirni*, but the colonial estate was more invested in selecting a reliable population of peasant settlers for this region to close this nomadic frontier. The openness of this region to Central Asia made it susceptible to the possibility of

Afghan and/or Russian expansion. It needed to be enclosed with a settled loyal population, but the prevailing land administration systems proved to be untenable in such a sparsely populated and mostly nomadic region.[20] The colonial state introduced the Mahalwari system of revenue in this region, which transferred the responsibility of revenue collection to the representative group. Thus, the colonial state designed Central Punjab according to its own image of a productive modern Indian village, which was to be regulated by the colony manual and settled by a select group of peasants.

The construction of a large network of canals, based on perennial irrigation, transformed the arid plains of Central Punjab into one of the largest centers for commercial agriculture in South Asia. The military figured prominently in the transformation, as both a beneficiary and a benefactor of canal colonization and land allotment. Between 1885 and 1947, the canal-irrigated area in Punjab increased from less than three million acres to around fourteen million acres (Ali 1988, 9–10). The political rationale for the development of canal colonies involved the forcible settlement of nomadic communities into year-round cultivators (Paustian 1930, 27). After the administrative takeover by the British Raj from the East India Company, the logic for canal colonies evolved into a broader project of cultivating new habits, new property arrangements, and new labor relations to create a more "benevolent" and paternalist form of colonial governance. The canal colonies represented a new social and legal space through which novel forms of private property were implemented and other claims to space were reduced. However, as I show in Chapter 3, these new arrangements were reworked by preexisting customs and ethical beliefs that the colonial, and now the postcolonial, state had to contend with.

Unlike most irrigation projects in British India, the canal colonies were established in a dry, sparsely populated region of Central Punjab. The irrigation and settlement of this vast agrarian space brought into being a new hydraulic society where the state controlled the source of agriculture: canal water. The colonial state had complete power over the manner in which the land was disposed, the kind of person (dependent on caste, religion, and loyalties) who was allowed to settle in the area, to whom the land was to be allotted, and the type of tenure rights that would prevail (Ali 1988, 63; Darling 1925; Fox 1985; Gilmartin 1994; Paustian 1930). The creation of canal colonies required massive in-migration of peasants and the forced settlement—and criminalization—of formerly pastoral communities (Arnold 1986; Major 1999).

The Okara district was one of seven large colonies that were shaped out of the canalization project. It was allocated over 1,192,000 acres, the largest distribution of land in this period in colonial India (Ali 1988). As I show in greater detail in Chapter 3, land grants were offered to select groups as an incentive to recruit peasants into enlisting in the British Indian Army. The increasing share of land allocations to the military reflected a major shift in the post-1858 British Raj policy of recruiting soldiers from the newly annexed territories of Punjab and the North-West Frontier province. This militarization of Punjabi society was also encouraged by British colonial ethnographic representations of Punjabis as a martial race (Fox 1985). The political-economic legacy of militarization and its overdevelopment as an institution in the region that is now Pakistan started with the conscription of Punjabis in the British Indian Army. The Cold War and most recently counterterror funding has led to the concentration of commercial and industrial interests in the hands of the military establishment. The Pakistani military has used its extensive land holdings to carve out a position in the public and private sectors, in industry, business, agriculture, education, scientific development, health care, communication, travel, communication, and transportation (Rizvi 2000, 233).

The settlement of the Indus Plain in Punjab, Sindh, and Khyber Pakhtunkhwa in the late nineteenth century resulted in closure and settlement of the North-West Frontier, or what is today's Punjab. The closure and settlement had two major effects in this region. The most immediate effect was that the mobile livelihood of itinerant peasants, nomads, traders, and hunter-gatherers was seen as a vestige of a primitive way of life that was slowly being criminalized. However, a more indirect and profound cultural impact of territorialization in South Asia was the expulsion of Muslims and Christians as indigenous claimants to Indian civilization, whereas the Hindu (or Brahmanic Arya, to be more specific) and

Sikh populations were taken to be indigenous by both the colonial state and the Indian nationalist elite.[21] David Ludden (2003) expresses this point when he writes about the cultural fallout of nationalist historiography that naturalized cultural borders and raised doubts about the claims of Muslims, Christians, and other peripatetic communities.[22]

THE POLITICS OF PLACE

Punjab did not become a hotbed of Indian or Muslim nationalism, despite the outsized role it would play in postcolonial Pakistan. The All India Muslim League had little or no organization presence in Punjab before the mid-1940s, and the Indian National Congress was unable to break the hold of the Unionist League, which consisted of prominent Muslim, Sikh, and Hindu landlords and gentry who were sympathetic to British Raj and ambivalent about nationalism (Talbot 1998). The Congress Party and Muslim League were also not very popular in rural East Bengal, where a mass farmer-peasant political party, the Krishak Praja Party (KPP), had come to power. The KPP made an alliance with the Muslim League in exchange for the promise of land reforms for Bengal's predominant Muslim peasants (Bose 2014). The veteran Bengali politician Fazlul Haq presented the Lahore Resolution calling for Indian Muslim nation-state(s). The resolution pieced together disparate interests of Muslims in South Asia ranging from the salaried professional classes (especially in UP and Bihar) to the wealthy landed groups in Sindh Punjab and Khyber Pakhtunkhwa, with appeal to the princely states.

Early forms of anticolonial nationalism in South Asia first emerged among English educated-elite circles. The late Pakistani sociologist Hamza Alavi (1998) refers to this class as the *salariat*, or individuals who worked in the colonial state bureaucracy, such as revenue clerks, lawyers, teachers, and administrators. The members of the salariat accepted the ideological and spatial presuppositions of Liberalism even as they challenged the colonial state's use of historical and cultural reasons to exclude them from self-rule and appropriate the surplus generated by British India. The nationalist elite popularized a homogenous image of India as Mother Goddess, a female deity that had been violated by a history of conquest. The cultural and physical homogenization of the national geo-body through the creation of physical borders (boundaries, checkpoints, the Durrand Line, etc.) and images (Bharat Mata, the national personification of India as the Mother Goddess) also differentiated and marginalized minorities and social groups especially for religious, cultural, and linguistic reasons, who were either ignored or, worse, represented as the reason for national weakness or impediments to national unity.

Muslim nationalism was doubly derivative insofar as it emerged from a subsection of a larger Indian nationalist movement but could not become one with it. The idea of a separate Muslim state was unimaginable for Mohammad Ali Jinnah, the founding figure of Pakistan, and most Muslim League leaders until the late 1930s, but it captured the imagination of Indian Muslims by the 1940s. The certainty of British departure after World War II created a competitive atmosphere and uncertainty among Indian elites and political parties, including communists, Hindu nationalists, the Indian National Congress, the Muslim League, and princely states, about the absolute dominance of the Congress Party. "Pakistan" emerged as a floating signifier in the late colonial period that meant different things to different people. Jinnah initially rejected the term as a concoction of the "Hindu press" (Jalal 1995; Chatterji 2018), but it came to capture the imagination and different ideals among a cross section of South Asian Muslims. The call for a Muslim nation represented land reforms to Bengali Muslim peasants, sovereign citizenship to Muslim minority League supporters in UP, regional provincial autonomy to state administrators in Sindh, and the assertion of a Muslim majority in Punjab. Ayesha Jalal (1995), David Gilmartin (1988), and Ian Talbot (1998) have argued that the Pakistan movement articulated vague and at times contradictory messages about its objectives or ideology, but it was brought together under shared concern about representation and fear of marginalization. The failure of British colonial administration, the All India Muslim League, and the Indian National Congress to come to a power-sharing agreement resulted in the bloody partition.

The Pakistan movement promised provincial regional autonomy to Muslim majority provinces like Punjab and Sindh, and it offered sovereign protection to Muslim minorities in Bihar, UP, and Tamil Nadu, who feared becoming a permanent minority. The Muslim League promised to respect the sovereign autonomy of princely states and create a joint defense, foreign policy, and market relations with them. These proposals were seen as a measure of securing national recognition in a federated system where Pakistan and Hindustan could share power in a federal government of India rather than a unitary centralized government. This vision of a looser center and shared governance was accepted by the Muslim League in the Cabinet Mission Plan in 1946, and rejected by the Indian National Congress. The Congress sought to establish firm authority over the central government to undertake major reform and development policies. The rejection of the Cabinet Mission Plan power sharing resulted in growing distrust and intensified calls for partition among the supporters of the Muslim League, who rallied around populist slogans like "Islam is in danger."

The end of British imperial rule was ushered in by mass civil-disobedience protests but negotiated at round-table conferences, with elite men who had been recognized as the emissaries and ambassadors of ethnic, religious, and caste groups, and many multitudes numbering more than the total population of the UK. These men were tasked with deciding the fate of millions who didn't have much say in their own destiny, or in many cases the right to simply exist in the house of their birth, and their town and village. This was the culmination of the two hundred years of colonial rule and modernization programs that ripped apart communities that had coexisted for hundreds of years and resulted in one of the most violent forced migrations in modern history (Pandey 2001; Talbot and Thandi 2004). The violence that was unleashed at partition was most severely experienced in Central Punjab, especially in canal colonies, because these regions had been most recently settled by the colonial state and were home to some of the largest number of retired soldiers. The land allotments in this region had been made on the basis of their affiliation with a specific community (*biradari*), military service, and reputation of industry. The colonial frontier had been designed along the lines of the ethnological science of colonial state.

This suppression in the Okara Military Farms has rekindled memory of partition among older tenant farmers, especially those who made their way to these farms after escaping the violence in Jullunder, Amritsar, and

Gurdaspur. The partition was a constant reference in my interviews with tenant farmers, who invoked its legacy, the sacrifice of ancestors, and the aspirations for Pakistan as refuge. The imposition of cash contract farming, the possibility of eviction, and state repression has shaken up the tenants' identification with the state. Instead, many tenants see the state question the very premise of Pakistan for the poor and the landless. Busra Bibi, an elder of the AMP, wistfully concluded an interview with me in 2014 by stating, "We are human beings just like the military officers. We want the same things: for children to go to school, get an education, to get married, and be happy. We never imagined that our asking for our right to bread [*roti*], our demand to have a little parcel of land so we can feed our families, will make us into 'terrorists.' It's up to them to let us live or not; we only ask for this land to make a living. How did that become a crime?"

METHODS AND MOBILIZATION

The research for this book started with a preliminary trip in 2004 and was supplemented by extensive fieldwork between 2007 and 2008 and then with brief follow-up trips in 2012 and 2014. It has been a complex task to keep an eye on the moving parts of a social movement in the ever-changing political climate of Pakistan. Since 2000, Pakistan's political landscape has shifted many times. The neoliberal dictatorship of General Pervez Musharraf was overtaken by a broader movement against military rule (partly inspired by the AMP); the restoration of democratic parliamentary rule was overshadowed by the rise of militant attacks; the assassination of Benazir Bhutto, who was leading the opposition to General Musharraf when she was killed in December 2007; and the feeble rule of two elected governments, which, since 2008, have been beset by violence and increasing fallout from the wars in Iraq and Afghanistan that have exacerbated ethnic and sectarian hostilities. During this period, the AMP evolved from a militant grassroots peasant mobilization in Okara Military Farms to a Punjab-wide movement spreading to other military-related farming estates between 2005 and 2007, when the AMP achieved provisional success in occupying the farms. The police and the paramilitary forces withdrew from those farms after growing public pressure and negative headlines in both national and prominent international press. The period saw a consolidation of the AMP leadership, but it also was the time when the movement split along the questions of tactics and leadership.

The bulk of my fieldwork research occurred during 2007–2008, when there was an uneasy détente between the AMP and the state authorities. The mobilization had plateaued, and there were few signs of active mobilization in the villages. The tenant farmers were in control of their land, and the military personnel were on guard at the nearby military cantonment, storage areas, and their other sites of operation. It was possible for a journalist or a visitor to spend time in these villages without knowing they had been the heart of a radical mobilization only two or four years before. The *chaks* (villages) prospered greatly during this time, as more and more tenants turned to more-intense cultivation by digging new tube wells, investing in tractors, and even renting land from other tenants. The collective ethos of the movement was less visible as the tenants started selling their produce in nearby markets for great profit. This turn of events was distressing for many key participants in the movement, especially women leaders, who played a major role in the movement but were not included in much of the leadership meetings.

I established contact with AMP leaders through student activists and political parties who were working closely with the movement to spread the word about the protests to NGOs and reluctant cable channels and new media. Much of my initial fieldwork involved interviewing AMP leaders, participating in political rallies, preparing materials for rallies, and traveling with AMP leaders to various meetings and villages to spread the word about the movement. It was a moment of immense activity in the villages, as the tenants had just gained de facto control of their land after the military personal and the Rangers paramilitary forces were withdrawn from the farms. The initial successes of the AMP mobilization created generated great optimism among leftists, students, and other progressives, who sensed that the AMP's de facto victories might galvanize a wider movement for land reform and bring issues of class and livelihood back into the mainstream.

How does one assess a social movement as an ethnographic object? This question followed me into the field. I wanted to take what I thought would be a critical stance toward the AMP while remaining in solidarity with the movement. My interest in the movement was motivated by my affinity toward a shared goal for greater redistributive, democratic, and grassroots politics, which seemed so rare in Pakistan. The AMP base is made up of peasant farmers who themselves belong to different patrilineal groups (*biradaris*) and religions. The tenants also have a wide range of difference in their personal stakes in the land (some have twenty-five acres; others are landless), their genders, and the generation they belong to. They come together around a shared sense of history, a shared identity. The significance of the AMP does not lie in the number of people it mobilizes or its concrete achievements; instead, the central force of this social movement is ontological: it ushers in a way of seeing and relating to the world that make long-standing injustices suddenly become insufferable and intolerable. In the AMP's radical slogans and actions we see a clash against long-held assumptions about spatial power in Pakistan, where the army takes Central Punjab as its base of support and patronage. In this sense, the study of the AMP not only reveals injustices carried out by the Pakistani military as landlord but also illuminates the historicity of power in practices and meanings of rights tied to territory and subjects.

Chapter 1 gives an ethnographic sketch of the AMP and tenants' testimony about life under *battai* and the spontaneous beginnings of the AMP mobilizations. Ethnographic scenes focus on the variegated meanings of land for the tenant farmers as a source of subsistence, a place of belonging, and relative freedom. I focus on the political agency displayed by the tenant farmers to resist the Pakistan army in retaining control of the land.

In Chapter 2, I turn to the material history of canal irrigation and the infrastructure of roads and railways in Punjab to understand the conditions of possibility that gave rise to the AMP. I develop the classic theory of gift exchange to analyze the personalized relationship forged between peasant settlers and the colonial state through canals and large and ostensibly impersonal infrastructure projects. The AMP's land rights claim to the farms is also tied to the expectations of state paternalism, through which Punjab's large infrastructure projects unleashed intensely personal relationships between people and institutions through public works projects.

In Chapter 3, on land relations, rights, and property, I build on my historical and ethnographic survey of the environmental transformation of the Indus Plain to examine the afterlife of colonial rule in the military farms in Pakistan. I look at what the Punjab tenants' struggle illustrates about the formation of land rights and how land relations figure in conjuring ideas about community, ecology, and national belonging.

In Chapter 4, I focus on the affective, performative, and pedagogic acts of resistance employed by AMP farmers to make these moral claims, and how these became widespread. The farmers' defiance of the Pakistan army's unilateral decision to change the sharecropping system quickly became a full-fledged movement. As one tenant farmer observed, before this event no one dared to talk back to farm managers, but chants like "Ownership or death" and "Whoever sows the seed shall reap the harvest" became common refrains repeated by young and old. The expressions coined by the AMP, the tenants' testimonies, and poetry provided a moral prism through which to reevaluate the relationships between property and propriety, servitude and freedom, state and society. The AMP's understanding of land rights is not exclusively about individual possession, but also about common rights that are conceived as moral entitlements. The tenants conceive of land as a question of belonging in terms of a continuity of self through the century of working these lands. Tenants claim rights by invoking dense histories of struggle and the debt owed to them by the state.

In Chapter 5, I sketch out the historical-political vocabulary of protest in these villages, while also paying attention to the translocal links forged between the AMP and civil society actors as represented by various NGOs, urban activists, and left-based political parties. In seeking to examine these relations, my aim is to pursue answers to the following questions: What is entailed in translating local livelihood struggles over land into a coherent sociopolitical movement? On what basis did the tenants forge alliances with NGOs and political parties, and how did the farmers grapple with the influx of civil society actors in their villages and in their struggle? To what extent did the political vision of the tenants differ from the one represented in the pamphlets, brochures, and literature produced by the movement as it was funded by NGOs and leftist parties? What were the promises and pitfalls of such alliances?

Sherry Ortner questions a pattern of "ethnographic refusal" in the anthropological literature on resistance movements (1995, 175). Ortner points to the wide gulf between how social movements are depicted and the actual formation, factions, and internal differences that pervade them. Certainly, some level of ethnographic refusal is strategic, as it might be required to sustain the symbolic unity of a peasant political movement in the face of real differences, but this tension offers a challenge to anthropologists' and activists' sensibilities of what qualifies as politics. To what extent can activists, or scholars, efface real differences and tensions "for the sake of the movement"? Protest movements might be rooted in local memories, injuries, aspirations, and struggles, but also they are routed through a transnational discourse of rights and NGO networks that affect the ways in which local demands are represented and made legible to the state, the military, and international civil society. The manifestation of subaltern politics in rural Pakistan, I argue, is a product of colonial land settlement and ongoing processes of dispossession and is shaped by a particular notion of rights connected to a history of settlement and tenant sharecropping, which itself is inflected by notions of caste and territory. A close examination of the AMP illustrates the historicity of power relations in Pakistan and shows us the conditions of possibility when a subaltern movement can challenge a formidable state institution like the army.

CHAPTER 1

POLITICS AS PROCESS IN OKARA
MILITARY FARMS

THE PUNJAB TENANTS' ASSOCIATION (AMP) was entering its
fourth year of struggle when I made my first trip to Okara Military
Farms in the summer of 2004. The movement had already done the un-
thinkable by defying the Pakistan military's orders to sign on to the new
cash lease system. The tenants stood their ground in the face of police
suppression and military siege of their villages in the summer and winter
harvest seasons of 2002 and 2003. The state authorities were forced to
withdraw in response to critical international news coverage and public
outcry. General Musharraf's military government was trying to project
a moderate image of Pakistan in the aftermath of 9/11 as it partnered
with the United States in another war in Afghanistan. To outside observers, like me, the tenant farmers' movement seemed inconceivable when it
first emerged in July 2000, just six months after the military coup, yet by
2003 the AMP was challenging the military's narrative of technocratic
and benevolent governance. I wanted to find out the story behind the
movement and the growing mass opposition to military rule in what had
been perceived as a conservative, prosperous, and pro-military region of
Punjab.

I started following the news about the AMP through online news
articles in 2002. At the time I was living in New York, where I was working as a computer network technician and finishing my bachelor of arts

in political science as a part-time student at Brooklyn College. My family had moved to the United States in the late 1980s to escape the ethnic-sectarian strife that had engulfed Karachi in the aftermath of the first Afghanistan war. I was expected to follow a safe career path like medicine or engineering as the eldest son of an immigrant family. However, I was drawn to the study of political science, history, and literature in college. I joined the City University of New York anti-austerity student activist groups like Student Liberation Action Movement (SLAM!). I was introduced to many different community-based organizations through student activist networks, and I met cultural anthropologists who were documenting the surveillance and harassment experienced by immigrant communities right after 9/11.

I joined the PhD program in cultural anthropology at UT Austin to work on a project about the rise of sectarian politics and the demise of labor organizing in Karachi, Pakistan. However, my interest in the AMP grew as I started following the news about rural protests in Okara Military Farms. The rise of the AMP ruptured the popular expectations about the Pakistani state and opened up space for popular dissent in Punjab. It also inspired pro-democracy activists and leftists who were reeling from a decade of defeat, the dissolution of international socialism, and the suspension of parliamentary government in the wake of General Pervez's neoliberal style of dictatorship. The two main political parties (Pakistan Peoples Party and Pakistan Muslim League–Nawaz) were quick to support the AMP and spoke on behalf of the tenant farmers. However, both parties had suffered major defections as their leaders were imprisoned or forced into exile. Both parties also faced large-scale defections to the military. A network of civil society human rights groups and nongovernmental organizations (NGOs) for women's empowerment, like Shirkat Gah, and workers' rights, like the Pakistan Institute of Labour Education and Research, was formed to support the AMP.

A series of high-profile news articles in Pakistan's English newspapers, like *Dawn*, and international media, like the *Washington Post* and BBC, raised awareness of the AMP by transforming the protests into a symbol of resistance against the military's growing political and economic power (Lancaster 2003; "Pakistan Military Rejects" 2004). In a short time span, the AMP had gathered major importance in the national discourse. The AMP mobilized tenants all over Punjab, but it was most closely associated with Okara Military Farms, which went from being a place to a symbol of resistance. The AMP was characterized by newspaper articles, press reports, government briefings, and other outlets in multiple ways, including as a grassroots land struggle, a criminal conspiracy, and an NGO creation.[1]

The Pakistan military was struggling to justify its suppression of the AMP. The state portrayed the AMP as a "criminal" organization (briefly as terrorists) funded by outsider "anti-state" agents. I followed the news through online news reports, cryptic government press releases referring to "miscreants" and disturbances in Okara Military Farms, and the Khanewal Seed Corporation. The tenants were routinely described as gullible or misled villagers, and other times they were cast as violent and crafty criminals; for instance, one report said, "We know that there are all sorts of miscreants, proclaimed offenders and other criminals hiding in villages . . . who could take advantage of the confusion and create a law-and-order situation we might not be able to control on our own" (IRIN 2003). I saw the AMP as in line with classical uprisings described in early works by Subaltern Studies Collective scholars who questioned the idea of spontaneity of peasant rebellions to take account of the missing voices, narratives, and "lost" causes that came into view through peasant insurgencies and uprising (Guha 1999; Chaturvedi 2000). The Subaltern Studies Collective's approach highlighted the political demands of the *un*imagined communities whose existence is acknowledged only as a problem of development and governance.

The NGOs and civil society groups tried to defuse the conflict by framing the AMP dispute as a human rights issue. For example, in a widely circulated article titled "Terror in Okara," Pervez Hoodbhoy gives a detailed testimonial of the violent repression in Okara. He concludes by framing the Okara peasant struggle as a nonpolitical human rights issue: "For all practical purposes, the nearly 1 [million] people of Okara are under military occupation. Peasants have no political agenda—land is about livelihood and physical survival" (Hoodbhoy 2003). Hoodbhoy's representation of the AMP echoes the attitudes of many urban activists, intellectuals who saw the AMP as not necessarily a political movement in itself but rather a "prepolitical" mobilization for subsistence. This distinction between politics based on ideology and politics that emerge on the basis of subsistence became a dividing line between the AMP leaders and the urban activists.

In Austin, I met Asha Amirali, one of the main organizers from the People's Rights Movement (PRM), a Rawalpindi-based activist group. Asha was on a tour of American college campuses to give talks about the PRM and its work with the AMP struggle and other grassroots movements.[2] The PRM activists put me in touch with Latif Ali, one of the key AMP leaders who worked closely with the PRM. Since 2001, there had been a regular flow of journalists, civil society members, and fact-finding missions coming through the chaks to document the conditions in the villages. The solidarity trips peaked after the military operation in 2002–2003 to highlight the dire conditions of the besieged farmers. Hence my initial interactions in every village took on the quality of a briefing where most people perceived me as a journalist before I could explain my project. It was only after my return visit to the villages that people started to share more-personal stories with me, even if they veered away from the movement or the official script of the AMP.

The AMP's ability to forge unity among peasants from different backgrounds, across *biradari*, occupational castes, and religious divides, was remarkable. Women leaders' prominent role in the movement also generated great interest in civil society organizations to support the AMP. This cross-sectional solidarity in the AMP had a lot to do with creating a shared sense of purpose based on the common need for land to ensure basic subsistence. The aim of my research was to get to the ordinary sense of place and experience of the people in these villages. My questions had to do with the story that was being left out of these reports, such as the history of mobilization in these farms and the tenants' changing perception of the state and the military. I was interested in documenting the kinds of changes that brought about the rise of this farmers' movement; and, last, I wanted to see how different communities, varying across castes and religions (the majority Muslim and a high percentage of Christians), overcame internal differences to organize around their material interests.

I wanted to understand the tenants' understanding of land rights and their ability to mobilize around a moral claim to land. My path into the military farm villages (chaks) influenced my interaction and initial rapport with the tenant sharecropper (*mazarin*) community.

My initial goal in following the AMP was to understand the significance of this struggle and the local perspectives about land rights. I was interested in the tenants' mode of deliberation, their agency and subaltern understandings of rights. The tenants' mobilizations speak to the dual meanings of subalternity, as in the literal sense of being the subordinate class in a military organization and the more widely used conceptualized meaning that refers to the marginalized poor, those who are talked about but rarely heard from. The timing and the location of the tenant farmers' reaction also added to the element of surprise, given the fact that most Pakistanis view Central Punjab as being especially amenable to Pakistani establishment. I became interested in the (un)timeliness of this movement, as the rise of the AMP coincided with the American rapprochement with the Pakistani state in the aftermath of 9/11.

A compendium of books (some trade, some academic) with alarming titles like *Descent into Chaos* (Rashid 2008), *Making Sense of Pakistan* (Shaikh 2009), *The Paradox of Pakistan* (Jaffrelot 2015), *In the Line of Fire* (Musharraf 2006a), and *Pakistan: Between Mosque and Military* (Haqqani 2005) were published in the wake of 9/11 to explain Pakistan to a Western audience. Almost all of these books repeat the same epithet about the praetorian nature of the Pakistani state: "All countries have an Army but in Pakistan the Army has an entire country" (Rashid 2008, 38). Therefore, these books do not contain much about the day-to-day lives, dreams, aspiration, and fears of an ethnically and linguistically diverse population of over two hundred million people. The books do not tell the reader much about the history of the political activism and the social movements that have challenged the state and toppled military regimes since the founding of the country (for notable exceptions to this trend, see Ali 2015 and Toor 2011).[3]

The history of peasant protests and broader social movements in Pakistan has not been recorded, yet these movements have left a rich archive of symbols, signs, slogans, literature, poems, and personalities who struggled for other possibilities of reform. Many of the key figures in student movements, socialist parties like the Democratic Student Front, National Students Federation, Mazdoor Kisan Party, Communist Party of Pakistan, and Pakistan Peoples Party, went on to become educators, lawyers, media personalities, and artists. Thus, much of the rhetoric of land reforms, ethnic nationalism (multinationalism), socialist internationalism, and feminism remains alive even if it is posited through songs, poetry, TV dramas, or news editorials. These ideas break out into mass protests and spontaneous mobilizations in times of dictatorships. This book historicizes and contextualizes the overlooked story of subaltern resistance and resilience, and the challenges faced by the AMP as it upended the status quo and struggled to maintain its gains in the face of stricter counterterror discourse and restrictions on public assembly.

My first trip to Chak 33 L in June 2004 coincided with Punjab Chief Minister Pervez Elahi's trip to the military cantonment in Okara City. There was a heavy presence of army patrol vans, military police vehicles, and a strict patrol by the paramilitary Rangers forces. As the local newspaper explained, there was a "strict inspection going on in every village to protect from any unpleasant activity" ("Strict Inspection" 2004). Ranger forces and police personnel patrolled the bus stop and surveyed the crowd.

My preliminary research trips to the villages in the summer of 2004 were characterized by grave concern about making it to the villages without attracting police attention or endangering friends who might facilitate my travel. The police and Ranger forces patrolled the Multan Road highway and roads surrounding the AMP villages to catch AMP leaders when they ventured out of their village.[4] Initially I took extra precautions by not using voice recorders or taking any pictures and avoiding biographical details to the best of my ability in writing field notes. I traveled to the military farms in smaller vans that run through rural backroads to avoid the main bus depot in Okara City, which was under constant surveillance during my preliminary research, and I tried to keep a low profile in general.

In 2007, I found the situation to be dramatically different. The tenant farmers and the local administration were settling into an uneasy détente when I started the bulk of my fieldwork research. The AMP leaders were traveling between the city and the villages, and even the local district government offices, as they were running for local elections. My cautious fieldwork approach was routinely upended by tenant farmers, who took me to the dairy farms, to police stations, and to the sites where they had been held during the siege. During these forays, I was introduced to local police and military personnel, and some of my interlocutors were already acquainted with local police and farm managers. The media paid little attention to the AMP between 2007 and 2008, as the news cycle shifted to other pressing topics.

In selecting a field site, I chose a village that was less caught up in the AMP leadership squabbles, as I aimed to be in a locale where Muslim and Christian village leadership were still working together. Through my conversations with different activists and tenants, I decided that Chak 33 L would be the best place to start, because this village was a bit more isolated from other farms and the AMP leaders there were staying out of the leadership squabbles. I was already in contact with Latif Ali, one of the AMP leaders in Chak 33 L. Latif had gained wide respect among urban activists for his easygoing personality, his sharp wit, and his facility in translating when breaking down critiques of global trade policies to tenant farmers in concrete local language. Latif extended an invitation for me to stay in his village and offered to make the arrangements for my initial stay and travel.

Soon after I arrived in Chak 33 L, I was taken to a guestroom in Wasim's house. Wasim was a young AMP activist who ran a small bicycle and farm-tool repair shop. The shop faced the village center, and the villagers used the back room of his shop as a meeting place on scorching-hot days. As I settled in at Wasim's place, I heard an announcement from the mosque's loudspeakers about the arrival of a "guest," and soon a large group had gathered at Wasim's. I did not get a chance to properly introduce myself, and most people in the room probably assumed that I was a journalist or NGO worker. Latif was keen to point out that the assembled group varied across *zat* (caste) and religious lines. Latif introduced me to Farid Daula, the village elder and former military veteran who is respected for being part of earlier protests in the military farms. He is the eldest of the AMP leaders, while most of the other leaders are significantly younger. Farid was elected president of the AMP at the Lahore peasant convention in 2002, after which he was abducted and imprisoned for a month. When I met him, Farid was tall and slim, with thick gray hair and a well-groomed beard that made him appear a patriarchal and distant figure. Latif's self-deprecating humor made him seem more accessible.

Latif noted, "Now that people have become more aware, the differences between *zat* [tribal caste or community based on descent] and religion are not important" (interview by the author, June 20, 2004). Latif's opinion about the community's political consciousness and its diversity had changed by 2007, when he decried the tenants' criticism of AMP leadership. The tenants gave testimonies about the working conditions in the villages before the rise of the AMP. I tried to dispel their impression that I was reporting for a newspaper, explaining my research as a study of social movements. The AMP's story had been published, the military had backed away, and I wanted to find out about the history of the movement and all the work the tenants had done to build a sense of solidarity and common purpose across *zat*, religion, and Pakistan. I was interested in how the movement worked and what lessons it could teach to others facing similar issues.

Farid testified in 2007, "Life under the *battai* system was miserable. The villages were administered under 'corrupt law' [*kala kanoon*], by which people were held like prisoners." Repeated references to "unfair law," "British law," and "corrupt law" signified that the AMP leaders did not have complete faith in the law; they viewed it as the same as the law of the colonial state and the groups that benefited from it.

The tenant leaders wanted to give me a more authentic version of the struggle than those I found filtered through NGO narratives about the movement, which the tenants said were based on taking words from a few select members to make money for themselves. Farid proceeded to tell me the history of the *mazarin*. These testimonials were addressed to me as much as to the assembled group that had gathered to hear the retelling of the conditions that had brought about this movement. These meetings were powerful and emotional events that served to shape a collective narrative of the movement at a time of heated internal debates and growing questions about the direction and meaning of the AMP. Using "we" and "our" to speak for the whole village, Farid told the history of life under *battai*. Pointing to me, he described how the system of evaluating crops and estimating harvests was set up in such a way that the chak-in-charge (farm manager) would inflate the estimated harvests so the farmers had to surrender a greater portion of their share during sharecropping:

> They would inspect the fields and make projections for the harvest crop. These evaluations were always inflated, so when the time came for harvest and *battai*, the government would demand a greater share of the harvest. They were supposed to take 50 percent of our harvest, but in reality, they would take as much as 65 to 70 percent or more of our harvest, and the chak-in-charge would demand some more. If there was a drop in the harvest due to bad weather or disease, they wouldn't lessen their evaluation. There was so much poverty in these villages before. People were so poor that there were times when they didn't have enough to eat; they would dip *roti* [bread] in *lassi* [buttermilk]. . . . The landowning farmers used to come to our village because they knew we were poor. In those days, there were fewer machines, and there was a lot of physical labor involved in preparing fields. People did anything to feed themselves. People used to go into the army. We couldn't cover our costs; some would go enlist in the army. There was only hunger here. People didn't like going into the army. In the army, we were sepoys [noncommissioned soldiers]. (Interview by the author, 2007)

The farmers alleged that the farm administrators stole most of the harvest collected, and only sent a fraction of the revenue to army headquarters. Farid went to describe how the farm managers required every peasant household to sit in the same *maidan* (common area) where the chak-in-charge held daily assembly. Latif turned to me after Farid's speech to give me an example: "The military officials abused their powers and profited by stealing from the *battai* that was collected. Even the village guards [*chowkidars*], who had very small salaries, would be driving new motorcycles and building houses in Okara City soon after working here."

The tenants had developed a testimonial nature in the meetings. Farid said that it would be good to introduce me as a guest who had come from

America. It would boost the morale of the tenants to hear that news of the tenants' movement had been heard across the world. I agreed to speak at the meeting, but there was considerable discussion among the leaders on whether to make the announcement on the "hooter," the local term for the mosque loudspeaker. In this region of Punjab, the hooter is used to broadcast messages, such as announcing a birth or death, in addition to its use for call to prayer. During the siege, the loudspeakers had also been used to alert the village about approaching Rangers or police. Latif cautioned that making an announcement on the mosque hooter meant that the authorities would be tipped off, but in the end, the AMP leaders decided that it would be safe to make a public announcement calling for a village meeting after evening prayer (Maghreb).

These village meetings were held regularly in the first few years of AMP mobilization to update everyone on any progress that had been made and also to ask for more donations for the movement. The meeting was held at 8:00 P.M., after most people ate dinner, and the smell of wood-burning stoves and food was still in the air. A sizable number of people had gathered at the meeting area by the time a few AMP leaders and I arrived at the field. A row of chairs was set up for us and the rest of the crowd was seated on the floor waiting for the meeting to start. I found it a bit distressing to be seated on chairs after hearing all the stories about how farm administrators used to sit in that very spot to give commands to the farmers. The moment made me think once again about leadership of the AMP and the challenge faced by the movement to stay true to its grassroots base.

During the meeting, Latif gave a heartfelt speech about the state of the movement and warned against the tendency of the peasant farmers to slow down or back down when the military authorities retreated. He said that the state was trying to put the tenants to sleep and to sow discord, and the tenant farmers needed to take more initiative in keeping the movement going by donating some money to the AMP and coming to the meetings. Then he turned to me to introduce me as a friend of the movement who had traveled all the way from America to meet them. These attestations to my intentions by the leadership of the AMP left me uncomfortable, as I struggled to explain my motives in studying this movement. Having arrived just a few hours earlier, I was at a loss for words. Moreover, I was still uncertain about the role of this leadership and the possible splits that were reportedly taking place within the movement. I tried to keep my statement to a minimum; I said something about the uniqueness of the *mazarin* struggle in Pakistan, that word about the AMP had reached far and wide, and that the farmers had completely shaken up the elite establishment through their brave struggle. I ended by reiterating that the movement could continue to grow if it learned from what it has gained and stays united.

The AMP's president, Farid, spoke last. As he talked, I kept thinking about my exhortation for unity, wondering if I had spoken too soon. My apprehension stemmed from the fact that I knew there were internal differences in the tenants' movement, and I was struck by how the leadership criticized people in the community for slacking off. Among the reminders that the battle was not over and that the army was trying to put people to sleep, there were warnings that some people wanted to create a level of friction in the community.

After the meeting, the AMP leaders described the stakes of the movement by drawing comparisons to the abject hunger faced by the indigent poor in Karachi who have no independent means of getting food except by buying it or begging for it. Many of the tenant farmers had spent time as laborers in Karachi or had relatives who lived there. The tenants also knew that I was from Karachi. The potential loss of land meant not only loss of a livelihood but also displacement, dispossession, and the breakdown of families, as the example of hungry children in Karachi streets was supposed to evoke. The tenant farmers emphasized that people in cities might consider them poor, but there was no hunger in their village even among the poorest families. The poverty in the village in this agriculturally productive region of Punjab was different from the abject poverty in the big cities.

We went to Farid's *bhetak* (gathering space), which served as nightly meeting space for village elders and resolution of disputes. My conversation with Farid turned into a broad discussion about the meaning of land with other tenants who had gathered at Farid's place. The tenant farmers argued that in contrast to the extreme poverty in the cities, even the poorest groups in their village had a *marla* (small plot) where they could grow enough food to survive, whereas being destitute in the city meant having no place to sleep, no land to grow food, and no kin to rely on. The tenants emphasized that the land was more than just a means of subsistence. Latif said that he viewed the land as a mother. Farid joked that he had probably heard that line in a film, and Latif ignored Farid's comment as we he went on to say that city people who get their food and milk from the village should view the countryside as a jewel rather than a backward place. Farid interjected that most families in his village have family members who live in cities now and that some villages also have a great number of people working in Dubai, Bahrain, and Saudi Arabia. However, he argued that land remains an important source of connection for these families with loved ones working abroad; the village is a place that ensures mutual care, and it is the source of one's standing and reputation. While tenant farmers are not exclusively dependent on the land for making a living, their access to land defines the way in which they live and see themselves. Access to land offers a degree of autonomy and social recognition and connects farmers to other modes of making a living. For example, one's landholding or tenancy in the case of the AMP can be used to secure loans or get a sponsorship for apprentice work in Lahore or Faisalabad. And it was the potential of eviction and the cash contract system that compelled the tenant farmers to challenge the undisputed hegemony of army rule in Punjab.

MILITARY-STATE SPACE

The relationship between the tenant farmers and the army is more complex than it may appear from afar. The tenants take a nuanced view of the army by differentiating between the army as an institution, army officers, and noncommissioned soldiers. Many AMP leaders, like Farid, are retired soldiers, and most tenant households have family members who work for the military dairy farms, as gardeners in the nearby cantonment, as barbers, or as hired hands to supplement household income. The AMP leaders underscore the importance of the military in their public speeches, pamphlets, and private conversations by citing the plight of Kashmiris and Muslims in occupied lands. They offer examples of the 1965 war, when tenants volunteered to fortify the defenses against possible Indian ground invasion in Punjab. However, the tenants' identification with the army is combined with criticism of army generals, brigadiers who betray the national interest for personal profit, corruption, and Western alliances. According to Farid, the army officers behave like British colonial masters, or, as he phrased it, "Kalay Angraiz" (the Black Englishmen). He argued that the officers oversee the same system of sharecropping, rules, and protocols that were exploitive and humiliating to tenant farmers. He claimed that the military retained a colonial attitude toward the tenant farmers: "Occasionally, when a brigadier or VIP would visit, everyone in the village was ordered to clean the streets for days, water the plants, and whitewash the walls and tree trunks with a coat of limestone [*choona*]. Old men would be sweeping the streets for days" (interview by the author, June 24, 2004). Farid offered a terse response to my follow-up question about good officers or farm managers, who I had gathered from my interviews, by stating that good officers were exceptions rather than the rule.

Farid shared his own experience as a young soldier in the early 1960s to give me some perspective on the army's changing relationship with the public. He stated, "There was great respect for the army in the early days of Pakistan. People made many sacrifices during the creation of the country and admired soldiers. I joined the military as a *sipahi* [sepoy] in 1962, and I was posted by the Indian border in East Pakistan. The Bengalis were very patriotic, but they wanted greater democracy, and elections, while the military didn't want to give up its control over the country" (interview by the author, June 24, 2004).[5] Farid was demobilized in 1967 and got a job as a truck driver for the military dairy farms in Okara, where he learned about the corruption and profiteering in the farm operations.

According to Farid, the army changed drastically in Pakistan after the 1965 war, becoming heavily involved in land acquisition, commercial dealings, and real estate. The military established a string of large cantonments in Punjab, including one in Okara, which was made by acquiring land from six military farm villages and displacing hundreds of tenant households in the late 1960s and into the 1970s.[6] The Okara cantonment was established as part of a string of new cantonments in eastern districts bordering Indian Punjab, with an eye toward creating new border towns that would be settled by military officers and military institutions, in giving them greater incentive and logistics to defend those lands in time of war. As I discuss in Chapter 3, a vast portion of the Okara cantonment consists of agricultural lands that were taken from tenant farmers and given to military officers. However, it is not uncommon to find laborers who had exclusive tenancy rights to the farms where they now work as hired hands on what used to be their own fields. Many military officers have in turn sold these awarded and subsidized plots to developers and emerging middle-class residents who want to live in the comfortable environs of the Okara cantonment.[7]

Farid argues that the expansion of land allotments and cantonments compromised the army, turning it from a disciplined institution into one corrupted by military officers who use their official position for self-gain. Farid recalls that he was able to escape the unforgiving poverty and sharecropping by joining the army, but younger noncommissioned soldiers might find themselves laboring in the fields for military officers on the public exchequer. A new agrarian class of retired military officers leverages their links with the army to receive subsidized electricity, inputs, and labor from noncommissioned soldiers on their lands, especially if they are located in the cantonments. The Pakistan government reclaimed some nine million acres of land in the mid-1960s with the construction of small dams (Guddu Barrage, Kotri Barrage, and Ghulam Mohammad Barrage in Sindh). One million acres of this land was allotted to military officers. General Ayub Khan, the military dictator at the time, received some 247 acres of land during this time.[8] Moreover, the military used the 1894 Land Acquisition Act to claim agricultural lands for the construction of new cantonments, practice, and camping grounds, and to post the Defence Housing Authority in Karachi, which have expanded to Pakistan major metropolitan cities like Lahore. The military is the only state institution that can convert state-owned land for official purposes and later distribute it for private ones. There is a nexus between the acquisition of public and private lands for the military's official purposes; for instance, running parade grounds, practice runs, storage facilities, and allocating adjacent lands for military officers' private personal and/or commercial investments.

As Ayesha Siddiqa shows in *Military Inc.* (2017), the allocation of land to military officers created a new class of land barons. The rise of the AMP opened up the debate about the Pakistan military's real estate and business interests, or what Siddiqa has aptly termed "Milbus" (2007, 35). However, the critique of "Milbus" or *Military Inc.* has resulted in a vocal defense by military officers who brand terms like "Military Inc." to be disingenuous regarding the history of infrastructural development, land reclamation, and town planning in Punjab. Indeed, the tenant farmers viewed the contract system, with its built-in weakening of their claim to the land in lieu of this recent history, to be land development through dispossession. The AMP challenged the military's claims to be an efficient, disciplined, and technocratic institution.

The Pakistan military has dominated the state structure since the first decade of independence. Recent scholarship on Pakistan's independence suggests that the Muslim League leadership was caught off guard when the Indian National Congress and British Indian government granted Pakistan's independence outside of an all-India power-sharing framework. The political leadership of the nascent country was more concerned about preserving a centralized nation-state than risking division or dissent (Bose and Jalal 1998). Thus, Muhammad Ali Jinnah dismissed the provincial governments in the North-West Frontier Province formed by the Awami National Party (which had run in a coalition with Indian Congress Party), and the Sindh government was disbanded on charges of corruption. A combination of domestic, regional, and international factors tilted the balance firmly in favor of the nonelected administrators rather than empowering elected institutions of the state. The constitutional framework stalled following the successive dismissals of chief executives, and General Ayub Khan formally took over the reins of state power in 1958 with the approval of the Pakistan Supreme Court. The state's direct links to the broader vision of Jinnah's Muslim League were extinguished with Jinnah's death in 1949 and the still-unresolved execution of Liaqat Ali Khan. On October 16, 1951, Liaqat Ali was killed by Said Akbar while addressing a public rally in Rawalpindi.[9] The tentative start to a parliamentary democracy and assembling the constitution was aborted in 1958 after the military coup led by General Ayub Khan. The chief justice of the supreme court sanctioned the military coup by invok-ing the "doctrine of necessity" to justify the exceptional measures. The military intensified its grip on the state structure, which was meant to be federal in form and unitary in substance; the military's authoritarian character went against the grain of politics in its constituent regions.

The military-led government was concerned about growing influence of anticolonial, socialist, and democratic populism throughout the 1960s. The Pakistan military, business, and bureaucratic elite shared mutual dis-trust of popular representation and ethnic nationalism, which threatened to undo the growing alliance between the Pakistan military, bureaucratic, and industrial elite and American foreign policy objectives in Asia and the Middle East. The Pakistani elite saw themselves at the center of the geostrategic alliances of the Southeast Asia Treaty Organization and the Central Treaty Organization. However, this strategic vision lacked con-sideration of the uneven development and growing sense of injury felt by the Bengali middle classes, whose numerical majority and interests were not recognized in the cultural, political, and economic vision of the state.

The military was caught off guard by the rise of mass mobilization against the Ayub Khan government that spread throughout the country in the late 1960s. Some of my elder interlocutors in the different branches of the military described the wave of protests and political activity that swept through Pakistan for the first time in their living memory. Ayaz Masih, of the Punjab Seed Corporation farms in Pirowal, smiled when he recalled the secret meetings to demand land rights. Ayaz recalled hearing fiery speeches by Maulana Bhashani in Khanewal as he toured through Punjab in the year after Fatima Jinnah lost the election that was based on a restricted franchise. He recalled the fear and excitement in the village as people started to believe that institutions could be challenged. The tenants in the military farms mobilized and rose up to demand bet-ter working conditions and fairer practices of sharecropping with an eye toward demanding land redistribution as part of Zulfiqar Ali Bhutto's promised land reforms. The history of these protests might seem like an aberration and blip to the political administration and elite classes, but these protests have lived on in the memory of tenant farmers as impor-tant moments of possibility and reminders that powerful institutions can be challenged and dramatically altered, especially when it comes to the basic question of survival.

The AMP's rise came as a major shock to military officers and local landlords who saw the mobilization through the lens of "law and order," or at worst a plot by a hostile state. For instance, Sajjad Haider, a top civilian bureaucrat in Okara, told Integrated Regional Information Networks (IRIN) that the tenants' demand for land rights was ridiculous: "It is a totally ridiculous and malicious agitation inspired by certain frustrated political elements, some NGO's and human rights groups." He went on to say, "I will not transfer proprietary rights to these people, even if the army succumbs to their pressure. The whole edifice will crumble if the provincial government gives the land to these people. That's why it will not" (IRIN 2003). Thus, the Okara movement created grave concern among the military and civil administration about a greater radicalization and demands for more substantial land redistribution in 2002–2003.

I was careful to limit my discussions with military, civil, and police officials while I was doing fieldwork in the Okara district in 2004 and 2007. However, I interviewed retired army officers (three majors and a retired lieutenant colonel), a police sub-inspector, and retired civil servants in Karachi and Lahore. These officials had served in the Okara district or were familiar with the military farms, having trained in the nearby cantonment for military exercises. The military officers' personal responses matched the military's official statements that rejected the possibility that this agitation could have been self-organized or instigated by the tenant farmers themselves. Instead, the military officers saw the mechanisms of political parties, former activists who worked for NGOs, and one retired officer whom I called Major Khaliq. He spent four years in Okara in the late 1980s as part of the fourteenth division, and he mentioned the naïveté of peasant farmers, or the possible duplicity of some of their leaders, in what he believed was an espionage mission by a foreign hostile state to create disturbances in Punjab and stem the prosperity that would have come from the contract system. I also interviewed Sub-Inspector Shezad Malik (a pseudonym), who served in Okara from 2005 to 2006. He was transferred out of the district after complaints were lodged against him for mishandling criminal cases against AMP leaders (interview by the author, April 23, 2007, Lahore).

Many police officials in Okara were transferred out of the district or even punished for not being able to squash the movement. Shezad's tenure in the Okara district started in 2005, when he was told to report for duty in the fields surrounding Hanif's village, where the station house officer of the police was laying siege on the village to confiscate the wheat harvest as a punishment for the tenants' refusal to pay their rent in cash or in kind. According to Shezad, the situation was tense because the peasants were armed and had taken up position along the perimeter of the residential section of the village. The police had received orders from the lieutenant general to confiscate the harvest to make up for the losses from civil disobedience. The police had marked out and gathered the wheat crop, and tractor trollies had been arranged to transport the crops, but the police were also ordered to avoid any bloodshed or firing. The situation stuck the police in a quagmire between the army and tenant farmers. Shezad claims the military has taken a soft approach toward the AMP.

I also interviewed retired Lieutenant Colonel Imtiaz Akbar (pseudonym), who was trained as a veterinarian and managed the Okara farms in the 1970s when these farms experienced the first wave of protests (interview by the author, November 9, 2007, Karachi). Akbar disagreed with the army's official statement that the protests did not represent the tenants' will. Akbar recalled the unrest taking place in the military farms in the mid-1970s, when the tenant farmers started a movement demanding greater oversight in sharecropping and crop evaluations. There also had been some talk about redistributing the government land to the tenant farmers. Akbar blames the AMP protests on this history of populism, which he dates back to Zulfiqar Ali Bhutto's populism that dislodged the sense of national duty in both the public and the army ranks. Akbar is a prominent member of the Ahmediya community, and he connected the banishment of Ahmedis with the rise of populism as part of the broader mechanisms of populist politics that has been used by politicians to channel resentment and to grab power.

Akbar argued that the tenant farmers' demands for land rights hides a stark fact that most tenants will turn around and sell their lands at inflated market prices, and that is indeed their agenda in taking out this instigation against agrarian reform. He argued that the Pakistani military occupies a unique position as a force of modernization, and land development that goes back to the colonial times. I followed on Akbar's contention about the military's historical role of development by asking him about the rationale for the massive use of public lands for private gains for retired military officers and military-affiliated luxury housing development associations, like where his own house is situated. Akbar countered my argument by explaining that the army is unable to pay its trained engineers and qualified officers the high salaries offered by multinationals and Pakistan's banking and professional sectors. Therefore, the land allotments and awards are offered as a form remuneration for officers who would most certainly earn more in the private sector. However, he added that growing wealth disparities in the country are resulting in a situation that could endanger the country and the army.

The tenants vehemently opposed the military's official claims of being a force for modernization and improvement. The tenants claimed that the military farm management has been pilfering greater shares of the harvest for decades. Moreover, the military has institutionalized the policy of accumulation through dispossession of the poor, especially those who reside on state land under precarious terms. The military's broader role in defending the ideological boundaries was also discussed in my conversation with Farid and Latif. This conversation emerged when I asked if they thought that the land rights struggles waged by ethnic-nationalist groups and parties, like the then-growing struggle in Balochistan led by Akbar Bugti, would get the tenants' support and, more important, if the tenants felt that these movements were the same as their own. Farid and Latif held very different positions on this question. Latif had gone to Dera Bugti along with a group of leftist activists as a gesture of solidarity with Akbar Bugti, the elder Baloch statesman who had been killed in a final standoff with the Pakistan Army (interview by the author, July 2007). However, Farid refused to see common ground with the Balochistan movement, which he saw as spearheaded by feudal tribal leaders who wanted to gain greater autonomy to secure control over their tenants and laborers (interview by the author, 2007).

POLITICS AS PROCESS: THE RISE OF
MAZARIN POLITICAL SUBJECTIVITY
IN THE MILITARY FARMS

The tenant farmers of the village, both leaders and residents, consistently brought up the term *shau'r*, meaning awareness or consciousness, to explain the rise of the AMP. The success of the movement is attributed to growing *shau'r* in the villages. *Shau'r* is a polysemic term, referring at different times to increasing awareness through education, worldliness, political consciousness, or connections with the outside market or material world. Here is one comment by Latif that reflects the sentiments widely shared in the chaks: "The movement didn't start before 2000 because people didn't have the same consciousness [*shau'r*] before. . . . We were scared and servile. There were a few protests, but leaders always cut their own deals with the farm managers. But now the leaders know that the people are aware and that they will have no place to go to if they sign on to the contract system, and their lands will be eventually taken. Also, this time the leadership hasn't cut a deal with the army. It's mostly younger educated people who made sacrifices" (interview by the author, June 12, 2007).

Many younger leaders like Latif blamed themselves or the previous generations' lack of education for enduring so many years of brutal repression without rising up sooner. As Latif put it, "Our biggest fault is that this movement should have started a long time ago. Our biggest mistake is that our ancestors should have started this work. We sacrificed ourselves for the army, we have served Pakistan, and that is why we have gotten kicked by Pakistan [*juti khai*]" (interview by the author, June 12, 2007). Latif's comments echo the prevalent ideology of development and progress in explaining the rise and success of their movement as evidence of their own development. They blame the lack of awareness, or worldliness, for the century of exploitation. Latif grew up in Chak 33 in a refugee (*panahgir*) family that had migrated from Eastern Punjab (India) at the time of partition. They were allotted twelve acres of land that had been split among four brothers and a sister. Latif left farming to work in the fruit and vegetable wholesale market in Karachi and became a vendor in smaller cities in Sindh in the 1980s, but he returned to the village after the breakout of ethnic riots in the 1980s. For Latif, the rise of the AMP meant that young men like him would no longer need to leave the village to make ends meet. Most of the key leaders in the movement have experienced circular labor migration to the cities, and many others like Farid had served as noncommissioned soldiers in the military.

There was a generational aspect to this reasoning, too. Older tenant leaders like Farid rejected Latif's assertion of a new political consciousness by emphasizing the history of protests and resistance in the past. Farid recalled, "Our ancestors told us about the past, that this land is ours and that the original settlers were promised this land in exchange for settling this land" (interview by the author, July 3, 2004, Okara Military Farms). These narratives are especially potent for the Christian tenant families, whose ancestors were the earliest settlers in Chak 10 (the oldest of the military farm AMP villages).

The last major protests on the military farms took place in Okara in the mid-1970s. As Farid recalls, it was the first time that many people had felt they were entitled to some respect, and there was a lot of talk about equality and redistribution: "Things improved a little in '73, when Bhutto ruled that new seeds and fertilizer should be given to tenants. People started to wake up [during] Bhutto's government. They started to demand fairer *battai.* . . . At the time, no one had a proper brick house, and people used buffalo plow carts [*bail gari*] to prepare fields" (interview by the author, July 3, 2004). Latif's most enduring memory about the impact of Bhutto's administration at that time—he was ten years old in 1973—was that even the poorest people in the chaks started wearing sandals [*chupals*] called "Bhutto *chupals*" as a sign of greater dignity. But there were many other changes in the early 1970s. The first elementary schools in the chaks opened, and there was a growing sense that institutions could be challenged.

At that time, the tenants were mobilized under the prospects of land reform and/or redistribution. They started participating in the rallies held by local Pakistan Peoples Party (PPP) stalwarts like Rao Sikander, who

hailed from a large landowning family in Okara. The prospect of land redistribution in the military farms was so strong that the Retired Veteran
Military Farms arranged a meeting with Ghulam Mustafa Khar, PPP's
Punjab minister, to make a case for preserving the military farms as a
national asset by describing the many sacrifices made by the staff to keep
the system functioning. Bhutto's government complied with the army's
wishes by not breaking up the farms, but the populist government man-
dated changes in the military farm administration, such as providing new
commercial seeds and fertilizers, and carrying out the weighing and *battai* harvest revenue in the presence of the farmers, providing the tenants
with receipts for their work. This era of reform and oppositional politics
came to an abrupt end on July 5, 1977, when the military, led by General
Muhammad Zia-ul-Haq, overthrew Zulfikar Bhutto's government. Tenant leaders like Farid were arrested in Okara Military Farms in a sweeping wave of arrests, in which hundreds of thousands of student leaders,
tenant farmers, and PPP party members were arrested on the same day.

Farid is widely respected for his lifelong commitment to the tenants'
struggle. He was elected as the president of the AMP at a famous AMP
rally in Lahore, which was held to showcase the AMP's wide network of
support among civil society and urban activists. He was arrested as he left
the stage at the rally. He was immediately put in a police van and taken
to the nearby Kasur border (one hour away from downtown Lahore),
where the police agents or officers he thinks worked with the intelligence
agencies who accused him of being an Indian spy, an agent for the Research and Analysis Wing (RAW) agent. Here is how he described the
situation: "I was arrested the day I became the AMP president. I was
taken by the ISI [Inter-Services Intelligence] to the Kasur border. They
told me that the governor had given orders to shoot me at the Kasur
border, and they accused me of being a RAW spy. I told them that I am
a representative of the poor people; I am from Okara and not a RAW
agent. I was blindfolded, hands tied. They took me out, and they said that
they would shoot me. They asked me to face the qibla [the direction of
Mecca, toward which Muslims turn at prayer]. I asked them how could
they expect me to face the qibla when my eyes, hands, and are tied, and I
don't know where I am? They asked me if I had one last message for my

family. I said something. I thought they were going to kill me there, but then they put me back in the van and took me to jail" (interview by the author, July 3, 2004).

Moments like Farid's arrest, or the brutal attacks in the villages, also radicalized the tenant farmers into action and garnered greater sympathy in the villages for the movement and the activists. Younus Iqbal took the leading role in the movement in terms of spreading the word about the AMP protests and forging connections with civil society organizations, NGOs, and other influential entities. Younus is the energetic leader from the AMP who had been sidelined after being accused of corruption in terms of taking money from NGOs without consulting the movement. Younus went into training to become a Catholic cleric, because, as he put it, "I didn't want to live a life of servitude in the chaks" (interview by the author, March 3, 2007, Chak 10/4 L).[10] Younus Iqbal's career as a political leader can serve as an important illustration of the modes of resistance, the alliances, and the divisions within the movement. As a young man in the early 1980s, Younus opted to join the clergy to escape from sharecropping and the clutches of the military farms' authorities. During his training, he became involved with several NGOs and civil rights organizations that were working with Caritas, a Catholic charity organization, including Pak Kisan and several other organizations primarily working on bonded labor issues in Southern Punjab and Sindh. Younus left his clerical training to work with several NGOs as an organizer for the Bonded Labour Liberation Front (BLLF). He later returned to Chak 10. In 2001, when the tenants' movement was targeted by military authorities, Younus lobbied AMP leaders to not rely on longtime political representatives and local influential men like Sajjad Haider and Rao Sikander. He urged tenants to instead contact NGOs and especially those with international connections to spread the word about the AMP. He told me:

> I had experience working as an organizer for BLLF in Okara and Sahiwal. The Bonded Labor Act was passed in 1992 because of the attention and international pressure from overseas, not from internal pressure or a movement. So I was convinced that when they feel the pressure from outside, they

will themselves make a law for us, they will themselves pass legislation in the national assembly, and they will themselves implement these laws. Whenever we have worked with politicians, they have only used us for their own deal making, and then they made deals with the establishment. When we contacted NGOs and people started visiting us from Karachi and Islamabad, that's when people gained reassurance and became confident. . . .

We knew that NGOs gain funds and reputation for supporting our cause, but we felt as long as our message is getting out, that's fine. . . . I brought this issue to the NGOs; no one else knew about this thing [the AMP movement]. Then our message got out throughout the world. The media played a great role, but before we were able to bring these people from Karachi, Lahore, and Islamabad, no one would even put a line in the newspaper about our movement. The local journalists were scared to put anything against the government in the newspaper. (Interview by the author, March 3, 2007)

I had this conversation with Younus in Chak 10, a predominantly Christian village with a sizable Muslim population. In 2000, Chak 10 was the site of the first confrontation between the tenant farmers and the military farm authorities, an event that catalyzed the farmers' movement. But some AMP leaders criticize Younus Iqbal and his dealings with NGOs, and leveled allegations of corruption pertaining to his acceptance of donations and gifts for the movement. Yet it was Younus who acquired the documents about the disputed and contested right of the Pakistan military on this land. The debate over the leadership of the movement has garnered a lot of energy, but one consistent factor that has been noted then overlooked has been the role of women leaders and members in the AMP.

My interaction with female leaders was more constricted than with the males, because public gatherings were mostly male or divided by gender. Over time, I was able to meet some prominent leaders through my friendship with their family members. That allowed me to forge friendly relations with Nazira and Busra. They were most vocal in their disappointment with the AMP leadership, who largely ignored them now that there were no confrontations. Nazira had joined the mostly Christian camp of Younus's AMP, because she was given an honorific title of president and reassurance that she would play a central role in the movement. But Nazira felt sidelined and often was left out of the key decision and tactics. The women activists in the AMP across the spectrum were critical of the leadership, which had largely been absent from the villages during the confrontations then had come back to make deals and cozy up with the government officials. Women took a leading role in the protests, especially in confronting the police as they made their way into the villages to arrest AMP leaders. Busra, one of the AMP "political workers" (active members), took me to task for being too cautious when I confided my hesitation to talk with women leaders. Busra was one of the most dynamic leaders of the AMP. She helped organize the "Thapa force," which comprised a group of older women who carried "traditional laundry bats" to "greet and welcome" any soldiers or police personnel who tried to enter AMP villages to arrest a leader. Busra noted that she was radicalized after the October 2002 murder of Suleyman, a young man, as he raced to reach a village that was coming under siege by the police.

As Busra put it, the police and later Rangers forces thought that they could just come in and pick up the men and lock down the villages. They tried to torture the men and force them to sign the contract. But the women villagers decided that they could not let that happen. They organized and confronted the officers, thinking that they would not hit or beat up women or abduct them. They were wrong—the officers shot at them and hit them, but they could not hold them back. The women fought. The officers called in more female police officers to intimidate them, but the women felt that they had nothing left to fear: "We left our children at home crying, so what was there to fear now? . . . They would cry the same if we died." The women felt that if they had to die, then it was better to make a lot of noise, go to the highway, so that at least people would know that something was going down in Okara (Busra Bibi, interview by the author, June 23, 2007).

She noted that prominent female leaders were pushed aside, as most of the discussion about the movement took place in men's gatherings in *bhetaks*. Nazira joined Younus's AMP faction, and she was honored with the office of AMP president; but, as she confessed, this turned out to be an empty title, as she was not consulted in the planning, included in strategy, or kept informed about the funds received by this group. Younus's AMP group remained a one-person show (Nazira, interview by the author, July 1, 2007).

The arrest and intimidation of AMP leaders like Farid and Younus also gave rise to younger leaders like Mehr Abdul Sattar, who replaced Younus as the chairman of the AMP. Sattar barely has an acre of land to his name, but his reputation stems from the fact that he quit his master's program in veterinary science to come back to his village and advocate for the *mazarin*'s land rights. Sattar, unlike Younus, came from the traditionally influential Arain caste, and he took a more conservative view of the movement. Ironically, Sattar's moves to replace Younus as the chairperson of the AMP were supported by the leadership of the PRM.

I asked Sattar if the AMP would consider a plan that will improve living conditions for the landless laborers (*kammis*) in the village. Sattar sensed that I was talking about redistribution, and he replied that the AMP was not a communist organization, and the only reason the movement has been successful was the will of Allah. Sattar went on to note that Pakistan was slowly becoming a non-Muslim country under the policies of General Musharraf. He protested that the country's resolve on Jihad was weakening with the influence of NGOs and education reforms. Going back to my question, he said that if land was given to *mazaras*, then the laborers would benefit because greater prosperity would bring more work in the village (interview by the author, October 7, 2007). The answer I commonly got from other AMP leaders was that following the success of their demands to land ownership, the next major campaign by the AMP would be to fight inflation, and the rising costs of farming that is hurting small farmers. Sattar's orientation was different from Younus's, who had been instrumental in organizing the AMP and spreading the word about the movement.

Initially most leaders, like Farid Daula, minimized the differences between the factions by stating that all sides agreed on the fundamental things and neither side would accept the contract system or any deals with the military. Yet in passing conversations, there were many allusions to the greater influence wielded by the Christian community through the church and other nonprofit organizations, which were seen by some

AMP leaders as the apparatuses of Western governments. Influential Muslim AMP leaders reminded me several times that the Christians are poorer and they come from certain scheduled castes (formerly the sweeper or leatherworker castes). According to Farid, the lower-caste groups had converted to Christianity to escape their caste status. The Muslim AMP leadership's suspicion of Christian tenants often falls in the double bind of sectarian prejudice, where the "other" community is seen as both inferior and more powerful. The greater influence of the Christian community is offset by their lower caste position. However, it is important to note the schisms between different camps of the AMP that came so prominent in Okara Military Farms were not shared.

In this chapter, I show how the tenants' experience of historical suffering, poverty, and exploitation, as well as their fears of dispossession, forged a shared political subjectivity regarding the politics of survival as subsistence tenant farmers. I also discuss how within this movement the tenants' mobilization was fraught with lines of divisions about funding, divergent notions of community, and certain forms of hierarchy that reasserted itself in the course of the mobilization.[11] In Chapter 2, I show how the tenants' passionate attachments and their sense of belonging to the land are informed by a moral ecology of land rights that has been forged through a specific form of spatial practices that were put in place during the canal colonization of this region at the turn of twentieth century.

CHAPTER 2

THE AFTERLIFE OF COLONIAL
INFRASTRUCTURE

BERNARD COHN (1961) has noted that there is no singular past when it comes to the history of an Indian village. The political significance of Cohn's insight struck me when I started looking into the histories of the disputed military farms. Take the history of Chak 10, the oldest settled village of the Okara Military Farms and the site where the Punjab Tenants' Association (AMP) mobilization started when the first confrontation between the tenants and the state authorities took place in October 2000. Chak 10 was known as Anthonyabad when it was established in 1908, and it was supposed to be the first of several Christian mission villages planned by the Catholic Church to settle a growing population of lower-caste converts from Capuchin Jesuit missions in Sialkot and Narowal. The Capuchins priests were allotted land in the Lower Bari Doab to settle the newly converted Catholic peasants who hailed from landless service castes. The canal colonies were going to offer the Capuchin missionaries a space to inculcate Christian values and promise both "moral and material" progress to its new flock in the newly irrigated regions of Punjab (Harding 2008, 121). However, this project of social uplift for new convert communities ended abruptly with the outbreak of World War I in Europe. The church funds, which mostly came from northern Belgium, dried up when Belgium was occupied by Germany. As well, the British Indian government was wary of Jesuit Capuchin missionaries from Belgium, which was part of the Austro-Hungarian Empire at that time, and they expressed a desire to use the newly irrigated lands for military recruitment, cavalry runs, and regimental requests (Harding 2008). The bishop of Lahore returned these lands to the Punjab government in 1913, which in turn transferred the farms to the British Indian Army. The village underwent another transformation around the time of the partition of British India in 1947, when all Hindu and Sikh inhabitants (both tenants and farm managers) left for India, and Muslim peasants and farm managers took their place. This long-forgotten history of Chak 10, similar to that of many other villages, gained new salience with the rise of the Punjab Tenants' Association (AMP). The AMP invested great significance in the overlooked history of tenant farmers and their suffering on this farmland to make claims to the land.

My inquiry into the history of the Okara Military Farms started out with the objective of finding some clear documentation of the legal status of these eighteen villages established at the turn of the twentieth century. I decided to look for the land title deed, a file that became all-important in 2000, when the military unilaterally changed the land tenure system on its vast commercial farm estates from *battai* (rent-in-kind sharecropping) to a cash-contract-based tenure system. The missing file dates back to 1913 and lays out the lease details about the allotment of oat-hay farms to the British Indian Army for a twenty-year period. The tenant farmers had tracked down a mention of the land title allotment for the farms, which clearly states that the government of India (British India) would make a recurring payment of 15,000 rupees per year to the provincial government of Punjab for the loss of "land revenue and *malikana* [occupancy] charges in respect of the land which it is proposed to allot for an oat-hay farm in the Lower Bari Doab Colony" (Executive District Officer Revenue 2003). The summary report does not give any further details, but it demonstrates that the land belonged to the civilian government of Punjab and not the Pakistan Army. The file is missing in the Punjab Revenue archives but is known to exist, as it has been cited by other revenue reports dating back to the 1920s.[1]

In my search for the missing document, I was surprised to learn that most tenant farmers did not emphasize their technical legal claims on the land. After all, there was clear evidence that the land was technically the property of Punjab civil government and the military's lease on the land had long expired. Moreover, the military had not paid any rent on this land or shown any revenues. The nongovernmental organization (NGO) community and civil society emphasized these legal cases, whereas the tenants invoked a moral claim to this land based on an archive of their experiences, sentiments, and memories of suffering while working on the land. The AMP stakes the tenants' claims based on their history of laboring and cultivating this farmland, and the group used this history of settlement to resist the army's imposition of the cash contract system.

In this chapter, I examine how the legacies of canal colonization shaped the political subjectivity of tenant farmers and established the conditions of possibility for the rise of the AMP. I use historical narratives as relayed through documents and stories about the different kinds of worlds that were opened up by colonial engineering—and other possible worlds that were foreclosed—at the turn of the twentieth century.[2] Canal colonization had far-reaching impacts in structuring the cultural, economic, and political spaces that brought new forms of communications. I argue that the AMP's claim to land rights is based on a moral economy tied to the politics of infrastructure integral to the agricultural settlement of this region.

More specifically, I analyze the material-semiotic agency of infrastructures like roads, canals, and railways in shaping a politics of place in Punjab. Overall, I trace the tenants' changing relationship to the state, from the initial settlement of the farms (territorialization) to the current state of uncertainty engendered by the military's effort to commoditize land relations (deterritorialization). This history of settlement and commoditization shows how governmental power is embedded in the politics of land and livelihood. As Talal Asad has argued, the point of application of modern power is not necessarily the body of the subject but the conditions in which that body is to live and define its life (Scott 1998, 199; see also Asad 2003).

Recent anthropological and historical scholarship on infrastructure has highlighted the important role of public works projects in the formation of the modern state and political subjects (Klingensmith 2007;

Larkin 2008). This body of scholarship examines the constitutive yet often concealed role of infrastructure projects like roads, canals, railways, and telegraphs in giving shape to the everyday experience of the state and the making of political subjectivities in the modern era. Cultural anthropologists study infrastructures as ethnographic objects and systems to analyze the points of connection through which the modern state entered the ordinary lives of people in remarkably diverse regions, tying them to modes of association and material-semiotic exchange. While this literature focuses on postwar and contemporary relations, I am interested in how infrastructures personify multiple layers of reciprocity between the paternalist colonial state and the peasantry and how in Punjab this enabled the AMP to make a moral case for tenant farmers' land rights. I approach this region and land rights movement as neither "an accomplished fact" (modern Punjab, pro-establishment Punjab) nor a "formless tendency" (an inevitable propensity) but rather as "an occupied space of contingency and desire" (Stewart 1996, 90).

Unlike the other major irrigation projects in colonial India (such as the irrigation projects in the Ganges River basin in current-day Uttar Pradesh and the Kaveri River in Madras), which took place in settled agricultural areas, the Punjab canal colonies were unique in that the irrigation projects took shape in a place without a permanent settled population, and as such were not constrained by the considerations of local populations. The entire infrastructural network of canals, roads, train stations, villages, towns, and central districts of the Indus River basin was being laid down at the same time as a select migrant settler peasant population was moving in.

While rivers have been the source of intensive agriculture and urban formation in different parts of the Indus Plain for millennia, the colonial irrigation projects were different in that state engineers far away from villages, rather than the local community, controlled these canals. The canal colonization schemes closed the open Indus frontier by settling migrant farmers and nomadic indigenous tribes there. The 1853 *General Report upon the Administration of the Punjab Proper* contrasts this region with the verdant regions of eastern Punjab in 1851, two years after the annexation of Punjab. The report offers an account of the scrublands or the jungle, which is overgrown with grass and bushes, threaded by sheep-walks and cattle footprints. The inhabitants of these parts are nomadic pastoral tribes, who know "neither law or property"; they are said to collect herds of cattle stolen from agricultural districts. The document goes on to note that their odd sights of hamlets in the wilderness that are farmed by "a semi-barbarous population" who come from the same group as the aforementioned "aborigines." There are signs of previous cultivation and wealth because there are ruined cities, villages, temples, tanks, wells, and watercourses. As early as in 1853, the colonial state saw this region as a strategic asset to supply firewood, pasturage, dairy supplies, and gigantic projects that would take in lots of capital but produce. "Indeed the Punjab could ill spare its wastes: they are almost as important as the cultivated tracts" (Government of Punjab 1853, 4).

Fittingly, the lands irrigated by canal colonies were referred to as "command areas," with branches flowing out across rectangular plots, each of which was to become a chak, or designated village site. Slowly the entire Indus basin became an interconnected network, as the engineers turned the river into a machine, with centralized water control and command (Darling 1925; Aloys 1967). The bureaucratic nomenclature of village names in the region, as in Chak 33/3 L (where 33 is the unique number of the village on a certain branch of the canal, and 3 L tells us that this village is the third on the left side of that branch), is a testimony to the engineered history of this landscape. Regional modernity entailed a transformation that involved routing the rivers and connecting the irrigated plains to the cities via railroad tracks to port cities and imperial networks of trade.

Initially, it is important to note, the irrigation works were not planned with the stated objective of creating modern Indian peasants or collecting large sums of revenue. Instead the initial irrigation works came out of more-immediate considerations for security "by finding some kind of work for the disbanded Sikh soldiers, who immediately after annexation were demobilized and left without any settled mode of earning a living in a peaceful manner" (Paustian 1930, 27). The biblical proverb of "turning swords into plowshares" was invoked in the earliest projects, such as the extension of the Mughal-era Huslie canal that served Lahore and

Amritsar (27). However, the great success of new public works projects, coupled with the general orderliness of Punjab following the 1857 Indian mutiny, gave impetus to a more ambitious vision of irrigation along the lines of a paternalistic approach to government that became widely known as the Punjab Tradition (van den Dungen 1972; Michel 1967). In his influential book *Irrigated India: An Australian View of India and Ceylon, Their Irrigation and Agriculture*, Alfred Deakin, the distinguished Australian statesman, summed up his admiration of Indian irrigation works in terms of a political vocation: "What the soldier begins the irrigation engineer continues" (quoted in Gilmartin 2015, 69).

The former grazing grounds of the Indus Plain were parceled out ("killabandied" in Anglo-Indian bureaucratic language) in twenty-five- to twenty-eight-acre squares that were allotted or auctioned to a select caste of peasantry and retired servicemen (noncommissioned officers). The dramatic success of the early canal colonies resulted in growing requests to reward army veterans, appease tribal chieftains, and restore the prominence of caretakers of Sufi shrines and notable families of influence who served as intermediaries for the British colonial state. Mixed with these new allotments were other considerations, such as institutional grants related to military needs like the allotment of large mare farms, and charitable grants to reformist religious organizations (like Christian missionary societies, the reformist Arya Samaj dharamshalas, and the Ahmadi missions).[3]

Encouraged by modest early success, the colonial state embarked on more-ambitious projects. As early as 1887, the colonial state dramatically expanded the scope of the irrigation works with the Chenab project that watered two million acres of scrubland. By 1900, it was successful in repaying the entire cost of construction. By 1946, it is estimated that the Chenab colony had repaid the original investment by more than 1,100 percent. However, with the expansion of these projects came new considerations, as occurred in the planning of the Lower Bari Doab colony, the last major canal colonization plan and also a central site of struggle for the AMP. The military farms located in the Lower Bari Doab were the last and most ambitious of the eight canal colonization projects taken up by the British colonial state. The success of the canal colony schemes

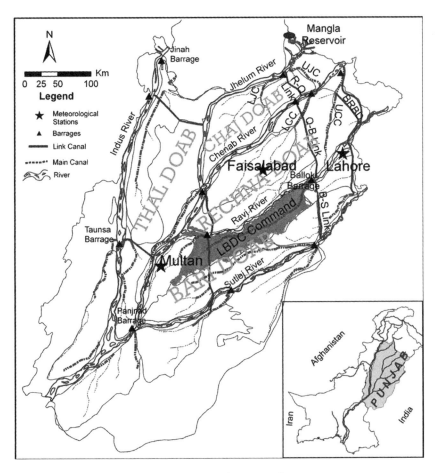

Lower Bari Doab Canal Colony. Command scale integrated water management in response to spatial climate variability in Lower Bari Doab Canal irrigation system. Source: Basharat, Umair, and Azhar 2014.

opened up over fourteen million acres of land in the late nineteenth-century and early twentieth-century Punjab.

DIFFERENT WAYS OF SEEING A PLACE

While, roads, trains, and canals carried means of progress and modernity in Britain, they took on added significance in British India, where these technologies were used to justify the beneficial or even redemptive aspects of colonial rule, while also establishing the crucial difference between the colonizer and colonized. These technological wonders and the dreams associated with them gave rise to a colonial gift economy. Scholars argue that a gift economy creates personalized relationships between people through objects; the exchange of gifts generates mutual recognition, while at the same time incurring debts and obligations to reciprocate in kind.

In his foundational essay on gift, "Essai sur la Don," Marcel Mauss argued that the gift object takes on part of the personality of the giver (Mauss 2016). "Gift" creates a personalized relationship between people through objects. The exchange of gifts generates mutual recognition while instantiating differences, incurring debts, and creating obligations. Mauss quotes a Maori sage, Tamati Ranapiri, to argue that during this process, part of the donor's soul becomes entangled in the gift, and through its wish to return home, compels the recipient to reciprocate the gift. The anthropological literature on gift exchange hence distinguishes the personal exchange of gifts in precapitalist societies from the impersonal market exchange. This formal distinction creates an analytical division between premodern gift economies of custom and modern capitalist societies wherein social institutions are separated from the formal market sphere of "economy."

I argue that in the case of Punjab, the canals, roads, market towns falling in the canal colony area like Lyallpur (Faisalabad), Montgomery (Sahiwal), and Khanewal became "object examples" or "totems" of British colonial rule. The rich landscape of Central Punjab is still indelibly connected to British colonial rule, yet it is also subject to the moral and material unequal exchange that is based on forms of patronage, and set of obligation expected from the state in the form of protections, sharecropping, and food security.

Hence, a gift economy is not always reducible to premarket conditions alone.[4] The reciprocal relations that establish mutual recognition and obligations between the giver and receiver take on different meanings over the course of exchange. Thus, in colonial Punjab, the landscape-altering and society-changing projects of canal building, along with roads, rail, and model villages, elicited a politics of mutual recognition that was carried out through material and symbolic exchange. Further, these exchanges resulted in what the anthropologist Christopher Gregory has called the "efflorescence of gift exchange" in the colonial period, by which gifts turned into commodities and commodities into gifts (Gregory 2015, xxii). In writing about the political economy of Papua New Guinea, Gregory contends that "the colonial imposition of a commodity economy from above did not destroy the indigenous gift economy but created unintended conditions from below" (xxii).[5] As Richard Fox has shown, the market penetration of Punjab's agriculture forced landlords to maintain or even revert to collecting rentals in kind rather than cash from their best lands (Fox 1985, 222n30). Rentals in kind based on a fixed share of the harvest were a rational extension of market agriculture in the sense that they cushioned hard-pressed peasants in times of bad harvests. These emerging markets were tied to the global circuit of cotton or wheat, and thus they were a form of agricultural commercialization, even if they were organized through rent paid in kind by tenants exercising their usufruct rights. Similarly, the massive transfer of land allotment in colonial Punjab was done on the basis of preserving customary rank as well as intensifying cash crop agriculture.

By discussing the symbolic gift exchange of colonial infrastructure, I do not dismiss the extractive and exploitive aspects of colonialism. Instead, I foreground the symbolic exchange between customary Punjab and the emerging modern paternalist state that occurred through infrastructure projects from the period of canal construction to the present era. This distinction is clear in the case of military farms, where the notion of reciprocity is central to the facilitation and contestation of identity and land rights. In this instance, there are multiple actors who are anxious to claim land that was made fertile through infrastructural projects and where the landscape-altering projects of canal construction, road building, and railways are weighted in the moral economy of reciprocity. The breakdown in the sharecropping arrangement brought this tension to the surface in the form of subaltern histories of canal colonization.

In this context, the reciprocal relationships established by infrastructure projects forged a hierarchical structure of state patronage and land allotment in the form of subsistence, as well as agrarian industry and belief in improvement. These arrangements were imbued with the ambiguity inherent in gift exchange because of the colonial nature of the enterprise, which promised radical change and also reestablished traditional modes of authority within modern frameworks of government.

A TALE ABOUT A FAKIR AND AN ENGINEER

Keeping in mind these spatial presuppositions, consider the politics of nature, space-time, and government that can be gleaned from a thin booklet, *Youngest Punjab Canal Colony*. The Government of Punjab printed the pamphlet in 1920 to publicize the opening of Lower Bari Doab, the largest of seven canal colonies and home to the disputed farms. *Youngest Colony* sets the stage with a mythic fable about an itinerant fakir who was roaming across the tract now known as the Lower Bari Doab that lies between the Ravi River and the Beas River. According to the legend, the fakir was insulted by the prosperous, arrogant inhabitants of the towns on the banks of Beas River, and he emptied the Beas with his *lota* (a round water pot used for ablutions) and diverted its water into the Sutlej River at point three hundred miles above the old confluence of the rivers. Hence the blight and hideousness of the land, which only a twentieth-century miracle could redeem (Government of Punjab 1920, 2).

With these opening words, the pamphlet orients the reader to visualize the landscape of Gunji Bar, the high plains of Central Punjab, through the intimate device of narrative. In the pithy sentences and vivid images that typify the (fictive) nonfiction colonial writing and travelogues, the pamphlet foregrounds the experiential and aesthetic modes through which the reader comes to see the Indus Plain as "wastelands" that can only be redeemed by modern irrigation technology.

The pamphlet offers a reclamation narrative wherein the colonial state restores back to life what was once a prosperous land, cursed by a roving fakir (a Sufi mendicant). It rehearses the millennial vision of water's restorative powers in making the desert into a garden by directing the reader to visually orient himself (the subject of this testimonial is always *he*) as an "average passenger in the Karachi mail, as he travels space and time to the youngest canal colony, [he] may perhaps notice where there used to be solitude and crops where there was nothing but caked mud and sand, but it is doubtful if he has any idea of what the reclamation of the desert means" (Government of Punjab 1920, 4). The reader is invited to witness the work of canals with related modern infrastructure, such as roads, railways, and the telegraph, weaving the arid expanse of Central Punjab into the fold of modern colonial administrative institutions. The historical documents on the settlement of Punjab share the visual simplicity of the image where the barren landscape of Lower Bari Doab spreads out like a map before the reader's eye. The pamphlet instructs the reader to imagine taking a trip on the Karachi mail train ten years prior to canal irrigation, when the entire region was a collection of sand hills and barren plains full of dreary emptiness broken by "the vivid mirage of water and trees which for mile after mile form ahead and vanish as the train approaches" (Government of Punjab 1920, 1). The only signs of life were occasional wayfarers mounted on camels, or an encampment of nomadic wanderers moving across the desert brush.

Soon a new landscape came into view as the train made its way into the young canal colony: "as far as the eye could see and stretching back for miles on either side, rich fields of cotton, maize and cane or, in the spring, great expanses of wheat, relieved by bright yellow scarves of mustard, greet the eye" (Government of Punjab 1920, 1). In this idyllic image, one can see "flourishing towns, each with its mills and factories ... and every station is thronged with a crowd of prosperous peasants" (1). The booklet makes it clear that no revenue report can ever do justice to the sublime transformation under way: "One could fill a stout Government report with details of distribution and figures indicating the nature of the change that water has brought to land, but statistics, however illuminating to the initiated, convey little to the man on the train" (2). The changes in the land had to be seen to be believed. Indeed, the sight of this landscape was so powerful that one of the most ardent critics of the expensive irrigation works, the British commissioner in Sindh, was completely disarmed after witnessing the geometric regularity of the new fields of the Chenab colony (Gilmartin 2004, 6).[6]

The artful competition between the two different domains of authority that lay claim to this space, embodied by the fakir and the engineer, highlights the colonial encounter where the technological superiority of the British colonial state seen as giving it the right to rule. Hence, the irrigation of the youngest Punjab canal colony was "the latter-day miracle [that] transcends that of the Faqir though the Beas is still obedient to his spell" (Government of Punjab 1920, 1). In conferring legitimacy to the colonial state, this allegory also performs a subtler act of elision of the local technological history of waterworks and economic and information exchange carried on by the region's inhabitants, a key omission that makes way for the rule of experts, bureaucrats, engineers, and multinational aid organizations whose long-distance expertise is based on neatly demarcated technological models and projects that simplify local reality based on market valuation (Scott 1998). Things are divided in a binary of value and waste, instead of looking at the habitat as a whole; other community and human uses are ignored in favor of a utilitarian vision. Hence, these material projects come to be associated with projects of rule by indigenous communities.[7]

Canals and trains are part of the modern technological infrastructure that expands the reach of state institutions, connecting remote terrain in a network of administration, economy, and communication that Henri Lefebvre calls "state space" (Lefebvre 1991, 23). In the face of such rationalization (in Weberian terms), the train also incites a proliferating set of reactions of apprehension, awe, and fear. More than anything, the moving train stands as the potent symbol of modern technological progress and mobility, even as the canals deceptively meld into the ecological milieu of the landscape. But as we continue to learn, knowledge is a social product, and the promise of technological progress cannot ignore the social worlds that technologies come to inhabit.

The railway tracks connected places, however remote, in a network that compressed the distance between the high plains of Ganji Bar and the port city of Karachi. Karachi took the shape of a cosmopolitan city in relation to the growing volume of trade flowing out from the Indus Plain, as the canal colonies quickly became the largest producers of cotton and grains in British India and used Karachi as their seaport. With the advent of trains, the old trade routes over rivers became insignificant, and the overland markets in Shikarpur were passed over by the train.

In Punjab, as in the colonial world, modern trains, canals, bridges, and roads were "made into totems and placed in the center stage in society . . .

the material objects through which the relationship between the ruler and ruled were embodied" (Larkin 2008, 247). However, these "totems" turned out to be more than just symbols of technological prowess and dominance, as they were domesticated over time into the material and cultural worlds of the ruled communities through ballads, narratives, and short stories.[8]

This comes across beautifully in a short story by Ahmed Nadeem Qasmi (1973) about the coming of the train and canals to the arid region of Thal, which slowly found itself transformed with advent of irrigation and railway projects. The story gives an account of what the passing train means to the peasant farmers who reside in a place that is about to be connected to the infrastructural grid of railways and canals. In the typical brevity of an Urdu short story, Qasmi charts the life course of a young man, Misri Khan, who overcomes the desire for the prosperous life in a distant river valley to toil in the same place where his father and grandfather struggled to eke out a livelihood. Thal is a parched landscape of sandstorms and blazing sun, where the kikar trees whistle as the hot summer wind blows through the naked reed branches. Yet this very earth swells up with wildflowers with a rare hint of rain, and the kikars bloom with fragrant yellow flowers when torrents rush down from not so distant mountains. It is a place dotted by small homesteads where people's livelihoods involve livestock and scant seasonal farming, a way of life suddenly broken as irrigation engineers and railway tracks make their way into Thal.

In contrast to the pamphlet, Qasmi indicates that the emergence of trains and canals encapsulates different layers of meaning for the peasant inhabitants who struggle to make sense of these technologies. These challenges are realized through a set of symbols, beliefs, and fears that are embedded in different conceptions of space and authority. Here I paraphrase another section of this story. The narrative begins with an old man recalling the time when the first rail tracks were laid down in Thal. These tracks were approaching the sacred space of the Hazrat Pir (a local Sufi saint) shrine in Thal when a powerful dust storm covered the tracks with sand. On that very night, an army of jinns and goblins descended on the tracks and chewed up the steel rails like stalks of sugarcane. The

English engineer awoke the next morning to a strange sight: chewed-up peels of steel scattered here and there as if floating everywhere on sand. It was then that the British cooked seven large pots (*deghs*) of sweet rice and distributed it to the needy on that very site. This ritual of feeding of people (irrespective of need) is a traditional means of warding off the evil eye. The engineers had to set up a *langar*, a common customary offering of food to the community to atone for any wrongdoing, to seek protection from evil, and to propitiate the sacred order; another example of Sufi saints' supremacy in this story. The route for the railway station changed, and that is why the train makes such a steep detour to get to the next station (Qasmi 1973, 32).

Instead of severing two different life-worlds, Qasmi's Thal evokes the technological wonder of modern trains as it is embedded in the cultural world shaped by the charismatic power of the pir. Qasmi's story shows how preexisting modes of authority rework modern infrastructures into their own interpretive world. For example, the engineer atoned for violating Hazrat Pir's shrine and its surrounding sacred space by offering a lavish amount of food and a large *langar*, a customary practice of spiritual gain (baraka) by serving the needy and common people who reside in the area. More important, the route of the train was changed in order to steer clear of Hazrat Pir's wrath. For the residents of Thal, the sharp turn taken by the railway before the next station indicated the spiritual agency of Hazrat Pir.

In the end, the railway track was laid down, but the contest between the spiritual powers of the local pir and the English technology continued. Qasmi's story goes on to describe the contest in the following way. The English railway engineer was frustrated by the onset of massive sandstorms that covered the tracks. He wrote a pleading letter to Delhi headquarters complaining about the curse of massive sandstorms that deposited entire sand dunes on the tracks. The Delhi rail headquarters acquired an amulet, from the big pir (Sufi saint) of Delhi, which was hung on the shrubs near the tracks. The amulet tamed the extreme weather, as the sandstorms stayed clear of the tracks. But the local saint was more powerful, because a few weeks afterward, a large sandstorm gathered near the tracks and overpowered the amulet, leaving mountain of sand on the tracks. Hazrat Pir and the pirs from Delhi were locked in a tight contest for as long as they laid down tracks in this region. Hazrat Pir's jinns and goblins seem to be active to the present day, which is why local people acquire amulets from the local shrine before they get on the trains.

The accidents and dangers tied to trains, represented in Qasmi's folk story, speak of this technology's mysterious agency, a mystery that lessened over time as trains became a familiar sight and people learned to negotiate their associated dangers. The contest between Hazrat Pir and the Delhi pirs continued as people stayed on good terms with the local Sufi saint while also traveling on the train. Over time the residents of Thal came to depend on the convenience of the train but found it prudent to get an amulet from Hazrat Pir's shrine before embarking on a journey, to lessen its physical and moral dangers. The trade in travel amulets was a boon to the shrine keeper (Khan Bahadur), who was happy to comply with British designs for rail tracks that violated the sacred space of the shrine. The entire village changed with the coming of the train and canals, yet this change was indelibly local and subject to the history of culture-power that linked the train with colonial forms of rule as well as local forms of authority. Hence the train not only enabled more intensive agriculture, trade, and travel, but also served to underscore the powers of Hazrat Pir, as well as the existing hierarchies, fears, and agencies that were remade with the coming of this new technology. As the story shows, the onset of modern infrastructure does not eradicate the local; instead, these structures are layered on top of existing social worlds as an intense force of connection, a relay point that materializes through conflicts and collaborations in strange articulations.

COLONIAL INFRASTRUCTURE AS GIFT

With this discussion of the cultural life of technologies, I return to the social milieu described in the *Youngest Punjab Canal Colony* pamphlet as it introduces the cast of characters who inhabit the new canal colony. It begins with the vision of a crowded railway station platform in Montgomery, today Sahiwal, a city that the pamphlet labels "a microcosm of the colony." "Take the crowd on the [train] platform, it is the microcosm of the colony" (Government of Punjab 1920, 3). Among the crowd we meet "the Mohammedan peasant with the red beard and the bundle of sugar . . . whose land has been eaten up by the [River] Sutlej" (3). At times the pamphlet suggests that the crowded platform and the open vistas of irrigated fields anticipate a future world where this engineered landscape will dissolve caste hierarchies, reform criminal tribes, and promise uplift to peasant laborers, thus making way for a new public that owes its existence to colonial-era trains and canals. "The Christian, the ex-dacoit [bandit], the Pindi Lothario [absentee landlord], the sad looking Arain [Muslim agrarian caste] whose property has been devoured by the Sutlej occupy two or three square yards of the platform. Clean and unclean, primitive and evolved, touchable and untouchable are herded together in the press for the train." Even in this passage there is martial figure, a retired soldier whose need for space is noted on what is a crowded platform. "Among them there is one dominating figure a retired Subadar of the Punjabi Cavalry, whose military bearing would command a square yard to himself, if there were any corner for the crowd to disperse into" (Government of Punjab 1920, 3).

As this passage from the pamphlet demonstrates, the function of infrastructure cannot be studied as something with the simple use value of transport, communication, and trade, but must be seen within the context of preexisting cultural frames that shape their reception and modify their meaning and function. The pamphlet proclaims that the new canal colony with its colonial-era trains and canals that will dissolve caste and ethnic prejudice to produce an industrious and disciplined social body.[9] But the pamphlet's description of the crowded platform also tells another story of difference, one that is made up of different subjects who are affected by different forms of recognition. The crowd ranges from the displaced peasant to the Pindi lothario, from the Christian convert to the dominant figure of the British Indian Army veteran who had served in Europe during World War I. A survey of this crowded platform shows the "contingent nature of the state, produced out of the processes through which it constitutes its populations" (Ghosh 2006, 507).

The assembled public belies the all-encompassing unity that is expected of the modern state. Caste, religious identities, class rank, and military service determine the different modes of address and the kinds of governmental programs that apply, what capacities are to be enhanced, and what kinds of conduct to monitor. In fact, the crowded platform serves as a deconstructive case against the idea of modern civil society, where in theory the political domain is stripped of its particular histories into abstract universal categories of citizenship and civil society. Far from dissolving caste, or erasing premodern forms of association, the crowded platform shows how colonial governmentality relies on a much more paradoxical preservation of these distinct identities.

In a suggestive article, Kaushik Ghosh (2006) has outlined what he sees as two modes of governmentality, whereby the colonial state works to partly incorporate or partially exclude subject populations.[10] One is a process of gradual incorporation through which the rule of law and the market assimilate certain populations, who in the final instance can become good citizen-subjects, such as the Pindi lothario, the zamindar, or the army veteran. This "politics of recognition" also works through exclusion by emphasizing the exception of a given population from common law. Universal citizenship holds little weight where modern subjects are indelibly marked by communal identities, caste distinctions, and "traditional" modes of labor like the peasantry. Hence the domain of citizenship remains extremely fragmented and constricted.

Ghosh develops his theory of inclusive and exclusive governmentality with regard to the question of the Adivasi community, but his formulation can be applied to a wider question of customary identities as applied to ethnic, caste, and tribal categories. The missionary reform colonies for lower-caste converts, the carceral villages for the nomadic tribal groups, and the special protections for loyal gentry whose fortunes are fading all fit into the particular framing of "preservation" and "protection" of customary distinctions of cooperative nobility, collaborative religious who lend themselves to indirect rule by the government commissioner, Christian missionary, and designated tribal chief. Similarly, there were parallel projects of reform and uplift passed to improve the conditions of the downtrodden in the name of improvement. The religious missions and Indian reform groups were given preference for these projects. The British Indian Army also got a large section of land allotments in Lower Bari Doab. The settlement of Lower Bari Doab gave large "gentry grants"

(150 acres) to specific elite clans like Qureshis and Rajputs, while middle-size grants were given to capitalists or investors for capitalist farming, and the large section of the land was allotted as twenty-five-acre plots to traditional agricultural castes like Arain, Kamboh, and Jat. These policies strengthened traditional hierarchies, but the settlement policies did not allot lands to landless farm laborer *kammi* communities, which were generally restricted. There were some exceptions in Okara, like the Capuchin Catholic villages, where landless Christians lived, as well as Hindus and Muslims whose lands were given to certain charitable foundations or churches. This differential form of land allotment created an economy of expectations, obligations, and rights based on the ethnological praxis of the land settlement of the canal colonies.

The pamphlet presents the coming of trains and canals as a gift that borders on a miracle in its ability to reshape rural Punjab. However, as Mauss has illustrated, the "spirit of the gift" ensures that the gift is never simply altruistic: there is always some compulsion and obligation to return and reciprocate (2016, 132). The spirit of the gift lies in mutual recognition and exchange, where the promise of modern improvement and technical progress comes in exchange with state subjugation. The reciprocal relations entailed within the "gift" of colonial infrastructure involve "two opposite movements . . . contained in a single act—the gift decreases the distance between the protagonists as sharing but it increases social distances between them as debt" (Godelier 1999, 12).

Thinking about colonial infrastructure in relation to the gift focuses our attention on how these relations of rule may be formed around material objects like canals, irrigated land, and railways. The idea of colonial infrastructure as gift parallels Michel Foucault's theory of governmentality insofar as modern infrastructures aim to guide conduct among subjects whose agency is deployed rather than destroyed (see Gordon 1994). Further, the increase in capacity brought about by modern infrastructures fits into the larger schema of governmentality; as increased aptitude comes with increased domination, the increase in production came with the increase in total control. For example, in the pre-canal colonies, water storage techniques followed seasonal floods, and digging water tanks and the *cherr* system gave the more sparsely settled villages and communities control over their water directions. However, the perennial canals in canal colonies transferred the entire control over water to the state administration, which selectively allotted lands and village parcels to different communities based on its own understanding of utility and Indian custom.

Even before the establishment of the canal colonies, administrators like Richard C. Temple argued that agricultural settlement was important not only for establishing order but also, and even more critically, for encouraging a general "moral" transformation that would cause Punjabi peasants and their rural social structures to improve under the guidance of the colonial legal structure. Quoting Smetis Thorburn, a senior civil service officer at the turn of the century, Malcolm Darling writes, "In 1849–50 'we converted collective into individual ownership of land, plus the right to alienate it at pleasure. By so doing we made an *un-conditional gift* of a valuable estate to every peasant proprietor in the Punjab' whereby the value and profit of the land was not limited by the constraints of local customs" (1925, 97; emphasis added). Yet we know that land allotment and proprietorship were almost always refracted through local social realities, including customary laws that found certain rural populations and tribes wanting for actual proprietorship. Thorburn himself wrote an entire book, *Musalmans and Money-Lenders in the Punjab* ([1886] 1983), on the need to restrict land alienation among indebted Muslim peasants who were increasingly losing farmland to moneylenders in central-western Punjab.

As Ghosh notes, this "protection" of specific communities, while not compatible with market principles and capitalism, says something about how states come to recognize "different subjectivities that do not fully correspond to the homogeneous time of the citizen" (Ghosh 2006, 508). They have to be ruled according to their customary laws, which have to discovered and documented: "This is where the colonial anthropology of customary law emerged" (507). Here we see the colonial state working in two different modes of incorporation, through market and laws, while at the same time isolating and protecting certain attributes that are not seen as compatible with market principles. We can see this logic at work in the pamphlet, which, like most colonial texts, strides along the contradictory path of promising radical change and preservation, inclusion and exclusion, offering utopian possibilities of modernity while at the same time resignifying traditional identities, enumerating ethnicities, and sedimenting Punjabi hierarchies into entrenched modes of legal address.

Imran Ali, a historian of the canal colonies, observes the following in his preface to *The Punjab Under Imperialism, 1885–1947*: "The great agricultural colonization schemes undertaken in the western Punjab during British rule turned this area into a virtual human laboratory, as castes, clans and tribes from different parts of the province converged on the new lands" (1988, viii). Perhaps the analogy of the laboratory can also be used to describe the "ethnological" praxis deployed to discriminate between who received land grants and who did not. Ethnological surveys, census reports, land revenue reports, and consultation with local notables were used to make the diverse communities of Punjab legible to colonial administrators in terms of fixed "castes," customs (including the capacity for different kinds of labor), and "tribes."

Officials created a chart of habits and customs of the diverse communities that lived in Punjab to select the most "suitable" members to colonize these farms. Most of the land grantees were brought in from rich agrarian and "overcrowded" regions of eastern and central Punjabi districts like Jullunder, Lahore, Gurdaspur, and Hoshiarpur.[11] Malcolm Darling identifies two groups as the ideal candidates for settling the newly irrigated canal colonies in his survey of peasant debt in canal colonies: the Jat Sikh and the Arain. The Jat Sikh group, he writes, "has been described as 'the most desirable of colonists.' Grit skill in farming and a fine physique are characteristics common to all, and on his new environment the Jat Sikh has reached a point of development probably beyond anything else of the kind in India. . . . The Arain, the prince of market gardeners, is his only rival. As thrifty as he is prolific, from dawn till eve bent over cabbage and onions able to draw a living from the tiniest of plots" (Darling 1925, 136–137). The myth of the *abadkar* (or settler) peasant from central and eastern Punjab was instantiated by the infrastructural support and steady water access provided to these farmers in the canal colonies. The land development and irrigation policies have led to uneven development in Punjab, and they have also delimited the borders of Punjabi identity. The southern and western sections of Punjab that were under control of large landowners were mostly excluded from land grants. Hence both zamindari and *ryotwari* (landlord estate and individual peasant tenancy systems) coexisted in different regions of Punjab. The southern and western regions fell into greater poverty with the changing economy and lack of access to a regular water supply, which was required with the growing productivity of canal colonies and greater monetization of agriculture. The southern section of Punjab is technically part of the province, but the majority of the people here feel geographically, economically, politically, and ethnically distinct from central-northern Punjabis; instead they refer to themselves as "Saraiki." The denial of land grants and neglect of southern Punjab, especially following the Indus Waters Treaty between India and Pakistan that diverted water away from this area, has led to popular agitation and calls for greater autonomy.

Tribal, caste, and religious categories thus become characterized by a rigid boundedness as they transcend context and are not "fuzzy" (Ghosh 2006, 508). Other populations like nomadic petty traders, pastoralists, and plains- and jungle-dwelling tribal groups who did not conform to the model of settled agricultural and wage labor were either criminalized under the Criminal Tribes Act of 1871 or forced into settlements where they were disciplined into agrarian life (Arnold 1986, 85).[12] The nomadic pastoral communities include the "Janglis," who were mostly cattle herders; Bilochis, who were noted for their camel herds used for long-distance trade and transport; Hitharis, who farmed on the edge of riverbanks; and other local groups. These communities were mostly deemed unfit for the model villages that were built in the newly irrigated plains of Punjab. For instance, take the case of the reform and settlement of so-called criminal tribes into penal colonies, where they would receive colonial pedagogy. The pamphlet describes them in this fashion:

> [Of] the criminal tribes . . . whose reclamation is being undertaken by government with conspicuous successes . . . the more disciplined are collected in settlements under supervision. Their villages are laid out in the form of walled barracks with a single entrance, which can be without a pass. . . . An incidental result of the salvage of bad lands and thievish men is the increased security of property. (Government of Punjab 1920, 5)

The "criminal tribes" were classified as wandering tribes who were thought to be dangerous, especially in regard to respecting property and the settled tribes. Designated criminal tribes were held in a restricted area and could not leave without a pass. Entire communities or clans would be notified of their classification as criminal tribes and be subject to constant inspection and limited mobility. As a report on the administration of criminal tribes in Punjab noted in 1919, "The introduction of the scheme has not only resulted in the obvious transformation of criminal tribesmen placed in settlements, but the effect of it on the criminal tribes generally has been to make them anxious to find remunerative occupation in their places of residence for fear of being removed to settlements" (Government of Punjab 1919, 2). These penal colonies also became a source of cheap labor to "expedite the constructions of military barracks at a time when, owing to recruitment and other causes, labour was very scarce" (2).[13]

Land allotments were denied to indigenous wandering tribes, but there were handsome rewards for war veterans and distinguished soldiers, used as a tool for military recruitment. The *Youngest Punjab Canal Colony* paints the area as a home to soldiers: "As is natural in the premier military province of India, the Lower Bari Doab colony is associated in many ways with the army. By the cavalry in particular it will be recognized as a most important horse-breeding area" (Government of Punjab 1920, 4). The pamphlet gives the example of Gurbachan Das, who distinguished himself fighting in South Africa, settled in Australia, fought the Ottoman Empire as a volunteer soldier in Gallipoli, and chose to retire in the new canal colony, where he started a large farm.[14]

Another kind of land allotment was granted to preserve the fortunes of the landed gentry who remained loyal to the colonial state but found their fortunes fading because of primogeniture. Thus, the *Youngest Punjab Canal Colony* states, "Another important provision of the colony is the allotment of farms to the landed gentry when property has not kept pace with the growing wealth of the middle classes and the peasantry. This fine old stock, the real leaders of the country and the strongest support of the administration in the rural districts have lost influence and wealth. . . . They need help the government can give them to supplement their dwindling acres" (Government of Punjab 1920, 4).

Last, the *Youngest Punjab Canal Colony* pamphlet circles back to the military farms that are the source of inspiration for this historical detour. It mentions the early settlement of the oat-hay farm as well as the British Cotton Association in Pirowal, two leading centers of the peasant protest movement. The oat-hay farm, which today is known as Chak 10, was initially allotted to Catholic missionaries to settle newly converted Christian families who possessed no land. But instead of producing social uplift, these farmlands were leased to the British Indian Army at the onset of World War I. Hence, the promise "To the depressed classes the protégés of Christian missions, or of non-Christian service association, most of them decent law abiding citizens, the colony gives a chance of rising from the menial positions to which their hereditary occupation have condemned them" (Government of Punjab 1920, 5) never materialized for the residents of oat-hay farm. The case of the abandoned missionary project now known simply as Chak 10, and the exceptions and protections in the system of land allotment, together make clear the compromised nature of the colonial gift economy.

Peasant settlers. Source: File 20-1, Box 52, Waterhouse Pages, Center for South Asian Studies, University of Cambridge.

Colonial infrastructure was fashioned as a "gift" that consolidated relations among different populations, bringing mutual recognition even in incommensurable contexts. Returning to the politics of place allows us to rethink the question of power in terms of something that is constructed locally, where the forces of change are not solely the "modern" rationalization of the center or state, but local practical relations created by the gift of colonial infrastructure that not only remade the environment of Punjab but also rearranged the lives of many inhabitants. As Henri Lefebvre has emphasized, "Global space produces rather than subsumes, generates rather than negates, the local, regional and national" (quoted in Goswami 2004, 36). Lefebvre continues:

> The local does not disappear . . . [I]t is never absorbed by the regional, national, or even worldwide level. The national and regional take in innumerable "places"; national space embraces the regions; and world space does not merely subsume national space, but even precipitates the formation of national spaces through a remarkable process of fission. Myriad currents, meanwhile, traverse all these spaces. The hyper complexity of social space should now be apparent. . . . [It] means that each fragment of space subjected to analysis masks not just one social relationship but also a host of them. (Quoted in Goswami 2004, 36)

Taking my cue from Lefebvre's call to connect spatiality and political subjectivity across scales and contexts as a study of spatial practice, I turn to oral histories that tell the story of how the local Okara peasant farmers' movement (AMP) invoked the moral economy of place to reject the military's unilateral transition to a cash-based land tenure system. The tenant farmers used their history of suffering and their connections to governmental institutions to resist the military's attempts to liberalize the state-owned farms. Chapter 3 provides another register to think about social-spatial changes based on subjective experiences and memories, exemplified in how the peasant farmers challenged the state's narrative about land and property.

CHAPTER 3

WHAT REMAINS BURIED
UNDER PROPERTY?

The tradition of the oppressed teaches us that the "emergency
situation" in which we live is the rule. We must arrive
at a concept of history which corresponds to this.
                    —Walter Benjamin, *Theses on the Philosophy of History*

THE PUNJAB TENANTS' ASSOCIATION (AMP) differs from many
contemporary land rights movements in that it is not based on cultural
claims to origin or indigeneity. The AMP land rights claims are not based
on more-abstract notions of social justice, as exemplified by Movimento
Sem Terra, the Brazilian land rights movement that has championed
landless peasants' occupation of land unused by absentee landlords. Instead, the AMP shares much with classic agrarian subaltern mobilizations that rose up, to the surprise of urban middle classes, to resist
changes in land tenure—for example, those in nineteenth-century and
early twentieth-century South Asia and Africa. From the standpoint of
free-market orthodoxy, the AMP might be seen as a conservative movement in its stubborn refusal to give way to a cash-based tenancy system.

Among twentieth-century economists, Karl Polanyi was one of the
first to take the moral dimensions of land relations seriously. He questioned the impoverished modern understanding of land when he wrote,
"What we call land is an element of nature inextricably woven with man's
institutions. To isolate it and form a market out of it is perhaps the weird-
est of all undertakings of our ancestors" (Polanyi 1948, 1). He critiqued
the narrow vision of private property as one that reduces the wider network of relations and claims on land. Anthropologists like Parker Shipton (1994) have argued that land rights in Africa, and to varying degrees

throughout the world, come with a set of moral obligations, as in the right to grazing, the right to the water below the earth's surface, the right to a share of the harvest, the right to gather wood, and the rights of those who are buried and those who are yet to be born. Polanyi based his theories on the vast archive of land-market relations in Europe and classic anthropological literature on exchange relations from Melanesia. His assessment of land as something more than a possession—something that is a substantive point of connection of social relations, moral entitlements, and social reproduction—echoes the claims to land that are made regularly in AMP speeches and pamphlets and that characterize the rhetoric of most peasant movements regarding land rights.

The AMP mobilizes the language of rights based on a memory of suffering and obligations to challenge the Pakistan Army's hold on military farmland. In pushing against the liberal conceptualization of "rights" as solely tied to political citizenship through property or juridical citizenship, the AMP invokes ethical and moral claims to rights to land that are based on occupancy rather than ownership. Tenant farmers' oral histories and collective memories provided a means for the AMP to make claims, created a political community among peasant farmers, and ultimately disarmed the state. This example of the AMP suggests that "rights" are not an exclusive element of Western modernity but can be founded in other cultural expressions of ethical relations. Building on Sally Falk Moore's work, Ajantha Subramanian (2010) contends that rights-based claims are not solely tied to the juridical protection of property and "universal" personhood, but can be the articulation of expectations of patronage, relationality, and obligations, embedded in long-standing notions of justice based on idioms of reciprocity. She writes that "rights claims are embedded in dense histories of struggle and, in this sense, are not distinct from other cultural expressions of relationality and obligation" (Subramanian 2010, 20–21).

Similarly, the AMP makes land rights claims by invoking customary rights, as in the right to bread, clothing, and shelter that has been the cornerstone of popular politics in South Asia. Instead of separating the language of legal rights and the language of customary rights, it is more generative to see the dialogical relationship between claims and rights, and between client-patronage relations and postcolonial governmentality, in which making claims generates new understandings and subjects of rights. Peasants have a different set of claims to the farmland in Okara depending on when they arrived there; more specifically, whether they (or their ancestors) moved there when the Catholic Church settled these villages or after the upheavals of partition.

The great transformation of Punjab in the nineteenth century has been written about as a technological achievement of science and engineering. It is easy to forget that these irrigation projects were also heavily freighted with moral, religious, and millennial images of water's transformative potential. Irrigation's promise for social uplift and moral improvement enchanted peasant settlers, colonial administrators, and missionaries. Consider the following lines by Imad ud Din, a pastoral worker for a Christian Methodist parish, as he talks about the Chenab colony: "Now we are on holy ground. When these canals are running at their full pressure they are a wonderful sight, carrying the life-giving water to the parched and thirsty lands, turning a desolate and barren country into a veritable 'Garden of the Lord'" (quoted in Hares 1920, 7).

The irrigation projects captured the surging evangelical aspiration of Capuchin Catholic missionaries who were relative latecomers to Punjab. The Catholic Church itself was a latecomer to colonial Punjab, where mass conversion movements were taking place at the turn of twentieth century. There were over thirty Christian groups working in Punjab, which converted up to half a million Indians to Christianity by 1930. This missionary activity was matched by the efforts of Hindu, Sikh, and Muslim reform groups to gain influence among the downtrodden communities. The evangelical zeal of reform and conversion translated into land allotments for various reform and mission groups in the canal colonies. The Punjab government allotted a series of villages to several religious reform and missionary groups ranging from Hindu Arya Samaj and Ahmediya movement to the Protestant Christian Mission Society and Catholic Capuchin Jesuit groups. Some of the oldest military farms in Okara were originally established by the Capuchin missionaries, who were allotted lands to settle their flock of downtrodden converts hailing from Sialkot and Narowal districts. Unlike other English-speaking missionaries, the Capuchin Jesuit order in Punjab hailed from the region of Antwerp, Belgium. These priests were known to be zealous in preaching to the marginalized segments of rural Punjab, such as the sweeper castes and landless village laborers.

For Capuchins, Chak 10 embodied the transformative potential for social upliftment and redemption for the marginalized classes and castes in Punjab who were at the heart of their missionary activity. As discussed in Chapter 2, land allotments were denied to indigenous groups like petty traders and plains- and jungle-dwelling tribes. Most of these groups who did not conform to the model of settled agriculture and wage labor were either criminalized or forced into settlements. However, the missionary settlements were an experiment to channel aid to the moral and material uplift of the marginalized communities, as long as they adhered to projects of reform.

This project of social uplift for new convert communities, the establishment of Chak 10, ended abruptly with the outbreak of World War I in Europe. There was a drop of funds from Belgium for the mission activities and a rising suspicion by the British authorities of Catholic German and French missionaries. The Bishop of Lahore returned these lands to the Punjab government, which in turn transferred them to the British Indian Army.

Chak 10 shows the contingency of rule that has come to shape the village histories in this region. And as we will see, these connections remain significant as the memory of missionary promises to convert communities is still alive here. The tenants' mobilization started in this village, and it was also the site where the first clashes took place between the peasant farmers and the military farm managers. Chak 10 was originally founded as part of the missionary activity of the Capuchin friars, who supplied the manpower and gathered the funds to shepherd a flock of new converts in the wilderness of Gunji Bar, which had not been irrigated at the time. Young Capuchin missionaries brought the same zeal to their grassroots work in Punjab as they once brought to the nineteenth-century Belgian countryside.

If we rely purely on archival and textual sources, we get a very different narrative of the history of the Okara farms. Officially, the goal of these farms was always reform, even the philanthropic project to uplift weaker communities. As Malcolm Darling, one of the most influential colonial civil service officers of Punjab, put it, the function of the "co-operative" farms in the Montgomery district was to inculcate "reform" and instill a drive for progress in the native population: "Their [peasants'] welfare and the development of their resources is its only care, and all its energies are bent upon teaching the most skilled use of their land" (Darling 1925, 274–278). This statement by Darling points to the dangers of taking bureaucratic texts at face value, as they may render modes of governmentality with greater coherence, effectiveness, and finality than actually occurred. Moreover, such representations may elide the coercive practices that might have taken place in the attempt to create the smooth space of order and reform.

Given this history, I wanted to know what claims to *malkiyat* (possession, but also synonym for ownership) meant to the tenant farmers. Did they want ownership? Or guaranteed possession? Or simply a right farm there and provide for their families? Moreover, I wanted to know how the tenant sharecroppers traced the genealogy of the AMP political agitation. What enabled the organization to link up with urban activists and non-governmental organizations? How did they gain a level of recognition that made it impossible for the army to launch an armed operation?

Subramanian discusses vernacular claims to justice as "not just the re-constitution of law through the infusion of new cultural meanings or the production of culture through the generative power of law but also a shift in emphasis away from the encounter between law and culture toward the historicity of rights" (2010, 15). Popular mobilization offers a way to rethink law and rights outside the diffusionist European origin story of juridical law and rights, where later adoptions are deemed derivative. Instead, social movements may invoke rights as a *structure of feeling* in a dynamic cultural formation that encodes local understandings of justice and accountability that are not of Western origin but interact or intersect with them (Williams 1977; Harvey 1995). The realm of moral economy and vernacular notions of rights and justice created the conditions of possibility for the AMP to invoke a higher authority to make claim on land, which disarmed the Pakistan military every time it tried to suppress and

forcibly control the AMP. In tracing this history of land rights and patronage in Punjab, I tack back to the history of settlement of these lands
by sharing an oral history about the settlement of Chak 10.

SITUATING MEMORY IN STRUGGLE

I made my way to Chak 10 in the sweltering July heat of Punjab. It was
high noon and the sun was baking freshly watered fields. A few women
were at work in the field tying bundles of wheat. The air was still, and
the green blades of berseem fodder stood tall along the perimeter of the
square fields. I was delighted to take in these sights after a long, bone-rat-
tling rickshaw trip from the faraway bus stop. Chak 10 seems remote and
isolated, a space far away from anywhere, with no paved road connecting
to it. But looks can be deceiving. Despite its appearance, I came to learn
this village was as connected to faraway places like Antwerp and London
as it was to Sialkot and Lahore. As discussed in previous chapters, Chak
10, formerly known as Anthonyabad, was the first village in a cluster of
Christian colonies that were set up in this area when it was considered
a wilderness. More recently, Chak 10 was the site of the first confrontation between tenant farmers and military farm authorities, which would
become a Punjab-wide movement. With these two facts in mind, I was
looking into the relations between the recent land rights struggle and the
social memory of this place.

I was going to this village to talk with Khushi Baba, who, according
to my sources, was one of the few surviving elders who could know about
the early days when these villages were established. I was doubtful even
as I made my way to the village. I had never heard of anyone with the
name of Khushi in this village, and the fact that these farms were first
established in 1913 made it unlikely that I would meet someone with
a firsthand account of those days. For weeks I had been pestering my
friends in Chak 35, the village leaders of the AMP, with questions about
the past, such as "What existed here before settlement? What grew here
before irrigation? What did the indigenous inhabitants [the so-called
janglis] eat?"

Most people simply replied that there was nothing here before; it was
all jungle, a scrubland. However, a few more questions revealed that most

of my interlocutors, who like me are Muslim (a majority in the villages), came here as refugees in 1947 from Amritsar, Jullunder, and Hoshiarpur, districts in Indian Punjab. My informants did not know much, or care to know much, about the historical transformation of this landscape by canals and railroads and missionaries' villages in early twentieth-century Punjab. If anything, the canals were an example of the visionary planning of the British engineers, which stood in contrast to the mechanisms of the army that wanted to take these lands away.

Chak 10 is home to an impressive church and two adjoining school buildings that conform to the metric standard. As it turned out, there were two Khushis in this village, and the elder I was looking for was not at home but at the *dera* (storage and cattle shed) by his fields. A young boy accompanied me to the outskirts of the village, where I saw Khushi resting on a *charpai* (a traditional rope woven bed) under a tall peepal tree. We sat there for half an hour getting acquainted. Khushi asked me about my *biradari*, my background, and my reasons for asking him so many questions. Khushi mentioned that he would tell me everything he could recall, but only after lunch. After a few hours, Khushi told me the story about his father and uncles when they first settled this land:

> The missionaries first brought people from Sialkot. My family came from Sialkot, and they had promised that the land would be given to the *mazarin* six years after the land was settled. At that time, this land was called Gunji Bar, and people in Sialkot still know this land as Gunji Bar.... The living conditions of the *abadkar* peasants were very tough. Christians, Muslim, Hindus, Sikhs, and Rah settled these lands together, and there was nothing here but jungle. At first there was no water here, and it was very difficult. I remember that old women used to sing, "We left land with water and rain to come to jungle with no water." Our ancestors told us about the past, that Father Herman had brought us here. The land belonged to the *mazaras*. Missionaries settled Chak 104, 11, 10, 9, 6, and 8. Those people who settled these lands have all passed away....
>
> The canal came to this area in 1913. My father worked on the canal; he dug the canal and removed the rubble in containers [*tokrya bahar kardi*]. Soon after the jungle was settled, two of my uncles died fighting snakes. One

of my brothers also died because of the snake. There were so many snakes, thousands; my father use to kill ten to twenty a day. . . . There were no animals besides snakes. . . . Slowly the snakes died out, but even now, some snakes come out. . . . After Pakistan was made and the Muslim government was formed, the Hindu and Sikh left. New chak-in-charge came. They were reasonable in the first year, but then they started abusing us, asking for more *battai*. In the evening, they would make us sit out on the floor like insects, and they would tell us what to do the next day. Talk and command, they held us hostage all these years. (Interview by the author, August 2, 2007, Okara Military Farms)

Khushi's feeling of betrayal by Father Herman, the farm manager, is an important counterpoint to the dominant history of canal colonization as the arrival of greater freedoms or as a story of deliverance for low-caste Christian converts. Having recorded Khushi's story, I started looking into the history of the village. I was able to confirm that this village was indeed owned by the Catholic Church, which acquired the land in 1908 in anticipation of canal irrigation. The village was founded as Anthonyabad in 1908 by the efforts of a charismatic Capuchin missionary named Father Felix, who had been active in the construction of new Christian colonies for new converts around Lyallpur and the Toba Tek Singh area. The first settlers traveled from another Christian colony called Maryamabad, near Lyallpur, the current-day Faisalabad (Rooney 1986). These tenants' long, arduous journey through the wilderness is still part of the oral narrative, and it is often expounded on in the biblical terms of exodus.

Soon after its founding, Anthonyabad suffered two major setbacks. One month after its founding, the Great War in Europe broke out, and the Capuchin missionaries were cut off from their financial support in Belgium. This meant that commitments to the Anthonyabad settlers could not be honored. The other setback was the removal of the charismatic Father Felix from Punjab. It was alleged that he had gotten into trouble for naming one of the largest Christian colonies after himself; the colony was named Khushpur (Khushi being a translation of Felix in Urdu), and it remains a major center of Catholicism in Punjab. Second, during World War I many German and Austrian citizens, including missionaries, were placed in internment camps by the British colonial state. The Catholic Bishop of Lahore relinquished his lease on Chak 10, along with Chak 9, and a few other villages were given to the Punjab government, which leased them to the British Indian Army (Harding 2008).

Political analysis based on just tracking governmental processes through textual and archival analysis privileges the "effectiveness" of certain institutional "rationalities of rule" (Moore 2005, 170). Looking at political technologies through the layers of multiple village histories gives a better view of the contentious political landscape and the limits and effects of power. For example, most of the earliest tenants of the Okara Military Farms came from lower-caste communities in Sialkot (a major city in northern Punjab) who had converted to Christianity. These peasants were lured by the missionary church with the promise of permanent land grants in exchange for the cultivation and settlement of this land. However, the land grants never transpired, and the peasant farmers remained subjugated in a sharecropping system where the military became the new landlord after taking over the estate in 1913.

THE GRID VILLAGE

All of the villages in the military farms are laid out in a dense grid formation for both the residential section (*gaun*) and the surrounding fields (*khait*). All the houses are adjoined to each other; most houses comprise a small, enclosed courtyard with one or two rooms in the corner. In slightly more prosperous villages like Chak 34/4 L, there are a few families (usually with relatives working abroad) who reside in brick houses with two or even three floors. The center of the village is a hub of activity with small stores, a mosque, and a church, almost resembling a *kutchi abadi* (slum neighborhood) one might find in a large city. It is tightly packed in narrow lanes, while the perimeter of the village opens up to an otherwise sprawling landscape of wheat, maize, and yellow mustard greens; in the case of Chak 51, outside of town one finds a neighboring army cantonment, which is flanked by fences, checkpoints, and spacious airy streets.

The grid layout of the villages in this region gives a full view of the entire street to a person standing in the middle of the street. The contrast in village layout in this region made a big impression on Paul Paustian, an American economist who lived in Lahore in the 1920s. Paustian characterized the traditional Punjab village as "generally quite bereft of order, its streets wandering crookedly about in order to miss the mud huts and walls of the various individual compounds of which the village is composed" (1930, 98). In contrast, these modern villages had boundaries that "had been settled by the engineers, the main streets and general plan of the settlement were determined upon, keeping in mind the needs of the Punjab village in the matter of grazing grounds, accommodation for the village servants and land to be devoted to communal purposes growing out of caste customs and traditions" (65). Even today, despite the population transfer of partition, the most marginalized groups in the village hierarchy, like the scheduled castes and the landless laborers, are located on the periphery, while the most prominent families or those with the greatest number of land tenancies have historically resided in the center of the village near the administrative offices of the military farm managers. As we shall see, the villages' spatial layout shaped people's experience of undergoing constant inspection and being watched by the farms' administrators.

Today, there is only a faint memory of pre-irrigation desert plains, which is preserved in fragments and folklore one hears from the descendants of the Biloch, Kharral, and Sial tribes. Stories and family histories about the pre-irrigation past persist, like the one offered by Majed Sahib, the headmaster teacher in Chak 51 and a descendant of the original Biloch inhabitants. "My ancestors," he remarked woefully, "didn't know much about property or land. They were scared of being penned in by the British" (interview by the author, May 12, 2007). They viewed year-round cultivation as a punishment, a form of slavery, and they fled their homestead when the British wanted to settle them on what is now the main city bus stop, prime property in the center of Okara City.

Majed muses about what it might have been like if his ancestor knew the value of land. Would they, the Biloch *biradari*, be like the Raos or the Wattoos who dominate the politics and businesses in the towns? A few years after leaving their homestead, Majed's family was forced to settle in a reform village for camel herders, which operated like a penal colony, complete with a school and grazing grounds. The initial restriction of movement on Majed's ancestors eased over time. Camels ceased to be in demand, and the later generations were encouraged to get an education to become village teachers.

The modern property regime, as exemplified in the canal colonies, is conceptualized as partitioned spaces linked by state infrastructures that promise to usher in new times and subjects (Blomley 2002). The natural appearance of the state is built out of distinct cartographic lines, standard plots, walls, and borders that seek to simplify the three-dimensional world onto the flat surfaces of maps, ledgers, and property deeds by etching a line into the ground, appropriating the history of these lands, and figuratively rooting the people in the soil.[1] But such efforts to impose the lines of property only go so far before clashing with local meanings, experiences, and politics that exceed these representations. These frictions are especially acute in postcolonial states where state fixations are brittle, where "measurement competes with memory, inscription with

Checkpoint in the field. Source: Author photo.

inheritance, and technical abstraction with social experience as arbiters of reality" (Craib 2004, 52).

Tensions between measurement and memory are ever present in the AMP mobilization, exemplified in the tenant sharecroppers' refusal to see land as an inert object that can be appropriated and alienated at will. Within this context, the army's move toward impersonal market principles clashes with the direct personal memory of debt and suffering that the sharecroppers have endured since 1913. Seemingly progressive policies like the shift from sharecropping to cash-based contracts mask the violence that threatens to dispossess tenant sharecroppers.

MEMORY VERSUS MEASUREMENT

The experiential sense of land relations and how they figure in ideas about community, "place," and belonging became apparent to me in conversations with tenant farmers. While land struggles often take shape through large-scale encounters, like that between the army and the tenant farmers, these struggles also have personal iterations. Technically, Chak 35, Hanif's village, was the last to join the movement, and a different wing of the army's corporate complex than the other villages managed the village. Hanif was a devoted AMP worker, which in local parlance meant he was a dedicated activist in the movement, but not a leader in the movement. Nevertheless, the tenants in Chak 51 were subject to the same unilateral change in land tenure to cash contracts.

I sat with Hanif as the sun slowly faded into a gray-orange dusk. It was cool enough for the mosquitoes to come out and feast on us. Most farmers were heading back to the village, and young children helped gather tools and load bundles of feed-grass before steering the buffalo-drawn carts back to the village. The evening calm was interrupted by the humming noise of the engine that pumped up groundwater from the new two-hundred-foot-deep well. The newly dug well (one of two in the village) was a necessity now that the villagers were working more intensely on their fields; the canal water was simply inadequate for thirsty winter crops like rice.[2]

Earlier that afternoon, I had helped Hanif and his two youngest sons dig a channel to link their seven-acre plot to the mouth of the new well.

I was happy to help Hanif, who generously offered to host me during my stay in Chak 51/4 L. Arif, Hanif's son, loosened the soil with a steel rod, and we followed him, digging a channel. Working with a plow, I thought about the immense labor that had been required to level these fields and dig canals throughout these plains at the turn of twentieth century. Having been used to talking all day and not working in the fields, I was exhausted as we sat and waited for the water to reach the tail end of the field. Resting there, I thought about the difference between my fieldwork and actual field work.

That evening, Hanif said something that brought me back to the present. He spoke after a long time, his voice heavy as he returned to an earlier conversation we had had about the past and potential of this land. "This land is like gold. God almighty made this soil rich, and the Angraiz [British] made the canal system to last a thousand years. . . . But look at our poverty here, our mud brick homes, our children in dirty clothes." He paused. "Look over there, where each bungalow costs two to three million rupees [$28,000]"—he pointed out the twinkling lights from the nearby cantonment—"where they [the military] use this precious land to march up and down and parade with their pipe band each morning" (interview by the author, March 1, 2008, Okara Military Farms).

Hanif's testimony brought up all the elements that have come to define the peasant movement in the military farms: the fertile soil, the foresight (or nightmare) of colonial irrigation, and the uneven growth that perpetuates the daily suffering of the poor and the wealth it affords the few who live in affluent army cantonments. I sensed something deeper in Hanif's expression that challenged the representation of soil and land as lifeless, that questioned assumptions about property. For him this earth, which includes all that has gone into it and all that has grown out of it, provides a moral prism through which to evaluate the relationship between property and propriety, servitude and freedom, state and society.

For Hanif, this land is a subject/object tied to distinct notion of rights as expressed in the common saying, *jeeray pahway ohi khaway* (whoever sows the seed shall reap the harvest). These claims are embedded in how this land is inhabited, labored on, and talked about in everyday idioms, making the language of rights not the exclusive property of modernity, the state, or some elaboration of liberalism. For the *mazarin* (sharecroppers), land rights claims are located in the densely layered histories of struggle and in cultural expressions of legitimate authority and moral obligations, not the least those expected from the state. These claims are based on a century of sharecropping that kept the tenant farmers like Hanif in abject poverty.

My mind wandered as I thought about my conversation with Hanif and the stories people told me over and over again to reinforce a personal connection to this land. I knew the broad history of canal colonies and the tenants' movement, but it was different to hear local accounts of life under sharecropping and the ongoing struggle to retain control of the land. These narratives mixed the past with the present, the suffering of past generations with the current fear of eviction, to tell the story of tenants' struggles in the military farms.

These moral and almost sacred understandings about the meaning of land fall outside of policy evaluations of agrarian structures, matrices of crop yields, and normative discourses of development and poverty alleviation (Zaidi 1999). Certainly, land distribution is highly unequal in Pakistan, with the top 5 percent of landowners possessing as much as 33 percent of all cultivated areas, while around half of rural households do not own any land (Gazdar 2009). Furthermore, land distribution varies widely, with large holdings in Sindh in Southern Punjab, and smaller plots with relatively more equitable distribution of land in canal colonies. However, some Pakistani economists have suggested that access to land and agriculture is less of a factor today as the rural economy matures toward formal employment, industry, and service-sector labor (Zaidi 1999).

Development-oriented theories of social change leave out the fact that access to land, and the social capital that comes with it, makes all the difference for both subsistence and informal work, as well as in seeking formal employment, accessing government services, and getting credit to participate in a diversifying economy, one in which the price of land has gone up with the expansion of roads, warehouses, and infrastructural development in the rural hinterland. This hypercommodification of land through price inflation creates new kinds of pressure on small-scale cultivators. As well, the data sets derived from commercial crop production are inattentive to the value of food security in terms of subsistence farming, small livestock pasture, and dairy farming. The subsistence needs of the poorest sections of the rural population disappear from the econometric picture of the rural economy.

Latif's family, like most households in this village, settled here after 1947 when they left their natal village in Jullunder in the aftermath of the carnage of partition. I learned later that his extended family is dispersed throughout Punjab and Sindh, as they were sent to different places from the Sahiwal (then called Montgomery) refugee camp where they were stationed at the time of partition. His own father only got to Chak 51, when he followed up on rumors in the camp that the army was looking for experienced peasants to work as tenants on its military farmlands. Lacking any documentation, Latif's father rented a buffalo cart to show proof of his agrarian roots and to claim his Arain caste. He rode down to the military farm headquarters in Okara, and later he had to produce two character witnesses, after which he received an allotment of 12.5 acres of land in Chak 51/4 L on a rent-in-kind basis (Latif, interview by the author, July 2, 2004, Okara).

DEVELOPMENT AND DISPOSSESSION

The prospect of dispossession resuscitated the feelings of displacement and the memory of dispossession, like the experience of partition, the everyday hardships of ancestors who toiled in poverty, and daily harassment by the farm managers. As Farid Daula, the elder leader of the AMP in Chak 33 L, noted, "Life under the *battai* system was miserable. The villages were administered under corrupt law [*kala kanoon*], by which people were held like prisoners. People lived in fear of chak-in-charge and the security guards [*chowkidars*]. People were scared of them, always tried to please them" (interview by the author, June 28, 2004). Farid recounted the time when General Chatha (who would eventually announce the change to the cash contract system) toured the farms to assess the lands:

He went around with his local touts as they went and looked and measured the land from every angle. They wanted to take twenty *murabay* [approximately five hundred acres] from each our farms for the jarnails to make plots, sell it, or rent it to some large farmers. These jarnails look at land, and they see money. They don't look at land as a mother; nor do they see it as having anything to do with them. We know this land because we have worked it and sacrificed for it so many years. We know how it has changed; we know how to keep it healthy and how it can be ruined. We know that the DAP Sona [a fertilizer brand] urea makes our crops grow, but it also takes the heat out of the land, and too much fertilizer can ruin the land. But if it was up to them, they will first exhaust the land, evict the people, and then sell the land in plots. (Interview by the author, June 28, 2004)

Farid's comments illustrate how tenant farmers experience land as generative source of fertility, habitation, and power. The fertility of the soil is self-evident with the vitality of its abundant crops and the fortunes it has created for *artis* (traders), landlords, and those who reside in the army cantonment, but the profits that come from intensive cultivation never go to those who actually cultivate the land. This sentiment echoed what Hanif and peasants in Chak 35 had emphasized, as the question of belonging and power is visible in the spatial contrast between the mud brick homes in these villages and the spacious airy streets of the nearby Okara cantonment.

The Okara cantonment occupies a huge chunk of the irrigated tracts in the district that are leased out to military officers, who in turn build real estate or cultivate the farmland by hiring tenants. The Pakistan Army established the Okara cantonment after the 1965 war with India, when it realized its vulnerability after a ground invasion by the Indian Army. A string of new cantonments was built in eastern districts of Punjab along the India-Pakistan border. Much of the residential land was allotted to retired soldiers and enlisted officers to give them added stake in defending these lands in the event of a ground invasion. Since 1970 these cantonments have expanded, as they have become a major source of real estate profits for retiring officers who sell their awarded or subsidized plots at inflated market prices. These "developments" come at a price to village dwellers, peasants, and sharecroppers, who suddenly find themselves behind the expanding fence of the cantonment. The experience of the villages that were razed by the construction of the Okara cantonment weighs heavily on the tenant farmers as they deliberate on the military's offers to monetize the land relations in Okara Military Farms.

The Okara cantonment was built by evicting six villages in the late 1960s. These displaced tenants were offered small plots of brackish land in compensation (on the outskirts of Multan). Most tenants moved to nearby villages where they had kin relations or became landless laborers. Since its establishment in the 1960s, the cantonment has continued to expand through the wholesale dispossession of entire villages like Chak 106/3 R, which was demolished in the late 1980s to expand the farmland encompassing the cantonment and gain more land to build a hostel for military recruits in training. The tenants of Chak 106 were also tenants-at-will who similarly practiced sharecropping in return for their permanent land use rights. However, these tenants were displaced in the first week of May 1989, when an entire truckload of soldiers and bulldozers showed up without warning. The tenants were instructed to leave the villages immediately and move with their carry-on belongings to their sheds (*deras*) in the fields when the cantonment authorities proceeded to demolish the village by razing tenants' homes and leveling the fields for agriculture and storage units.

Chak 106/4 L, Chak 104/4 L, and Chak 108/4 L were razed when the Okara cantonment was first built in 1972. These tenants did not join the AMP's campaign against the cash contract system because they felt too vulnerable and did not want to antagonize the army. "We did not want any trouble with the army because we had already endured the pain of evictions when our homes were bulldozed to build the cantonment," said Riaz, a tenant farmer who accepted the contract system (interview by the author, September 21, 2007). Hundreds of peasant households were forced to settle on the outskirts of neighboring farms, with some families settled in fields, animal sheds, and others opting to move to Gambor, a neighboring market town, where they continue make a living as day laborers. Others simply left the region.

These displaced tenants moved to the outskirts of Hanif's village, where they rented the land from one of the tenant farmers. Some of the displaced tenants from Chak 106 kept farming their old fields, but they accepted the cash contracts when they were announced in 2000. However, these tenants report that the cash rents have gone up from 500 rupees in 2000 to something like 25,000 rupees in 2014. The dramatic jump in the rent has made it impossible for many tenant farmers to rent and work the land themselves as laborers for others.

The dramatic increase in the cost of land is making it difficult for many households to subsist with farming, and many have gone deep into debt by borrowing heavily from *artis* (market traders who also lend money). By 2012, these farmers were having a hard time feeding their families and making it through the season. Each incremental increase in rent results in the loss of tenancy by poorer households, and subsequently the tenants' land is leased out on the market to army officers or higher bidders from neighboring towns. Serving army officers of all ranks in the Okara cantonment have been known to take up large section of the lands. For example, cash-paying tenants who were formerly displaced from Chak 106 are not allowed to build any proper shelters on the outskirts of Hanif's village, where they have been living since they were displaced from their native village. The expansion of the cantonment has also resulted in the loss of land for neighboring villages, say farmers. The army has posted fences and checkpoints on tenants' fields, thus taking their land into the jurisdiction of cantonment authorities and forcing tenants to pay rent for land whose ownership is disputed. It was this expansion and growing uncertainty faced by cash contract farmers that brought the cash-paying tenant farmers together with AMP members to jointly resist the cantonment authorities in a bid to secure some guarantees or to demand replacement land for tenant farmers outside the cantonment area.

CHAPTER 4

MOVEMENT AND MOBILIZATION

There is no room for pure spontaneity in history.
—Ranajit Guha, *Elementary Aspects of*
Peasant Insurgency in Colonial India

THE RISE of the Punjab Tenants' Association (AMP) is a topic of considerable debate among the small circle of leftists, progressives, and political activists over whether the rise of the AMP reflected the rise of new rural political consciousness, or whether the rise of AMP activism is based on long-standing notion of rights that have gained new urgency in the face of imminent dispossession. These questions go to the heart of agrarian theories of social change that are used to interpret the meaning of rural protest and peasant subjectivity. What makes social movements like the AMP happen? What is the broader meaning of the AMP?

As discussed in previous chapters, the AMP's radical rhetoric and actions clashed with long-held assumptions about Punjab, which was seen as the base of military recruitment, support, and patronage. The study of the AMP illuminates the contingency of governmental power in shaping the meaning of rights tied to territory and subjects in the region. In this chapter, I argue that the central force of a social movement is ontological, as in how it ushers in a new way of seeing and relating to the world so that long-standing injustices suddenly become insufferable and intolerable. Social movements have the ability to take particular issues and universalize them as a form knowledge and praxis. For instance, the AMP enlarged tenants' objection to cash contract farming into a discussion of land reform, citizenship rights, democracy, and human rights in Pakistan.

The AMP's critique of cash contract and its demands were not entirely based on legal precedents. Rather, they articulated political demands in ethical, economic, and emotional terms of subsistence in an economy dominated by the military-industrial elite. Most activist and journalists refer to the AMP as a grassroots movement but offer little analysis of the conditions that made the movement possible. For instance, Pervez Hoodbhoy's widely circulated and moving eyewitness account of his trip to the military farms after military crackdown characterizes the tenants' issue as a human rights concern and not a nonpolitical matter: "Peasants have no political agenda—land is about livelihood and physical survival" (Hoodbhoy 2003). Hoodbhoy depicts the tenants' response as a reflex rather than a political demand. Indeed, the AMP mobilization was hailed by civil society groups and nongovernmental organizations (NGOs) like Shirkat Gah, Action Aid, and Action Social Research as a sign of modernization that would dissolve backward forms of affiliation like caste and sectarian loyalties that prevented peasant farmers from mobilizing along their class interests. The civil society allies of the AMP marveled at its internal diversity, and the participation and cooperation of tenants across religious, caste, and gender differences.

For instance, Masooda Bano's *Breakdown in Pakistan*, a monograph on the effects of NGOs on institutional collective action, argues that the AMP came into being because of the presence of a few educated peasants and dedicated urban activists. Bano argues that most tenants were "Unable to read and write and possessing limited understanding of legal acts, the majority of the farmers initially welcomed the rent system." Bano confirms her preconception against uneducated farmers by drawing a contrast between the majority of tenant farmers and the few "who were slightly educated or had worked in the cities for some time and had some awareness of the legal consequences of this change, who issued the initial call to resist it" (2012, 101). This rendition of the AMP's history distorts the actual account of the tenants' resistance, which was initiated by the poorest tenants, who were the most skeptical of contract system based on cash payments and the dangers it posed for their tenancy status. Ironically, the more-educated and politically astute tenant farmers, like Farid and Sattar, who lead and speak on behalf of the AMP today, were initially supportive of the cash contract farming.

The Pakistani state, for its part, depicts the *mazarin* (tenant farmers) as naïve peasants who are being duped by NGOs, political parties, and/ or manipulated by criminals. For instance, in an interview, the spokesperson for the Pakistan Army's Inter Services Public Relations described the rise of tenants' protests this way: "Initially, the new contract system was welcomed by the people but on the instigation of certain land grabbers who alleged that the military wanted to evict them, the people were forced at gunpoint not to adopt the new system and pay the lease amount of provide fodder, to the army. Anybody defying was beaten up, socially boycotted and forced to leave the land" (Iqbal 2009). The military depicts the *mazarin* as manipulated, the civil society activists see the tenant activism as an epiphenomenon of privatization, yet there is little reflection on the risky and complex deliberation by the tenants themselves.

The military's and the urban activists' depiction of peasants as prepolitical subjects is similar to the elitist depiction of peasant struggles criticized by the subaltern studies project to challenge similar interpretations of poor people's struggles. In *Elementary Aspects of Peasant Insurgency in Colonial India*, Ranajit Guha sets out to underscore the history of creative political deliberation by peasants in out-of-the-way places (Guha 1999). He argues that the realm of subaltern politics remains illegible to national elites because it takes place in a domain that is organized along traditional idioms of customary beliefs and "horizontal affiliations" of kinship and territoriality (278). In other words, this form of popular politics had little to do with parliamentary procedures and the formal language of law. Guha's scholarship and the work of Subaltern Studies Collective have generated new ways of thinking about postcolonial politics that is not based on predetermined interests but rather on the experiences and memories of people who are cast out of the elite domains of history and politics. Here I look at some of the disjuncture between the theoretical directions (positions) of the subaltern project and my own findings.

The assessment of rural subaltern struggles from the analytical categories of consciousness and ignorance, development and underdevelopment, closes off the space of interpretation, deliberation, and the radical contingency where social change is a messier process. I don't dismiss the claims of greater awareness (*shau'r*) in the chaks as an important shift in the self-perception of the *mazarin*, owing to the role of new technologies of communication such as cell phones, the Internet, and satellite television. Rather, the greater awareness echoes Begonia Aretxaga's take on political agency as collections of moments and critical events, where "political agency is always moving in-between discursive possibility, grounded experiences, and changing conditions of possibility" (Aretxaga 1997, 9; see also Comaroff and Comaroff 1991; Gramsci 1971).

The measurement of social change by opposing poles of awareness and ignorance occludes the long history of passive resistance in the chaks, and the divergent ways in which power relations operate in the tenants' movement. Bano's conclusions are reflective of a problem of research design based on structured interviews and focus group discussions without spending time in a place long enough to get a fuller perspective. I found that the AMP leaders used the rhetoric of development, education, and consciousness to align the movement with the vision of urban activists. However, as I spent more time in the village, I discovered that there was an unbroken chain of suspicion about the military's ownership of the land, a history of protests and even everyday forms of resistance in these farms that predated the cash contract announcement. Some of the older leaders of the movement had been arrested in the 1970s for demanding fairer conditions for sharecropping; others petitioned political leaders or worked with human rights organizations to highlight the impoverished conditions in the military farms. However, this kind of insight was gained through informal discussion about the past, politics, and power relations in these farms. Otherwise, the discourse of "development" served as a powerful explanation for the rise of the AMP in more-formal interviews and speeches. Moreover, there were some important differences in the overlapping language of rights and development as they were articulated by the tenant farmers.

The AMP's language of rights is built on a web of obligations that might seem conservative in its demands for state patronage, reciprocity, and state protections for small farmers. This relational understanding of rights contrasts sharply with neoliberal policies that were being promoted not only by General Musharraf's regime but also by the planning regimes of the past that restricted the tenants in all aspects of their lives, ranging from whether they could repair the walls of their own homes, buy radios (until the early 1980s), or get No Objection Certification to leave the village for employment. This subaltern, reciprocal sense of rights is not exclusively something that is written down but rather something that works at an affective level. For the tenant farmers in the military farms in Okara (and also Pirowal, Bhelganj, and other sites of tenant organizing), this mobilization was not something calculated; nor was it based on recourse to law. Rather, the mobilization tapped into something visceral, a structure of feeling that is widely felt, or what the sociologist Deborah Gould (2009, 178) calls a shift in the "emotional common sense," which gains immediacy as it propels people into action. The army's unilateral change in land relations on its farming estates was a threshold moment when long-standing doubts about the army's ownership of the land and tenants' historical resentments about unjust work conditions set off protests. "Ownership or death," the AMP's defiant slogan, speaks of the life-and-death stakes for the tenants who see their struggle as the only thing keeping them from being dispossessed.

Cultural anthropologists have been trying to identify the breaking point that leads to political uprisings by hypothesizing about external factors, such as changes in economic relations, or internal factors, such as the violation of a normative threshold or moral economy. There are divergent explanations for any particular mobilization, but one thing they share is a sense of rupture, a break that marks an end and a beginning. These ruptures propel people to come together and unite around something, whether identity, ideology, or desire. The classical sociological literature on social movements emphasizes resource mobilizations, political opportunities, and rational choice scenarios. This kind of analytical framing was challenged by a new social movement literature that saw movements as driven not by preset ideology or clear vision of a utopian future but rather by collective aspirations for recognition—for the right to be equal and different, as exemplified by civil rights movements, third-world nationalisms, third-wave feminist movements, and gay, lesbian, bisexual, and transgender movements.

The overriding emphasis of social movements has been on how they represent a break from the past, customary rules, traditions rooted in hierarchies, and normative order that gave meaning to community. The literature on social movement sees mobilized communities as predetermined cohesive groups with a shared history of grievances, an identity that is explicit and complete. However, in the rise of social movements, there is also creative energy by which disparate notions of being and belonging shift toward new imaginaries and new collective forms. In such moments, there is a desire for change that is inchoate but also palpable, when it suddenly feels like institutions can be broken and it seems possible to create a different relationship to the world. However, new formations can also settle into sedimented forms, when political agency is linked to the articulation of a coherent past. To paraphrase Raymond Williams, emergent cultural forms remain open to new possibilities even as they are being reworked by preexisting histories of claim making: "In most description and analysis, culture and society are expressed in a habitual past tense. The strongest barrier to the recognition of human cultural activity is this immediate and regular conversion of experience into finished products. . . . [R]elationships, institutions and formations in which we are still actively involved are converted, by this procedural mode, into formed wholes rather than forming and formative processes" (1977, 128).

Peasant movements find themselves in an ambivalent position between these two broad categories of collective struggle, with one that focuses on either the politics of distribution or the politics of recognition. Peasant struggles for land focus on maintaining a livelihood with dignity, the ability to produce food, and social reproduction that is the continued existence of a community and its access to natural resources. The agrarian populism articulated by the AMP is based on a sense of community linked to bonds of obligations, reciprocity, and responsibilities. Environmental activists champion these values, but other theorists of political action like Michael Hardt and Antonio Negri (1999) characterize peasant movements as conservative because they seek to retain a space for community outside the logic of late capitalism rather than acquiesce to it. From this vanguardist perspective, peasant movements have always been seen as out of step with the inevitable expansion of capitalism.

SUBALTERN RUPTURES AND CONJUNCTURES

What follows is an account of the conditions in which the "*mazarin* identity" becomes more salient over and above other forms of difference. As I discuss in Chapters 2 and 3, access to land and natural resources in Pakistan is embedded within customary notions of belonging to a certain community, caste, and/or segmentary lineage. In Central Punjab, such customary relations were established at the time of the great transformation of this semiarid pastoral zone into permanent sedentary agriculture through canal colonization, which resulted in an unprecedented simplification and construction of "traditional village republics." In this schema, different agricultural castes and occupational groups found themselves in a regimented hierarchy.

In the military farms, agrarian caste members were not full proprietors of their land: they had to work under close scrutiny of farm managers who evaluated crops, collected shares, and arranged for tenants to do a great deal of labor on farmlands that was cultivated by the army itself. Many of these villages were anomalous in that they were home to a substantial population of Christian tenants who had access to land (even as sharecroppers), unlike most of their coreligionists, who typically served as landless laborers or worked in the service sector. These internal differences were not the main focus of the AMP mobilization; rather, it was a shared *mazarin* identity that became most closely associated with the movement.

Two weeks after the announcement by General Chatha (the general in charge of investigating the losses in the military farm exchequer) of the new cash contract system, the first major confrontation between tenant farmers and the authorities took place. It happened in Chak 10, which, as I describe in Chapters 2 and 3, was the first village in the military farms and settled by Catholic missionaries. After 1947, Muslim peasants moved to this village; as the Sikh and Hindu tenants fled, after independence, the new military farm managers arrived. Some villages became mostly inhabited, but Chak 10 remained predominantly Christian. Other villages have been absorbed into Okara City or lie next to the Okara cantonment, but Chak 10, despite its early origins, seems more out of the way and isolated. Out of the eighteen villages in Okara district, suspicion about the army's intentions and even its legitimacy as a landlord went deepest here. As I learned through interviews and family histories, there was a strong sense that this land did not belong to the army, that it was initially church land, and that ancestors in this village had sacrificed and toiled to clear this earth for agriculture.

The first confrontation between tenants and the military farm authorities started in July 7, 2001, when the farm authorities sent laborers to cut down the trees just outside the residential area of Chak 10. When a crowd of peasant farmers assembled to ask the authorities about cutting the trees, the farm managers offered little explanation, only saying that it was an order from the brigadier. The tenants accused the farms' management of profiteering by taking these trees to sell in the timber market. The village farm administrator, the chak-in-charge, arrived after the tenants surrounded the laborers. Unbeknownst to farm managers, there was already a great amount of talk about the possibility of evictions, and the tenants had been holding secret meetings about choosing a course of action. When laborers appeared to cut down the trees, it spurred the tenants to take action. The police were called in, but the tenants refused to cooperate, and the confrontation that followed resulted in the tenants evicting the chak-in-charge, the villages' guards, and their informants.

According to George, a participant in the first confrontation in Chak 10, the AMP leaders had focused on local developments inside their villages until this point, and they were afraid to confront the farm managers directly or even criticize the army in public. Younger leaders from Chak 10, like Younus Iqbal, had been working to spread the tenants' movement to other military farms in Renala, Lahore, Sargodha, Khanewal, and Multan to create a Punjab-wide movement. This way the military could not isolate the *mazarin*, and if they were to attack one place then other farms would rise up in protest. The military's hands would be tied because they would not be able to suppress the movement on a Punjab-wide level. This is precisely what happened after the initial uprising in Chak 10: other tenants heard about the event and started talking to each other. Villages who had said that it was crazy to take aggressive measures began giving some of the loudest speeches against the army.

Stressing the importance of the AMP's linkages with urban activists, civil society, and NGOs, George drew a comparison between the AMP and the 1980s resistance movement in Sindh: "I was thinking that during the 1980s General Zia had aerial bombed one *goth* [village] in Sindh and four hundred people died in ten minutes.[1] At that time, no one took any actions; they had suppressed all organizations, all NGOs. But NGOs have helped us so much that Musharraf once gave a statement that he will put restrictions against NGOs because they are giving unjustified support to the tenants" (interview by the author, April 19, 2007, Okara Military Farms).[2]

This kind of strategic essentialism, forging alliances based on a tenant farmer identity, worked well for a while, but the overriding structures of caste affiliation and religious identity also came to play a major role. Over time, the AMP saw certain forms of association become less salient and certain bonds of solidarity weaken as other forms of difference became more meaningful. Initially, urban activists and allies hailed the AMP movement as a sign of rising political, class-based awareness in the villages of Punjab, especially at a time when society was depoliticized and relatively indifferent to a military-led coup against the unpopular Nawaz Sharif presidency.

The government's move to shift from the *battai* or sharecropping system to a contract-based tenancy system came at a time when serious questions were being raised in the press about the military's expansive role in land speculation, corporate-sector investments, and involvement in private business interests. The farmers favored the existing sharecropping system because it guaranteed the tenants permanent rights to use the lands under the Punjab Tenancy Act of 1887. One newspaper article summed up the act's protections this way: "The Act stipulates that a tenant has the right of occupancy if he has been cultivating the land for more than two generations. He cannot be evicted from the land, and has the right to appeal to the civil court for redress" (Amirali 2002).

The Punjab Tenancy Act of 1887 is a good example of the protective clauses that were built into the settlement schemes of canal colonization. However, these measures have greatly eroded in Punjab with the growth of intensive commercial farming and cash-based land leasing and the demise of sharecropping. The contrast between the colonial-era tenancy law and the new contracts was not lost on the farmers in Okara when they entered into dealings with the army over the proposed changes to landholding rules. The military farms' authorities presented the new lease system as the first step in the development of "model villages," clinics, and schools. The new military regime promised to "end the culture of corruption" (*baimani*) and poverty in these farms. Here, the language of development was deployed to depoliticize the issue of land tenure and transform it into a question of proper management of resources.

Ali Cheema describes the details of the leases: "The lease period was originally set at 3 years but later changed to 7 years as a concession towards the tenants. As such this period is somewhat inconsequential as the contract is subject to annual renewal on the basis of the previous year's performance. The rate at which the land is to be leased out is currently set between a minimum of Rs. 2200 and a maximum of Rs. 3,600 per acre" (2003, 3). After a few weeks of deliberation, the tenant farmers rejected the new contract system (even though they had suffered greatly under the old *battai* system), because they feared for the fate of the land. The tenant farmers' mistrust of the military administration was reinforced after consultation with several lawyers and sympathetic local bureaucrats. The *mazarin* concluded that under the Punjab Tenancy Act they had greater protection as tenants under *battai* than as commercial renters.

News about these village-level confrontations was making its way into regional newspapers, but the narrative changed dramatically by the time stories made it out of Okara. The tenants' mobilization was discredited by planted stories in which respected peasant leaders like Dr. Chandio Munir Ahmad were quoted as saying that "leaders of the tenants being salary-paid [by] foreign based NGOs have been deteriorating the peace process [by] instigating the simpleton farmers against the Pak rangers to make their bosses happy" ("District (Okara)" 2003). The deterioration of law and order was ascribed to the local police superintendents, as the Okara police department saw a rotation of district police officers who were blamed for not being able to control the situation, while the army and Ranger authorities remained beyond reproach, and were depicted as the target of NGO machinations. In 2003, Okara's newly appointed District Police Officer Zafar Abbas Bokhari pledged to make police officials serve the people: "Touts have tarnished the image of police department hence their entries in the police stations will be banned completely," he told reporters ("District (Okara)" 2003).

The news about the AMP's initial protests and confrontation with farm authorities was first reported by local Urdu freelance correspondents like Sarwar Mujahid, whose brief regional columns about sit-ins and protests in rural Punjab were picked up by urban activists. Mujahid's report about the massive sit-in got the attention of a human rights delegation that then toured the military farms for a fact-finding trip. The Rangers' repression worsened in the days that followed the Grand Trunk roadblock, and many people were injured, arrested, and beaten. On May 11, 2003, Ameer Ali, an elderly farm laborer, was shot and killed while leaving a friend's house in neighboring Chak 5. Coincidently, a team of reporters and human rights groups from Islamabad was on a fact-finding mission in the chaks. Here is an eyewitness report by Pervez Hoodbhoy on what he saw:

> As I stood by the blood-spattered earth next to a wall pockmarked with bullets, grim-faced villagers pointed out the field from where they said the rangers had machine-gunned the village for over an hour. A tour around Chak 5-L followed. It is a fairly typical village with mud-covered huts, open drains, barefooted children, and scrawny chickens. Branches of trees felled in the shooting lay all around. Many houses, as well as the village mosque, had bricks broken or chipped by heavy bullets. They are there for anyone to see— but only if they can successfully navigate through the siege imposed upon the 70-odd villages in the area. Roadblocks are everywhere, manned by soldiers with automatic weapons as well as the lighter-armed police. Four-wheelers with mounted machine guns prowl menacingly upon the dirt roads next to the canals, raising huge clouds of dust. (Hoodbhoy 2003)

The Rangers descended on each village and forced the tenants (mostly women who stayed behind during the incursions) to put their thumb-print on lease contracts. The military blocked the water channels or *maindars* to two military farm villages for three months after the sit-in. In other villages, the tenant farmers also lost their crops because the military imposed a strict curfew and would not let them go out to water their fields or work on their farms. The blockade of eighteen villages from summer was lifted three months later following international condemnation of the military repression of tenant farmers. Several articles in prominent media outlets, such as the BBC, the *Washington Post*, and *Newsweek*, covered the story. These reports greatly undermined the Pakistani Army's image both domestically and internationally, and highlighted the increasing concentration of commercial economic interests among the top military brass. Moreover, these news stories also had the potential to jeopardize the Pakistan military's delicate relations with the United States, a big source of its funding since the September 11, 2001, attacks and in the war against terror.

For its part, the military has denied any wrongdoing. Speaking to a reporter from IRIN, a Kenya-based human rights news service, Okara district's Senior Superintendent of Police Muhammad Aslam Tareen denied all reports of police brutality: "Their claims and charges are totally wrong. Nobody is harassed or tortured. . . . [E]verybody is happy here. There is only a small minority of miscreants who want to create a law-and-order situation by protest and sabotage" (IRIN 2003). Colonel Saleem Khan, the commander of the Punjab Rangers deployed in the area, responded with an open threat: "Do you think it would be difficult for us to occupy the land forcibly? It would take no time, should we choose to do it, but we want to give them a chance to come around, to see the light" (IRIN 2003). Instead, the authorities tried to criminalize the tenant farmers, with Khan saying, "We are here to help maintain the peace. We are here to deal with the lawbreakers, not the people who respect the law" (IRIN 2003).

The drawn-out siege of the military farms also took a heavy toll on the Rangers. Some of the more humorous stories about the siege have to do with the times a Ranger unit was chased out of the village or stopped in its tracks. The unease of some paramilitary soldiers with laying siege on poor villagers during scorching summer months is revealed by an observation by Riaz, the young AMP activist in Chak 33: "Rangers had to sit in the heat, and they weren't provided water and food all day, so they would sometimes ask the villagers to rise up so they can run out of the village and leave. However, the townspeople didn't do that because they didn't want to provoke greater repression" (interview by the author, September 21, 2007, Okara Military Farms). The paramilitary soldiers who seemed so fierce during the initial confrontation seemed desperate as the siege on the villages continued through the summer months of 2003. The tenants were placed in an awkward dilemma by having to give water to the Rangers who were sent to lay a siege on their villages. The AMP leadership had to deliberate on whether to rise up and create a situation for the local Rangers to leave and thus spark greater retaliation or to just let things be.

The authorities were forced to suspend the siege because of popular and international outrage against the violent operations against tenant farmers, and Tareen was transferred out of Okara district. However, the slow campaign of intimidation continues with arbitrary arrests, abductions (when tenants are held without being charged for any crime), and torture. The list of those who have been abducted and tortured includes children, some as young nine years old. In 2004, Human Rights Watch published a report titled "Soiled Hands: The Pakistan Army's Repression of the Punjab Farmers' Movement." The report detailed that on May 11, 2003, Abid Ali was one of five boys (ranging in age from nine to fourteen years old) who were making their regular morning delivery of milk to Okara City when they were detained by Rangers. Ten-year-old Abid Ali described his experience:

> They snatched our milk and our bicycles. Gomi, the informer, took away the milk and bicycles. They blindfolded us and took us to Rangers' Headquarters. As soon as we got there, they started beating us with sticks. After a while we even stopped crying or screaming. Then they asked if we wanted food. We refused the food saying we were not hungry and wanted to go home. We were again beaten on our refusal. And this time were whipped as well. . . . There were sixteen farmers [already present when] we arrived there. [We saw them being] beaten badly with a flat leather whip by Wasim "Jallad" and Inspector Aashiq Ali in the presence of Major Tahir Malik. The farmers were bleeding and crying in pain. Some were weeping out of fear and sitting with their heads bowed. (Human Rights Watch 2004, 30)

The immediate purpose of such torture, according to Human Rights Watch, is to force the "tenant farmers or their relatives to sign the new contract and pay their cash dues according to these contracts" (Human Rights Watch 2004, 24). But as Michael Taussig has argued, the purpose of torture is not simply to carry out violence on a body to gain its compliance but rather to create an economy of fear—a space of death—through its many examples, recollections, rumors, and reports (1986, 3–37). In the case of the military farms, the work of torture is aimed at re-creating the symbolic capital of deference, obedience, and submission that vanished with the rise of the farmers' movement. However, the use of torture is always deficient in its effects-, because the victims make their own truth claims; tenant farmers utilize the sensory memory of pain to craft another narrative. For example, the names of Ranger officers Inspector Aashiq Ali and Major Tahir Malik have become synonymous with abuse. In every-day conversations, their names serve as sensory artifacts whose mention triggers strong emotions. As Nadia Seremetakis (1994) has elaborated in *The Senses Still*, these evocative recollections of pain create shared social meaning and articulate a political subjectivity based on a collective experience of suffering (see also Das et al. 2000). Moreover, the tenants have been able to resist the army's ongoing campaign of torture and intimidation by invoking a deeper fear of dispossession.

During the time of siege, 2002–2004, everyday activities took place alongside the latent fear of a Rangers attack or capture in the fields. As Mukhtar Lala of Chak 101 described the situation in 2007, "Now things are better here, but we can't go to the city easily; they will arrest us. Now we are trapped here. We even go to our [farm] land with fear. But people are not scared when they are together—only when they are by themselves" (interview by the author, September 5, 2007, Okara Military Farms). One's day, one's mobility, and one's work are defined by the political forecast that comes from reading newspaper reports, evening meetings, rumor and gossip about district-level politics, and information on the personnel operating the checkpoints on the country roads leading to the villages. The tenants mobilized along the lines of family and village networks. Things settle down, and people get caught up in routines of long days of tending to their farms in the early morning, cutting fodder, milking buffaloes, and threshing wheat. Days and weeks pass calmly and suddenly news arrives, like the day in July when Wasim, a young man from Chak 33, whose shop was the site of my initial meeting with AMP leaders, was arrested while on a trip to the market in Okara City.

Each arrest and abduction brings with it great consternation in the village. The news about an arrest would spiral out from families to neighboring villages and to AMP sympathizers. I was in Chak 33 when the news spread that Wasim had been arrested when he went to Okara City to buy and sell some pigeons. Wasim was charged as a bandit (*dacoit*), and the indictment was extended to other prominent activists in Chak 33. The police had called the AMP leaders and demanded that Wasim's family sign the new tenure contract and pay a bribe for Wasim's release. Wasim's mother wanted to go to the Rangers' office to secure his release. A large crowd had gathered at Wasim's house, and most people were trying to convince her not to give in to the officials' demands. There was a lot of debate about what to do. Everyone in the room knew precisely what Wasim was facing under custody. These moments and these discussions heightened a sense of dread or uncertainty, just when things had started to feel better, just when the tenants had begun to feel they had won. Wasim was released from custody six months after the arrest.

POLITICAL FEELINGS, PEASANT MOVEMENT, AND THE QUESTION OF SUBALTERNITY

Sarwar Mujahid, a freelance local reporter for the Urdu daily *Nawai Waqt* in Okara, wistfully recalled the first time he saw a large crowd of peasant men, women, and children marching on foot or riding on trailers hitched to farm tractors and motorcycles, making their way to the Grand Trunk Road.[3] He had cut through a long line of standing traffic on his ancient Vespa scooter to get a close-up view. Hundreds of tenant farmers were gathering on both sides of the road to join a sit-in on the national highway, a two-lane road that follows the ancient trade route all the way through Punjab's hinterland, cutting through fields and towns, linking large cities like Islamabad and Lahore to Southern Punjab and to roads all the way down to the port city of Karachi. The *paya jam* (the wheel jam) sit-in effectively closed the highway. Mujahid was struck by the size of the crowd; he had been to the military farm villages many times before but had never seen such a rally. There was no music blaring from loudspeakers, and only a few chants roared through the crowd. Within a few minutes, he learned that the rally was an improvised response to an attack that had happened just a few hours earlier.

That morning, on May 7, 2002, the Rangers paramilitary force had attacked Chak 34, one of eighteen villages that make up the Okara Military Farms. The Rangers and the police force encircled the fields surrounding the village while tenant farmers were harvesting their crops and then fired live ammunition into the air as tenants scrambled for shelter. Many villagers hid in the fields or took shelter behind trees as the Rangers closed in on the village. The attack ended as abruptly as it had started when the Rangers surrounded a tractor and arrested three AMP activists, all relatives of the acting chairperson of the movement. The three men were charged with the earlier murder of Suleyman Petras, who was shot by the Rangers in front of villagers on August 23, 2002, but the police pressed charges against the three activists.

The news about the attack on Chak 34 spread fast to neighboring villages through text messages and announcements on loudspeakers hoisted on minarets. As my acquaintances in Chak 34 told me, there was a sense of déjà vu because the tenants had lived through a three-month siege in 2002; that day's attack portended the beginning of another season of attacks. The arrest of three villagers in the murder case of a young man who was shot and killed by state authorities was interpreted as a brazen message by the state about what it could do; Mujahid cited the old proverb "*Jis ki lathi us ki bhains*," which translates to "Whoever wields the stick owns the buffalo," or, as another saying puts it, "Might makes right."

Minute by minute, the mood in the village changed dramatically, as fear turned to anger and even excitement. The apprehension of arrest was lifted as tenants from neighboring villages gathered at the edge of this village to march toward the Grand Trunk Road. By noon it was decided that the tenants would sit down and block the road, causing a spectacle, so the whole world would know what was going on in the village. They knew that the news about the traffic jam would be picked up faster and reach farther than did the shootings, rallies, or protests that had taken place within the villages. There was no guarantee that journalists would report on what they saw inside the villages or whether they would go with the army's version of events and press releases, as many local reporters had done in the past. But blocking the highway was a sure way of getting the message out and telling the local authorities that the movement was still very much alive. The tenant farmers had an explicit understanding of the value of connection and the circulation afforded by infrastructures and how subaltern communities can subvert these to force the state to engage with their concerns.

The *mazarin* waited for a large caravan to form before proceeding to the Grand Trunk Road. The police had been alerted about the rally, and they tried to intercept the marchers by charging in with batons and shooting bullets into the air, away from the crowd, but the tenants reciprocated with their strength in numbers. The police backed off as the crowd continued to grow for hours. The tractor pulled a trolley (a larger trailer) packed with people, and some carried large logs and shrubs to set up road barriers. Later in the evening, these barriers were set ablaze to prevent the police from clearing the protesters from the road. The tenants also blocked the railway tracks, thus obstructing both road and rail traffic. The momentum went back and forth as more police and paramilitary reinforcements arrived to regain control of the situation and clear the highway, but they were overwhelmed by the growing crowd.

By dusk, the sit-in took on a festive tone, as the police retreated and vendors from the nearby bus stop made their way into the crowd, selling everything from corn and roasted nuts to cassette tapes. Stranded passengers got off buses and stared at the spectacle from the side of the road. There were impromptu jokes and satirical poetry competitions in which village poets tried to outdo each other in making fun of the army generals. Then, a few hours later, the momentum changed again as dozens of jeeps brought in police and paramilitary reinforcements to clear the highway. The authorities encircled the protesters and fired tear gas canisters and aerial shots to disperse the crowd. The crowd fired back with rocks as the police clashed with protesters. The skirmish went on until the AMP leaders were able to secure visitation rights to the arrested men and the police guaranteed their safe passage. Altogether, the tenants occupied the highway until dusk before dispersing back to their villages.

Mujahid wrote an impassioned hour-by-hour account of the protest, which conflicted with the Rangers' narrative that blamed outside agitators for trying to manipulate and mislead the tenants. In one of our conversations, an interview held in 2004, he told me how the Rangers' administrators had bought off local reporters. He recalled that some reporters stood by the side of the Rangers, taking their statements, and that they later faxed their articles from police headquarters. Mujahid had been imprisoned for three months in 2003 for his reporting on the AMP movement; still, after his release, he continued to publish articles about the tenants' movement. He was arrested and tortured shortly after our interview in 2004.

RIGHTS: HISTORICITY OVER DIFFUSION

Partha Chatterjee (2004) has influenced subaltern studies by locating subalternity within postcolonial governmentality, rather than in autonomous or indigenous consciousness. He makes a distinction between civil society and political society in India, arguing that civil society is made up of the small percentage of the population that is integrated into the universal tenets of liberal democratic citizenship, while political society is made up of the vast majority of people who are not governed as individual citizen-subjects but as members of a particular caste, ethnic group, or religious group. Political society is governed by a politics of recognition that differentiates publics along an axis of primitivism and modernity, characterizing them as volatile or docile, mercantile or feudal. This politics of recognition has become institutionalized within government, and policies have to contend with forms of recognition and "particular demands of cultural identity, which call for the differential treatment of particular groups on grounds of vulnerability or backwardness or historical injustice, or indeed for numerous others reasons" (Chatterjee 2004, 4).

In Chatterjee's formulation of governmentality, subaltern populations are not entirely living in the margins of the state; nor does the national elite represent them. Rather, as nonelite actors, these communities use paralegal means, moral claims, and even violence to contest the state's policies and navigate through postcolonial modernity. Chatterjee writes, "As populations within the territorial jurisdiction of the state, they have to be both looked after and controlled by various governmental agencies. These activities bring these populations into a certain political relationship with the state" (2004, 36).

For Chatterjee (2004), the language of political negotiation and claims making is not based on a transcendental notion of right but rather on pragmatic and creative tactics by which groups in political society are able to make their way through uncertain terrain in the shadows of markets and the state. These communities engage in tactics like encroaching on state property to build homes, illegally tapping into electric lines or municipal drainage, taking over sidewalks as hawkers, and keeping the state at bay by bribing officials or ensuring mass engagement in elections. This happens in creative ways by seeking patronage from various political parties or even organs of the state, or at worst by issuing threats of unrest and violence. According to Chatterjee, this subaltern agency is distinct and different from the formal political realm of petitioning the state through the language of law and rights. Extending his analysis, I read the process of negotiation not just as a tactical maneuver but also as reflective of a different conception and language of rights.

An ethnographic understanding of subalternity, one that goes outside the textual analysis of historical archives, brings a different picture of peasant subjectivity. For instance, the academics and urban activists who work with the AMP paint a cohesive picture of *mazarin* subjectivity by underplaying the internal debates, diversity, and tensions in terms of who speaks for the movement and who is responsible for its success. Many urban activists and civil society organizations see the AMP as a symbol of a rural class struggle that overcame traditional loyalties or social affiliations based on caste, religious, and tribal differences.[4] But ethnographic studies show peasant subjectivity to be not only less coherent and more contradictory but also richer in understanding the relations of power at work (Tarlo 2001; Hansen 2002; Subramanian 2010).

THE BANALITY OF CHANGE

The banal work of making a living slowly evolved into changing relations between people and things, the market, and figures of authority in ways that generated a new politics of protest. The *mazarin* rarely attributed

increasing *shau'r* to formal education, because access to secondary school-
ing is still very limited in the chaks. Instead, other forms of experience
play a greater pedagogic role in the countryside. Some of the more prosaic
aspects of print culture in the chaks are tied not to reading (which mostly
preoccupies the leadership of the AMP) but to different forms of literacy.
Here I am referring to popular use of newspaper advertisements, posters, and pictures clipped from magazines as a means of sharing knowledge of the translocal commodity culture that is greatly present in the
villages. For instance, a list of decorative items hanging in a guest room in
a relatively prosperous home in Chak 33 L included the following items:
an advertisement for Tapal Family Time Tea, clipped from a newspaper,
depicting a contented middle-class family enjoying tea together; a 2002
Royal Fan calendar with an image of a happy couple in a trendy living
room; a poster of cricket player Wasim Akram; and a framed calligraphy
print of "Ya Allah" juxtaposed with a photo of Masjid an-Nabwi, or the
Prophet's Mosque, in Medina. Outside people's homes, there are far more
racy items: posters of Bollywood actresses, cricket heroes, and landscapes
(of a snow-peaked mountain, presumably K2, the tallest peak in Pakistan and also a popular iconic cigarette brand) are pasted on local grocery
stores in the villages. This economy of consumptive desire might find its
expression in objects and things in the villages in ways that might not
be intended, seen in the industry of knockoffs and imitation brands. The
appropriation of these images binds individuals to consumptive publics.
These symbols represent new forms of knowledge that are lurking in the
public culture of the village, rubbing shoulders with local worldviews and
resulting in myriad forms of meaning.

Within the chaks, there are many ambivalent feelings about the
changing character of the villages. As Dil Muhammad, a well-to-do dairy
farmer in Chak 34/4 L who formerly worked on a Greek cargo ship and
traveled throughout Europe, recalls, "Milk was never sold in my child-
hood. Such a thing would have been considered hurtful and shameful.
We mostly exchanged things like milk for wheat. People used to give
away wheat to the poor. People only went to the market for gold. There
was less difference, and everyone could eat" (interview by the author,
March 7, 2007). Bashir also remembers that up until the 1970s, no one

would sell or ask for milk, as it was not a commodity; people would just give it in times of wedding: "If there was a wedding, one would ask for some milk, and their containers would fill up. People didn't need money to go about" (interview by the author, March 7, 2007). The commodification of milk signals a change in interpersonal relations in the chaks. The increasing cost of subsistence since the late 1970s has increased the connections of the chaks with the market and has caused young men to move to the city to work as laborers, as land availability and the average family landholding shrink with every generation.

The structural adjustment reforms in the 1990s further deteriorated the economic and living conditions for small farmers. The tenant farmers saw the state protection and support for agricultural items like milk and wheat disappear even as the international market in food commodities remained artificially low, owing to the enormous subsidies handed out to corporate agribusiness in the United States and Europe (Oxfam 2005). Hence, the market value of small farmers' harvests and dairy hovered at (or sometimes below) the cost of their inputs. Slowly it became difficult to impossible for families with smaller parcels of land to survive in the Okara district.

Similarly, tenant farmers' livelihood practices are far more diverse than what one might think, based on the movement's militant land rights discourse. Many households (in the four villages where I did the bulk of my fieldwork) rely on family members who engage in paid work in the nearby cantonment or at village bazaars, or who reside and work in Karachi or industrial towns. Some families depend on remittance income from relatives laboring abroad in Dubai, Abu Dhabi, and Saudi Arabia. Many tenant farmers are directly or indirectly employed by the military as noncommissioned foot soldiers; as barbers, gardeners, and cleaners for the cantonment municipal service; as or dairy farmers. A few AMP activists had worked in cities either in Pakistan or abroad in the past, as well.

Many farmers I spoke to were more afraid of the arrival of multinational agribusinesses like Nestlé than the army or Rangers. The following is a telling exchange that was provoked by a conversation about the cost of things in a male gathering space in the AMP office in Chak 4/4 L in February 2007.

Latif: Before in all the villages, there was no Dalda [a brand of hydroge-
nated cooking oil popular in Pakistan]; people ate real ghee [clari-
fied butter traditionally used in cooking]. People used to say that
this Dalda is from America, and it is made from pork fat. People
did not go close to Dalda.

Sattar: Now people don't like their roti if it's not cooked with Dalda—

Latif: It's not that they don't like it; the problem is that they have no
choice, because desi ghee is so expensive.

Farid: But habits also change.

Latif: Habits change because of necessity. Desi ghee per kilo is much
more expensive than Dalda. No one would want to sell the ghee that
he makes after going through so much trouble to feed his cow, take
care of his cow. He makes ghee out of the milk he gets from the
cow. He wouldn't want to sell it if it wasn't for necessity. The small
tenant farmer is selling ghee out of necessity. This is not a business
for the person who might own only one buffalo. People who have
dozens of cows, they sell ghee for business. Few people used to sell
milk before. It really started since 1977. In the past, people in the
village rarely went to the market for gold. We have to go to the market sometimes, but things are too expensive now. The government
does not think about the poor.

Sattar: When we win this struggle, then we will start another campaign
about inflation. We will bring people together on this issue.

Farid: I have been struggling against inflation all of my life. We will keep
going. This inflation system will have to end. This Nestlé problem.

Latif: Let me talk about this, about Nestlé. This milk, the pure milk
that has all of the vitamins, they buy this milk from us at 12 rupees
per liter, but Nestlé sells it for 36 rupees per liter. They buy the milk
from us, remove the vitamins, and sell it in the city for 36 rupees per
liter. Why are people not buying fresh milk? Good milk that has all
the vitamins is available for 12 rupees, but why do people buy Nestlé
milk? People give 300 percent profit to these international companies. So what about our own people, our workers, farmers—why
don't we give profit to our local industries? The generals are making
these profits; those big *zamindars* [big land owners] who are making
their factories are making these profits.

In another conversation, Latif added, "Now everything is sold in the village, and with the exception of flour, everything is more expensive in the village than in the city. Our goal is that after getting this land, we will start building a movement for small farmers and not an NGO" (group interview by the author, February 27, 2007).

The most dramatic challenges for the AMP have been the unexpected turns during the course of the movement. Economically, the tenants prospered greatly during the period between 2004 and 2008 when the Pakistan military backed away from the farms. During that time, the tenants continued their civil disobedience campaign against cash contracts and even rent in kind. The AMP insisted that they would only negotiate with the civilian government of Punjab and not the Pakistani military. Moreover, the villages experienced a wave of tenants coming back to lease more land or work closer to home. Earlier, the tenants could only plant what the military farm authorities gave them in terms of seeds and inputs. However, now the tenants were planting, wheat, mustard seeds, potatoes, corn, and rice. The dramatic jump in tube wells in the villages and the tractors were other signs of wealth going back to the farmers. However, as the Chapter 5 details, this growing prosperity was accompanied by some discord, especially among landless peasant farmers who felt betrayed by the AMP landed tenants.

Yet land remains a significant source of social value and the basis on which people access different state services, take out loans, and arrange marriages. The ongoing infrastructural development of Punjab, through the building of new roads, bypasses, and industrial zones, has also increased the price of land. I offer this detail to highlight the indirect ways in which the value of agrarian farmland goes up because of its proximity to large-scale public works projects of infrastructure. However, this transformation does not mean that the villages cease to be villages or tenants will no longer identify with a rural ethos, but rather to say that there are different meanings of being small farmer, tenant, or small cultivator.

In contrast to the modernization narrative, the subaltern studies approach allows for the incommensurability of different cultures of common sense, without having to resolve them in some transcendent or unitary cultural or political logic. I echo Gayatri Spivak's early warning about describing "subaltern consciousness" in a way that reiterates a univocal notion of subalternity, posed either as a negation of the oppressors or as emanating from a preexisting indigenous response (2010, 74). A grounded perspective of subaltern social movements must position subalternity within existing hegemonies, locating it in relation to local and regional traditions, national and modern narratives, and a historical bloc of global trends. There also needs to be greater attention given to the spatiality of power; analyses should challenge essentialist ideas of indigeneity as simply rooted in place and outside of cultural flows, media circulations, and political changes that transform the meaning of community. In this vein, my analysis focuses on the differences of class, caste, gender, and religion that remain significant components within the AMP social movement.

These shifts occurred subtly during the course of events like the massive march and sit-in rally that took place on Grand Trunk Road in 2003, to which I now turn. This was one of many extraordinary moments in the AMP's history, and it affirmed that the AMP was intact despite state repression and the arrest of AMP leaders. The march to Grand Trunk Road galvanized the movement and altered the course of the tenants' mobilization by shifting the center of gravity from Chak 10 to Chak 34/4 L, bringing new actors into prominence. Once again, state repression failed to coerce the tenant farmers and their relatives to pay according to the new contract system, as tenants creatively responded with civil disobedience.

THE DAILY WORK OF MOBILIZATION

There is an AMP office in every chak, but the head office of the AMP is located in Chak 34/4 L, one of the more prosperous villages in the military farms. The AMP office serves as a meeting space where people gather to discuss current issues, share information, and resolve local disputes. Most AMP offices are makeshift places based in a house or granary that belonged to the chak-in-charge or their collaborators who were routed out of the village in the early days of the confrontations between the tenant farmers and the authorities. In some villages, the AMP office is simply a *dera* (sitting place where men gather) on the outskirts of the village. In Chak 34, younger AMP leaders—namely, Abdul Sattar,

Sadiq Amin, and Nadeem—have taken up residence in the AMP office, which formerly belonged to an informant of the chak-in-charge, whose family was hounded out of the village after the movement's rise. This building has a narrow courtyard with several *charpoys* (traditional South Asian beds) folded next to the walls during the day. Across the courtyard are two tiny rooms and a small kitchen that opens into the courtyard. The two rooms are rather bare, with little or no furniture. The main reception room is furnished only with a small side table in a corner that holds a heavy stack of newspapers, a fax machine that stays unhooked to the phone line, and a TV that only occasionally works. Several cushion pillows are dispersed throughout the room for visitors to lean on. There is constant activity with people coming and going from early dawn to late night.

The daily activities in the AMP offices involve resolving conflicts that appear in the chaks, reading newspapers, and corresponding with journalists and political allies. In replying to my questions about the burdensome task of resolving local disputes, Sattar, one of the AMP leaders, replied that there is no such thing as "the law" available to the poor. Referring to the state, he argued, "The law is made by [those] people to do what they want. It's their law, and they do what they want" (interview by the author, July 1, 2004). The local AMP village committee handles all internal conflicts; if they cannot resolve a case, or if a case is appealed, it is sent to the "supreme court," the AMP headquarters in Chak 34. Most ordinary cases are property disputes or personal issues. Latif said, "We don't have to go to the police or courts; we try to solve our problems here. If someone wants to go the police, we strongly recommend that they solve our problems here, because we don't do what they want us to do. They want to divide us into groups, in castes" (interview by the author, June 12, 2007). The AMP's juridical practice in the chaks gives the movement a quasi-sovereign status through which leaders of the movement reinforce certain normative rules that carry the force of community.

Although the AMP has claimed autonomy from the corrupt law of the state, the AMP leadership shares many precepts with the majoritarian legal morality of the Pakistani state. Unlike the traditional *panchayat*, a committee made up of elder village leaders, the AMP leadership mainly consists of younger men and leaders in the movement who enjoy a different kind of social capital. Most *chaudharys* (big men) are hierarchically defined or caste leaders who took initiative at the start of the movement but withdrew once the Rangers descended on the villages. Within AMP circles, the credit for the success and survival of the movement is given to younger leaders. Much is made of the fact that several younger leaders have sacrificed other opportunities or their higher education to work for the principle of tenants' rights.

INTERMEDIARIES

Working in solidarity with the movement, several prominent figures in Okara City routinely pass though the AMP office to catch up on the latest developments and channel information between the tenants and civilian authorities in Okara City. One of the notables I met during my stay included Chaudhary Iftikhar, the president of the local wholesale agrarian market (*mandi*) in Okara City. Iftikhar served as an unofficial liaison between the AMP (Muslim leaders in Chak 34) and the civilian administration of Okara City, including the local police. He was also important in providing the tenant farmers with vital links to merchants in the harvest seasons between 2002 and 2004, when the tenant farmers were under strict surveillance and could not take their crops to Okara City without having them seized or facing arrests. The merchants bought crops of wheat, maize, and potatoes in the villages at discounted rates, and then sold them at the market in Okara City.

Iftikhar also served as a liaison between the local police superintendent at the time, Zafar Abbas Bokhari, who, according to Iftikhar, was sympathetic to the *mazarin* struggle and who urged the farmers to keep things quiet. In exchange, he would try to reduce the criminal charges against some of the AMP leaders. In a group conversation in the AMP office in May 2004, Iftikhar said that the police felt a level of sympathy with the peasant farmers, but some of the tenants gathered there rejected such declarations by emphasizing the police actions, including their arrests and beatings by police officers, as well as the hated Rangers. Yet others said that the police are caught in the middle, their goal being to keep the army happy but also to maintain peace so that the Rangers leave.

Iftikhar also brought information about city politics, news about prominent traders in the *mandi*, and the rumors about the army's strategy in the coming months.

During the same conversation, Iftikhar pointedly asked me the "real reason" why the Okara farmers' struggle was able to succeed against the army. I told him that I did not know the answer, and I was there in part to study that very question. Without pausing, he offered me his explanation: "The only reason why the Okara farmers' case became an international issue was because of the Christian influence. They have influence." He argued that Musharraf could not carry out a siege in Okara because the Christian governments in Europe and America would not allow a violent operation against fellow Christians. Iftikhar's theory irked Sattar and the AMP's mostly Muslim leaders in Chak 34, who argued that the movement's success had to do with the will of God and the hard work of the *mazarin*. For the AMP, the idea of giving all the credit for the success of the movement to the Christian community or its connections was to nullify their own achievements and also to weaken their position next to Younus Iqbal and the other the AMP faction in Chak 10.

However, Iftikhar's assertion of the Christian influence did not condone the army's position, either. He shared the common resentment against the military actions in Okara by the local traders and businessmen. In that same conversation, he told me that people in Okara City were tired of Ranger patrols. He also reported that some of the army officers stole people's cars, disrupted their businesses, and took their milk containers, which are used by dairy company brokers to collect milk from small farmers, and that they harassed those who have family links to the villages (see Human Rights Watch 2004). As a result, there is much dislike of the Rangers' presence in Okara City. These descriptions of the military's arbitrary and extrajudicial authority were also the subject of popular discourse, as many newspapers and magazines printed stories about land grabbing, car thefts, and the dubious financial dealings of military officers. This state of exception of the military shows a complicated picture of sovereignty in Pakistan, where the official rights ensured by the state are deemed subservient to the might of the military regime.

Another local notable who was a fixture in the AMP's head office in Chak 34/4 L was Mr. Malik, a reputable local lawyer who represented AMP leaders. In addition to his legal expertise, Malik would also bring in the gossip from local courts, the news about local police officials who were about to be transferred, what people were saying about the movement, and the general idea of where the different actors were positioned vis-à-vis the tenants' movement. At the time of my fieldwork, he was preoccupied with tracking the whereabouts of Wasim, the young man from Chak 33 mentioned previously. The police had used the arrest to add additional charges against the AMP leaders.

In June 2004, in conversation at the AMP office with Malik and Sadiq Amin, a local AMP leader, and Sattar's friend and assistant, I brought up the arbitrary way in which the police were pressing charges against the tenant farmers (including sometimes children as young as four years old). Amin and Malik described their visit to the police station when they went to see Wasim:

> Amin: The police can arrest anyone to make money on discharge. They
>   hit people with doubled sticks. . . . They tie people's hands to their
>   calves until they accept guilt for something they didn't commit.
> Malik: The police had killed someone when I last went to the police sta-
>   tion. A body was being transferred. The police can kill anyone they
>   want, especially if someone confronts or stands up to them.
> Amin: It's open warfare on people, but these thinkers [*danishwars*], they
>   don't know what is going on. They keep talking about whether the
>   prime minister is retiring or not.
> Malik: I am caught in the middle, not here or there. . . . Local court
>   is better than high court, where they do as they are told. The local
>   judge is fair.

These conversations took place in the AMP office. The discussion and activity in the office would ebb and flow as the day went on. The legal and court (*kutchery*) system was one of the most repeated discussion subjects, because so many tenants had to go to court for the pending criminal cases registered against them for taking part in AMP protests. Everyone discussed the imperiousness of the police, and how they had little recourse or means to hold the police accountable. Yet men like If-tikhar, who enjoyed close contact with and the confidence of the district police superintendent, also attended these gatherings. Iftikhar would bring informal messages from the police authorities, and it was common knowledge that the police, Rangers, and other interested parties were well informed about the discussions and differences voiced openly in gather-ings like this.

In this chapter, I discuss how the insights from subaltern studies al-low us to understand peasant social movements' fragile alliance of dif-ferent peasants who come together at great risk to challenge the mili-tary farms' management. In the case of the AMP, certain leaders became the spokespersons of the movement, like Sattar, who spoke in ways that reflect the dominant hegemonic speech of the state. Sattar increasingly fashioned himself as a *chaudhary*, a patriarchal big-man figure who was in demand to settle disputes in the city. Sattar was positioning himself for the provincial assembly seat in the upcoming election.

This social movement also remained tied to certain customary notions of rights, justice, and difference. A newfound commonality of class in-terests allows agrarian Muslim castes to join up with landholding Chris-tians who raise questions about the new cash contract tenancy system. Yet as we see in the Chapter 5, the sudden growth and prominence of this movement also stirs rumors of imperial authority at work, as local media-tors worry about the effects of Christian influence on Pakistan and on the Okara farmers' movement through NGOs. Hence, these mobilizations are points of tension between vertical and horizontal sources of solidarity and belonging.

CHAPTER 5

SOLIDARITIES, FAULT LINES, AND
THE SCALE OF STRUGGLE

THE PUNJAB TENANTS' ASSOCIATION'S (AMP's) dynamics changed as the movement shifted from an early stage of militant activism (2000–2004) against cash contracts to a more centralized peasant organization trying to maintain the concessions it won from the state (2004–2014), and more recently (2014–present) one that is enduring a new wave of repression under the pretext of security and counterterrorism. Since 2014, the Pakistani state has used its new, harsher anti-terror laws to arrest AMP leaders and justify its policies of land monetization and privatization in Okara as well as in other disputed territories. I turn to these developments in this concluding chapter, where I describe the situation I encountered during my extended stay in the villages.

I conducted the bulk of my fieldwork research between 2007 and March 2008, when the AMP faded out of the national limelight, in part because of its own success in spawning oppositional politics throughout Pakistan. The rise of the AMP discredited the military's carefully crafted narrative of professionalism and accountability by raising questions about its land and real estate speculations. General Musharraf's grip on power dramatically weakened between 2006 and 2008, and the military government, which had seemed unassailable at the start of 2007, seemed untenable by the year's end. The tenants worked to gain attention during this period of upheaval, and they were brought up as an example of the Pakistani military's overreach by both the Pakistan Peoples Party (PPP) and the Muslim League led by Nawaz Sharif. However, the Okara Military Farms issue disappeared from the newspapers, and an uneasy détente had taken hold in the farms. The tenants were bracing for the upcoming elections that seemed inevitable as 2007 progressed.

The Pakistan military and paramilitary Rangers forces had withdrawn from the military farms, and the tenant farmers were comfortably cultivating their lands without much interference from the police or the army. The tenants experienced unprecedented prosperity when they did not pay any rent in cash or in kind. They could choose their own crops, dig their own tube wells, and keep as much livestock as they could sustain. However, this situation was not permanent, and everyone in the military farms was bracing for what would come next. The tenants realized that their occupation was untenable in the long run, but Pakistan was caught in a political impasse.

The AMP seemed like a historical footnote by the time I started my fieldwork. There were little signs of AMP mobilization in the villages, but there was a lot of talk and discussions in Pakistan's activist circles about the movement, its meanings, and its shortcomings. The AMP's success was offset by growing rifts within the leadership of the AMP, as some of the original leading figures like Younus and George were expelled from the leadership for alleged "corruption" by taking monetary donations from Action Aid and other nongovernmental organizations (NGOs) without clear transparency.

The AMP's success was attributed to the courageous resistance of the tenant farmers and to the AMP's skillful networking with urban activists and civil society organizations to generate wide publicity and recognition for the movement. However, little attention was given to the disjuncture between what was said about the movement and what was happening in the villages. The center of the AMP's political activism shifted to neighboring state-owned farms in Depalur, the Kulyana states, and the southern districts of Khanewal, where other groups of tenants tried to replicate the success of the AMP to make claims on farmlands originally settled and established by resident tenant families, which had subsequently been taken over by retired military officers (as in the case of the Kulyana farming estates), the Punjab Seed Company, or other state enterprises. Most of the direct-action protests and confrontations were taking place outside of the Okara Military Farms, and some of these actions or mass protests involved the tenant farmers from Okara, who went out to support the movement on occasions or major rallies. In Okara, the tenant farmers' leadership was pursuing a different strategy of maintaining the détente with the military officials while gaining political clout by participating in local politics with the aim of getting the AMP leader Sattar elected to the Provincial Assembly or the national parliament. The AMP did not function like a mass mobilization in Okara. There was a feeling of complacency among the AMP leadership, who were preoccupied with resolving village-level disputes, investing in their lands and livestock. The AMP leaders were in effect the new local *chaudharys*, local headmen, and Sattar was the figurehead of the movement.

Much of the work of the movement shifted to the headquarters, as Sattar had come to embody the movement in the district since our last meeting in 2004. The credit for the AMP's victory was increasingly attributed to its leaders, especially to Sattar. The Rangers' withdrawal from the Okara Military Farms and the AMP's provisional victory made Sattar into a local celebrity, a populist peasant leader who commanded influence over hundreds of thousands of tenants in the district, and he gained the respect of large landlords, businessmen, and district-level officials. A new narrative had emerged that saw Sattar as a college-educated reformer who started the AMP movement and raised the tenants' consciousness and emboldened them to fight for their land rights. Sattar had dropped out in the final examination month before obtaining his master of science degree in veterinary sciences at University of Agriculture at Faisalabad to come back to the village at the height of the conflict. Sattar earned great respect in the eyes of most tenant farmers for sacrificing a lucrative degree to come back to his village. However, the key figures in the movement realized that the movement did not originate with him.

In the same period, Younus and many other AMP leaders who were instrumental in the formation of AMP were marginalized. Younus and George were accused of financial impropriety, and questions were raised about their political affiliation. I was struck by the fact that some of the most charismatic and effective leaders of the AMP, such as Latif, the loquacious and sharp spokesperson for the AMP who had been my first point of contact, always insisted that I get the most reliable analysis from Sattar even though I found Latif's, Farid's, and Hanif's analyses and observations to be more sharp and compelling.

Sattar, who had been very approachable in 2004—I had spent a great deal of time with him in my preliminary fieldwork when the AMP leaders mostly stayed with their villages to avoid arrest—was less accessible in 2007, and most people in the movement had taken up the habit of calling him *chaudhary* (a big landlord, or a patron) as a term of respect, whereas other AMP leaders had retreated to their smallholdings. In 2007 Sattar was in great demand by the different power brokers in Okara City, who ranged from police commissioner to the local grain merchants. Sattar had taken on a big-man persona as a mark of distinction. He traveled in a big SUV with a driver (donated by Tahir Abdullah, an Okara sand and cardboard businessman who was good friends with Sattar and sympathetic to the cause of *mazarin*) and an armed security entourage. Local AMP leaders justified Sattar's *chaudhary* persona as a necessary posture when dealing with powerful men in the district like the local police superintendent, politicians, and landlords. Hanif explained to me that the local political culture in Okara required that Sattar take his SUV to meet with local dignitaries as an equal; he could not simply take a rickshaw or ride a motorcycle to meet local police superintendent. No one would take him seriously. Sattar was a leader of hundreds of thousands of tenants farmers, and he had to show it. Sattar was commonly invited to city functions; he enjoyed good relations with the district superintendent of police at the time, and it was an open secret that he was positioning himself for the next Provincial Assembly elections. I knew I would have to wait my turn to meet him when I returned to Okara.

The bulk of the AMP activity was controlled by Sattar and a host of new leaders who were trying to replicate the AMP's success in their respective state farms, such as Kulyana. I decided to visit Farid, the veteran leader of the AMP, and Latif, the loquacious AMP spokesperson. Farid and Latif reside in the same village, Chak 33 L, and both men have kept a low profile since the state and military authorities backed away from the military farms. Chak 33 L lies far from most military farm villages. This village was not part of the military farms at the time of Pakistan's independence, but rather it belonged to a local Hindu landlord and was allotted to the military farm authorities after independence. Chak 33 appeared to be more impoverished than other villages located closer to Okara City; however, the tenants in this village reported great prosperity (*khushali*) after reaping a full harvest without surrendering their crops to the army. Approximately eight hundred people lived in this village, belonging to many castes (Arain, Jat, Durray, Doggar, Machi, Sheik, Masih [Christian], Bhatti, Tirkhan, Nai, Kamboh, and more). A quarter of the population of 33 L was Christian. Less than half of the people had land; the rest were landless laborers or employees in neighboring dairy farms. The complex configuration of religion, *biradari* (patrilineal lineage), and occupational caste was both a source of conflict and solidarity in these villages and was a major factor for the movement to contend with during the course of the struggle for land rights.

On February 11, 2007, my journey from Lahore to Okara City took three and half hours. The bus picked up unsuspecting passengers like me, who had no way of knowing the extent of crowding, given that the windows are always covered with heavy curtains and the bus was blaring Naseebo Lal (a Punjabi musician) hit numbers. It took me an additional forty-five to fifty minutes to get to Chak 33 from Okara City. I took the makeshift Qingqi rickshaw vans that are quickly replacing horse carriages in rural Punjab. By dusk, I was sitting in the front guest room in Farid's house, his *bhetak* (a gathering place, also a sitting room). There was a sense of calm in the village as we sat wrapped in shawls and blankets; the sweet pungent smell of firewood fueled by dung cakes permeated the air. Wispy black plumes of smoke rose up from behind the courtyard walls where the chatter of TV and FM radio accompanied the everyday rhythms of gendered labor as *rotis* were prepared for dinner. Three years had passed since I had been to this village, and some of my acquaintances were surprised to see me again. "Things have really improved," said Latif. "Thanks to friends like you, we won, we chased them away. . . . After all, they [the Rangers and the Army] should be protecting our borders and not running these farms," he said when we spoke that day. Things had indeed changed, as there were no checkpoints to be wary of and no patrol jeeps. A general sense of calm had replaced the lingering fear I felt in my earlier trips.

Latif was being gracious when he kindly included me on the list of more prominent "friends," meaning the political activists and civil society personalities who highlighted the plight of the tenant farmers in 2003 and 2004. Latif reassured me that the movement was still very much alive, but things had changed for the better, so people had moved on with their lives. "Things have really improved; we have prospered greatly," he noted, using himself as an example: "Even with four acres of land, I have been able to refurbish my *kutcha gharib khana* [poor man's home; mud brick home] with cement bricks and paint." Pointing to his neighbors' tractor, he noted, "There are dozens of tractors in the village when there were hardly five tractors before, and now we have a traffic jam with so many tractors going to the fields in the morning. People are farming more intensely now that they are getting full returns on their harvest." People were not allowed to own more than one buffalo or two goats, and most could not afford to keep their own animals in the past, but now most tenants were buying two or three buffalos. Latif went on to admit that "with prosperity come other problems," complaining that "people become selfish and jealous, and they want more favors from their leaders" (interview by the author, February 11, 2007, Okara).

Latif's description of prosperity and how things had changed seemed incongruent with the radical slogans I had heard before, such as the chants of "Ownership or death" and "Whoever sows the seed shall reap the harvest," and the invocation of the hundred years of slavery, servitude, and debts to ancestors that had yet to be repaid by the army. The memory of the paramilitary siege was still fresh and just below the surface when brought up in conversations. Returning to the village after three years, I found it remarkable to witness how the rhythms of daily life had changed as a result of the détente. There was no obvious sign of a peasant mobilization, no AMP flags hoisted on rooftops, and no bullet marks or signs of the siege. No longer did one see people holding regular meetings to raise funds, or gathering at night to discuss what comes next. At first it seemed that the tenants had moved on. Some people had resumed working in the neighboring military dairy farms, the army's fields within the cantonment, and Okara City's large grain market as transporters and laborers.

Everyday life in the villages revolved around the sowing, tending, and harvesting of wheat, corn, sugarcane, potato, and berseem *chara* (livestock feed), with small vegetable patches grown for personal use. The case study of military farms would make a good case study for the viability for greater land reforms in Pakistan. Many of the small tenant farmers reported a dramatic increase in earnings and productivity from their ability to sell their entire crops, choose what to grow, and increase investments in livestock, all of which had been regulated and restricted by the sharecropping regime. However, the tenants' prosperity also exposed growing inequality between the landed families and landless laborers. Some tenants had started to rent out their land or to lease land from other tenants. The AMP leadership was mostly preoccupied with dispute and conflict resolutions.

There was growing sense of worry behind the outward appearance of prosperity. This was most frequently noted by ordinary tenants, those outside of leadership positions. The critics included women leaders who had played a significant role in the mobilization but were marginalized after the military withdrew from the farms. Everyone anticipated that the army would come back sometime in the future. The tenants commemorated the death anniversary of a martyr, and the annual peasant solidarity day in April. These occasions were a time to reconnect with journalists, activists and/or student delegations that would come by to meet people in the movement. Otherwise, there was little discussion about the movement between 2006 and 2008.

The AMP leaders seemed preoccupied by the fast-changing political situation in Lahore (the seat of the provincial government) and Islamabad (the seat of the national government). The AMP leaders paid close attention to news coverage of the growing lawyers' movement that sprang up in the spring of 2007, when General Musharraf summarily dismissed the supreme court chief justice, Iftikhar Chaudhary, for "misuse of authority" (Khan 2007; see also Traub 2008). The Pakistan military's leadership was upset with the chief justice's surprisingly bold rulings canceling the privatization of Pakistan Steel Mills, stopping the acquisition of forestland for a real estate project, and holding hearings about the disappeared Baloch activists, or "missing persons," abducted by state authorities (see Hashim 2017). The AMP's critique about the military's overreach and its meddling in commercial and land speculation did not seem so radical at this time. However, the tenants' movement was at an impasse because the tenants had gained de facto control over the land. The tenants debated if General Musharraf's growing isolation could force the military to strike a deal with them. The nightly gatherings at Farid's or Latif's *bhetak* were a time to discuss issues in the village, with joking and teasing that challenged or reinforced authority. The AMP leaders still gathered in the evening to smoke and chat, and many *bhetak* gatherings turned into dispute resolutions, where the moral force of the community was deployed to sort out domestic conflicts or issues as serious as theft of water.

In Chak 33 L, the gathering at Farid's house carried the most moral weight because of his age and his long history of struggling for the *mazarin*. However, Latif's satellite television was a big attraction for younger people, who arrived at his house to watch the news talk shows and then switch to music videos and Indian films. These gatherings were places to consume information and engage in gossip and share speculation, some of it quite prescient. Throughout my fieldwork in 2007–2008, I was routinely surprised to witness farfetched discussions in Latif's drawing room materialize into actual events. For instance, the outlandish talk about rapprochement between the PPP and General Pervez Musharraf actually occurred in 2007, but it seemed absurd when I first heard rumors about this possibility in a village in Okara more than a year earlier, in December 2006, when such rapprochement seemed absurd to most political observers.

A coterie of local journalists, local traders, lawyers, and party workers who were sympathetic to the movement passed through the chaks to take part in these discussions. Tenant leaders were also clued in to gossip gleaned from offices and drawing rooms in Islamabad, Rawalpindi, and Lahore by their urban activist allies. Besides national politics, there were many conversations about what the United States wanted from Pakistan. The AMP leaders realized that this exchange of information with guests was a two-way deal, and that many of the people coming through their *bhetaks* were also informing the Okara police authorities.

My presence as a Pakistani-American researcher in these gatherings was a subject of much curiosity and debate for the other visitors. I had been asked many questions about the US government, American people, and the war in Iraq. In a telling reversal of fieldwork expectations, the bulk of questions were posed to me: Where was I from? How did I come to know about the Okara farmers' movement? How did I get in touch with the movement? How many people knew about their struggle in the United States? And more general inquiries, such as who carried out the 9/11 attacks? These questions were a constant reminder of how local communities and politics are continually informed and formed in relation to global events and relations (and vice versa).

Indeed, the ethnographer is an object of curiosity, who is conscripted into local perspectives and asked to translate in both directions. At the time, the US war in Afghanistan was spilling over into Pakistan, and the villagers' view of the Pakistan Army's operations in its tribal areas was shaped by their own experience with the paramilitary forces. The tenants were sympathetic to Jihad but as a form of self-defense that they associated with the Taliban and Mujahidin. However, I saw this opinion change dramatically during the course of my research in late 2007–2008 as a profusion of bomb attacks rocked through Pakistan's urban centers. There was still great sympathy for the people of South Waziristan but also a growing xenophobia against Pathans and Afghans. Many tenants refused to accept that any Punjabis could be involved in terrorism. Christian AMP leaders expressed somewhat different sentiments: they saw war in Iraq as instigated at the behest of American imperial interests. They were careful to challenge the talk about the new crusades or a global war against Islam, referring instead to a war against the oppressed.

During these wide-ranging and disparate conversations about the goings-on in world historical events, the tenants' reiterated views about the Pakistan state being captive to and a client of American imperial interests; even district-level developments or the tenants' own struggle was weighted and debated in terms of its alignment or deviation from US objectives, intentions, and the possible workings of Pakistani agencies. However, despite these conspiracy theories, there was still great anticipation about the coming elections, and the political theater that accompanies campaign season in Okara City, which was already full of posters for Rao Sikander, the senior politician who had joined Zulfiqar Ali Bhutto's populist PPP in the 1970s and won several parliamentary elections for the PPP with peasant support and the backing of small farmers.

Rao Sikander won the party-less elections in 2003 by relying on his background as a key PPP member of the National Assembly from Okara, but after winning the election, he joined a group of twenty PPP elected senators who switched their allegiance to President Musharraf by splitting off into a PPP-Patriots bloc. Sikander was also appointed Defense Minister, a nominal position in Pakistan given the fact the military dominates the civilian government, but Sikander's ministry held great significance given that the military farmland dispute was taking pace in his constituency. Sikander had been a populist politician who sided with tenants in the 1970s, and was a staunch PPP leader from 1970 throughout the 1990s, but now he was pressing the tenants to accept the contract system. Sikander brought a populist approach to his public persona, in contrast to the distant and unapproachable position taken by major politicians.

The elections were scheduled for 2008, but there was no knowing if they would actually happen, or if the opposition parties would be allowed to participate in them. Locally there was great speculation on whether the opposition Peoples Party or Muslim League would repay their debt to the tenants' movement, given that it was the tenants' issue that challenged the army's grip on power by raising questions about their economic and political interests. There was great hope for the upcoming transition, but elections also threatened to exacerbate the tensions within the movement by exposing *biradari* and religious differences among the *mazarin*. Initially, most AMP leaders tried to avoid my questions about upcoming local elections, stating that the movement's goal was something beyond elections; it was to work with anyone who would secure the tenants' rights to the land. Still, the chaks were abuzz in the anticipation of Abdul Sattar's independent campaign for the Provincial Assembly seat on the basis of his leadership in the AMP.

Most of these conversations took place in Latif's newly renovated house that included a new *bhetak* now furnished with sofas, a large bed, and a small color TV connected to the satellite receiver (the only satellite

TV in the village). This room was now the most popular meeting place for influential AMP members. Most of the time I found Latif and his friends watching cable news talk shows, Hindi films, and Punjabi stage plays. Latif's new *bhetak* clearly led to some tension with the village patriarch, Farid Daula, who refused to put a TV in his *bhetak*. His gathering still consisted of a circle of men sitting together at night smoking, and most villagers turned to Farid to resolve small disputes.

Outside such gatherings, I sensed a much greater level of concern about the movement, as some tenants voiced disappointment with the leaders. A common complaint was that the leaders were betraying the sacrifices of ordinary tenants by furthering their own financial and political ambitions. The tenants noted that ordinary tenants and women had confronted the military while the leadership fled to Islamabad during the paramilitary operations. However, the leaders were quick to come back to reap the benefits of full harvests and to curry favors as part of their leadership positions. Furthermore, the newfound prosperity was spread out only among landed tenant farmers, and the village laborers who make up approximately 30 to 50 percent of tenants in any given village were left out.

The first person to speak candidly with me about the changed situation was Busra, Hanif's sister-in-law in Chak 51. Busra felt a great sorrow because of the lack of urgency in the movement and a sense that the leaders were now looking out for their own personal interests, which she perceived in Sattar's angling for the Provincial Assembly position. As Busra explained:

> The government has big policies. That is why they sent down these Rangers, they sent down the police, and then the army came. We beat them all back. Now the government wants to encourage traitors among us who are trying to demoralize us. As a result, there are some cowardly people who are secretly paying rent to the army, but I would rather see this land destroyed before I pay them rent on land that belongs to us. But most people don't have the strength to keep going, and they will give up along the way. (Interview by the author, February 10, 2008)

Busra's critique was a jarring contrast to the usual diplomatic dismissals of reports of any changes in the movement. In fact, Busra chastised me for taking so long to overcome my hesitation to ask her "tough questions" during the interview. With great relish, she recounted how the leaders who are hailed as *chaudharys* today, those who go around solving disputes or speaking for the movement, were the first ones to flee when the villages were under siege. Some went so far as to don a burka to escape the curfew and the siege. According to Busra, it was the women with their children armed with Thapa sticks and stones who faced the "unwanted guests" who descended on the village in 2003.

Women leaders played a central role in sustaining the movement throughout the siege and during repression. The AMP's male leadership was routinely targeted or arrested if they showed up at protests, but it was different with female protestors. The soldiers were confused when directly confronted by women and children who greeted them in kin terms, as mothers and sons, drawing parallels between themselves and the soldiers' own family members in other villages in Punjab. These situations were highly tense, and the army often backed away. However, as the siege went on, the authorities did not stop hitting the women, even if they were not targeted for arrest. The most violent episodes were when the Rangers entered the villages to arrest certain leaders and were confronted by the "Thapa force" of women

Thapa force. Source: Author photo.

armed with laundry sticks. Busra proudly recalled, "We didn't let them arrest our men. We chased them down and released our men even if it meant that we had to capture one or two of the soldiers. . . . We even went so far as to follow them to the precinct offices to surround the police station and get them to release our men. . . . Women showed more courage, and we fought more than men." Later in the conversation, when we were talking about the state of things at the time, she said resignedly that "these leaders, despite our sacrifices, they don't have time to consult with us or listen to us, but rather they spend all their time with these collaborators, selfish people. These leaders don't have any respect for the women and children [and what they have done], and for this they should be made to face a firing squad" (interview by the author, February 10, 2008, Chak 33/3 L).

My initial interaction with female leaders was constricted because public gatherings were mostly male or segregated by gender. Over time, I was able to meet some prominent female leaders through my friendships with their family members, and to forge friendly relations with Mukhtara Bibi and Busra Bibi. They were most vocal in their disappointment with the movement, though they were largely ignored now that there were no confrontations. Busra felt betrayed by the AMP leadership. Mukhtara had joined hands with the smaller faction of the AMP led by Younus when she was frustrated by larger AMP group. Younus promoted her to be president of the AMP, the same role as Farid, but Mukhtara's title proved to be just that—she had little say in the movement or tactics. She had gained wide recognition for her bold confrontation of a military major during the village siege in 2004, when she defied the military orders and marched to water her fields in Chak 101. She singlehandedly confronted and challenged the army officers to either shoot her or to release the canal water to the villages. Mukhtara felt that the new AMP leadership did not respect her contributions and sacrifices, as they failed to include her in important decisions or invite her to participate in the movement. She chose to work with Younus, who still claimed to be the guiding leader, the *Quaid*, of the movement.

Latif responded to criticism with a more general observation that the AMP was a large organization and many people had endured extraordinary hardships and sacrifices, and now just about everyone feels entitled to lead the movement or criticize the leaders if they do not get what they want. Latif conceded that some leaders had set a bad example by taking money from NGOs, but he went on to argue that the villagers were gullible to believe any rumors they might hear from government spies ("touts") or outsiders who incite them against the leadership. He argued that even the landless laborers were doing better, now that there were more tube wells dug in the village, more livestock to take care of, more homes renovated, and more work in the fields. They could work right here in their villages instead of having to leave their families and go to the city to find work. There were plenty of jobs in the villages and people had more things. Latif repeated that the overarching issue of land rights was not fully resolved, and he claimed that the authorities wanted to let things cool down so people would start bickering and fighting among themselves (interview by the author, February 14, 2008).

The multidenominational composition of the AMP, and the presence of a large number of Christian peasants in the movement with some in leadership positions, raised political activists' hopes of new forms of class solidarity. However, the growing prominence of the movement and its proximity to civil society groups also resulted in growing distrust, if not acrimony, within the movement. Sattar summed up the opinion of the AMP majority:

> Muslim, Christian—we have been together. This Younus Iqbal was eating money from other agencies. He went to all these places, and he publicized our misery; he gave out all these advertisements about what had happened to our people, our women, and he gave out all this big advertising. In China, Thailand, Japan, Germany, and America. Look at this: we are poor; the government doesn't give us bread to eat. . . . Those people gave them a lot of money. These people got so much money and ate it all. Naheed, George, Younus were eating the money. When they were arrested by the military, they quickly turned around and told us to surrender and sign the lease to the government. We said, "Why should we listen to you? You have made so much money." (Interview by the author, February 26, 2008, Okara Military Farms)

The tenants' prevailing apprehension of NGOs and urban activists was surprising, considering that civil society groups had played a crucial role in spreading the word about the Okara farmers' struggle. However, during my fieldwork I realized that this collaboration also changed the internal dynamics within the AMP.

The unprecedented nature of tenant protests captured the imagination of political activists who were baffled when they first encountered the AMP's mass rallies. Farooq Tariq, who was the chairman of Labour Party Pakistan (which subsequently merged with the Awami Workers Party), recalled in 2007 the first time he went to the tenants' convention in 2002 in Pirowal: "I was shocked to see such a large mobilization with people coming from afar. Sitting on the stage, I saw a large crowd getting larger, as tractors kept pulling in with lorries packed with people. I couldn't believe that such a large mobilization was happening and people didn't know about it [in Lahore]. . . . I contacted friends like Aasim and people in Action Aid about this mobilization" (interview by the author, July 10, 2007, Lahore). Initially, it was the mass scale of peasant protest along with Christian-Muslim solidarity that captured the imagination of many liberals and leftists in Pakistan. Starting in 2001, groups of activists, journalists, and civil society personalities like Asma Jahangir (noted human rights lawyer and former UN Rapporteur on Freedom of Religion or Belief), Mubashir Hassan (former finance minister and advocate of socialist development policies), Dr. Pervez Hoodbhoy (a physicist and public intellectual), and retired Navy Admiral Fasih Bokhari started paying close attention to the tenants' struggle. Several fact-finding missions passed through the villages after clashes and abuses were reported in the media. The struggle in the military farms presented an opportunity for urban activists to highlight the issue of uneven land distribution and to bring attention to the Pakistan military's growing appetite for land speculation.

The central question of land reform that defined leftist politics in Pakistan's early decades had been removed from political discourse in late 1970s by Muhammad Zia-ul-Haq, who instituted Sharia courts to declare land reforms and redistribution as un-Islamic. This controversial ruling, like many other religious amendments to the Pakistani state, became a sticky precedent that limits the legal avenues for social movements and advocates for land reform. However, the AMP revived the land question in a powerful way. The small cadre of Pakistani leftist parties gained a new foothold with the emergence of the AMP. The tenants' movement also revitalized left-oriented parties like the Labour Party Pakistan and the Maoist Communist Mazdoor Kissan Party (CMKP), which came out of the shadows after years of confusion and bitter disillusionment following the Soviet Union's demise. These parties were also joined by a new organization, the People's Rights Movement (PRM), a small network of activists who aimed to support and link up various place-based struggles throughout Pakistan in a coalition of social movements. The involvement of these groups created a broad network of NGOs and activists who helped turn the AMP into the preeminent symbol for land reforms, grassroots peasant activism, Muslim-Christian coexistence, and women's empowerment. However, this radical and progressive vision for the AMP was increasingly at odds with the internal dynamics emerging in the organization. I came to learn about the split early in my fieldwork in a conversation with Taimur Khan, an activist and college professor at Lahore University of Management Sciences, who told me that the movement was splitting along caste and religious lines.

When I was doing my fieldwork in 2007, there were no checkpoints and no Rangers. The tenants and the AMP leaders moved about freely in the countryside and in Okara City. Yet new barriers were emerging as the AMP split into two different groups. The divisions in the AMP are based on the different ways in which the tenant farmers allied with different NGOs and urban activists. The tenants recognized the importance of NGO connections, but they were also weary of being exploited by these organizations, which had different donor agendas. This issue first came to light when different AMP organizations accused each other of causing the arrest of AMP leaders Younus and George on charges of setting up an AMP office and launching a website detailing the abuses against the tenant farmers. Most tenants were unaware of this office, and they did not know about the source of funding, which had been exclusively handled by Younus and George, who also hired a small staff consisting of their acquaintances. Younus and George were arrested a few days after they launched a website detailing human rights violations against tenant farmers. Both men were tortured, and Younus was forced to go to the villages in Okara to formally ask the tenant farmers to accept the contract system. According to Farid, the funds from Action Aid and others were accepted without the consent of the larger AMP organization, and this gave rise to much speculation on how the money was being used (interview by the author, May 19, 2007). The controversy over the role of NGOs and outside funds quickly took on a sectarian character, because it was alleged that most of the money was received by Christian leaders like Younus and George. These two leaders had been the most active in spreading the word to urban activists about the Okara tenants' movement and also in forging stronger links and a united platform with the other eighteen military farms scattered across Central Punjab. This controversy over the funds also raised concerns about Younus's previous dealings with state authorities.

The tenants rejected Younus's appeal, and they also removed him from AMP leadership. Many ordinary tenants outside of the leadership became convinced that certain NGOs, journalists, and activists were amassing fortunes by selling the tenants' story abroad or by making and selling calendars, posters, or images of the tenant farmers. These impressions were reinforced by some tenants' visits to NGO offices in posh locations showing the lifestyle of well-heeled activists in Lahore, Rawalpindi, and Islamabad. I, too, was subjected to suspicion, being repeatedly asked about my income as a graduate student, my source of funding, and the possible profits from my book. These suspicions would also result in different forms of ethnographic refusal; for example, a young poet, whose verses about the tenant struggle were especially popular in Chak 33 and recorded on cell phones, refused to grant me permission to write down his verses or to record him. He was convinced that his work had been stolen by NGO workers who had filmed him earlier. My friends joked with me about my real motivations for studying the AMP.

Such inquiries were not new to me as a Pakistani American researcher working in rural Pakistan while the wars in Afghanistan and Iraq seemed to be proliferating, with no end in sight. I noticed an added layer of skepticism in the line of questioning directed at me in 2007 by tenants who were not well acquainted with me. The narratives of NGO exploitation and US foreign policy grew out of specific experiences of the AMP, but these interpretations were compounded by anti-NGO critiques that were motivated by other political agendas of the Pakistan state, Islamist parties, and Marxist criticisms of liberal NGO donor agendas. These all offered varying perspectives, but they also diminished the possibility for the AMP to work across differences, as much of the anti-NGO rhetoric became targeted against Christian AMP leaders.

Much of the rancor was directed at Action Aid. The Pakistan chapter of Action Aid has offices in Islamabad, Lahore, and Karachi staffed by veteran activists, former student leaders, and recent graduates from elite liberal arts schools. Yet in the village, the most common refrain I heard about the NGOs was that these organizations were set up by intelligence services, with the intent to "cool down" movements before they boiled over. Younus Iqbal and George John had received a check for 20,000 Pakistani rupees from Action Aid to set up a communications office on the outskirts of Lahore, though rumors at the time placed the figure much higher, even in the millions.

After several weeks of stay in Chak 33, I decided to return to Chak 10 and call on Younus to get his perspective on the controversy and the AMP split. Younus defended himself vigorously against a number of claims. He maintained that he was forced to ask the tenants to accept cash contracts under duress, and that his calls for a dialogue did not mean a cessation of the movement; rather, it was a deal to gain early release from jail. Younus and George both stressed that they had made it clear to their neighbors and friends that they were being forced to put on a show. As for the allegation of absconding with huge sums of money from Action Aid, Younus told me that the organization had provided an auditor for the grant and that he himself had a record of all the money (interviews by the author, August 10, 2007). One of Action Aid's major goals is to provide immediate relief in emergencies to help the most vulnerable people rebuild their lives.

Younus offered to give me a full account of how the AMP movement started in Chak 10. He summarized that in the decade before the movement started, the villagers had successfully apprehended a few farm managers who were stealing from their harvests and selling bags of grain in the market. They had filed complaints against the farms' management with the army headquarters. The tenants had mobilized in the 1970s for fairer and more transparent sharecropping. However, many of the leaders of this first mobilization had been arrested or put in jail when Zulfiqar Ali Bhutto was arrested and there was a crackdown against his PPP workers. The AMP leaders were strongly affiliated with the PPP at that time. The tenants started mobilizing after the end of Zia's regime as different tenant farmer groups approached Benazir Bhutto and Nawaz Sharif's government over the status of the land. Benazir Bhutto's PPP government counseled the tenants to start incrementally by demanding land titles for their homes in the villages, which technically belonged to the Punjab state government. Nawaz Sharif's Muslim League party also gave assurances that it would recognize the tenants' rights over their homes. Younus recalled:

> After Nawaz Sharif won the elections in 1997, we took two buses full of people to Lahore to ask the revenue board people about the lease file for these farms. They kept looking for the record, and they couldn't find the lease. We felt strongly that they [the military] didn't have a lease or any *patta* [legal land claim]. . . . All we had to do was stand up and fight, but people were too afraid. Six months later, we found out that there were three files that indicated that the army's lease had expired. I went to the revenue board and picked up a copy of those files Pakistani style [through bribing an official]. We showed these files to people and told them that all we have to do is to stand up and fight. (Interview by the author, August 10, 2007)

However, people were too afraid to do something while the sharecropping system stayed intact and their subsistence was guaranteed. Younus continued:

> We have been trying to start this movement since 1987. But people used to be very scared back then. . . . Some of us already knew that this land did not belong to the military because we were already in touch with the Punjab Revenue Board. . . . After Chadha's announcement [of the new cash contract system], people came together and created Anjuman-e Mazarin Punjab [the AMP], Okara.

The Catholic Church has officially kept a distance from the movement in order to not alienate the military government. However, the funds that Action Aid gave to the AMP, via Younus, were used to set up a communications office in Lahore. A website was launched, detailing the history of the tenants' struggle, along with photographs of the state's abuses of the farmers. The AMP office was in operation for only four months, from December 2002 to April 2003, before the army shut it down. The closure of the office, and the subsequent arrest of Younus and George, heightened speculations in Okara about the activities and motives of AMP leaders. During the eight months Younus and George spent in jail, they called on the tenant farmers to negotiate with the military farm authorities, which only increased suspicions about Younus's motives and commitment to the movement.

Younus blames the involvement of forces like the PRM, the Labour Party, and internal jealousies for the divisions in the AMP. He contends that the interference of activist organizations led to the dissension. The AMP Muslim leaders point out that many people have suffered long jail terms for not cooperating with the authorities, and that Younus's gestures of cooperation with the authorities make him untrustworthy of leadership. The question of trust is not exclusively a sectarian matter; several Christian leaders have also objected to Younus's dealings and have aligned themselves with the Muslims in AMP, whereas there are many Muslim peasants like Mukhtara and most tenants of the Pirowal farms who still accept Younus and George as the leaders of the movement.

In an August 2007 conversation with Younus and George in Okara, they told me that the urban political activists who are most critical of the AMP's contacts with NGOs are the very ones who put them in touch with the NGOs. For instance, Taimur Rahman, the energetic leader of the CMKP, confirmed in an interview that he helped fill out the application for the Action Aid grant for the Lahore office, but he also clarified that he advised against it, and he worked on the grant as a favor in his personal capacity not through the party (interview by the author, September 12, 2007). Similarly, AMP leaders noted that Aasim Sajjad Akhtar, one of the conveners of the PRM, was instrumental in putting the movement in touch with Action Aid at a time of dire need when the army had closed down all contact with the military farms. Action Aid then sent its first delegation with foodstuffs, first aid, and money to those isolated villages in Okara. According to Younus and George, people in the PRM had arranged this.

At the end of our interview, Younus offered to drop me at the bus station, but I was in for a major surprise when he suddenly changed our plans and swerved his motorcycle toward Chak 34/4 L. He was taking me for a show-and-tell session at the headquarters of his rival, Abdul Sattar, the leader of the AMP majority faction in Chak 34/4 L. The sudden detour complicated my earlier efforts to stay out of the partisan politics of the AMP leadership. For a long time, I had taken a position of solidarity with the peasant movement but not necessarily with the internal dealings of the leadership. I hesitated to write about the tensions within the movement, and I knew that my principled position was naïve in the present context and I needed to catch up with the situation on the ground. I could see that Younus wanted to show me his continuing importance, and use me to demonstrate that he had established contacts with translocal activists and journalists who played a significant role in getting the word out about the movement.

Things became awkward as we approached Chak 34 L. I spotted Haji Arshad waving as we drove onto the road adjoining the village. Arshad never missed a chance to remind me privately about Younus's lower-caste background, implying his untrustworthiness. Then I saw Amin George, my host in that village, who had warned me earlier about Younus's actions and intentions. Younus, seizing the opportunity, slowed the motorcycle to stop next to Amin, and we exchanged an awkward greeting before Younus abruptly pressed the accelerator and we were off to our destination in the village. I was left wondering if Amin felt betrayed by me, as he had hosted me multiple times at his home. Amin was a close ally of Sattar and very critical of Younus. I felt that somehow I had violated Amin's trust, even though I did not share his views regarding Younus.

These thoughts were circling in my mind as we made our way to *chaudhary* Dil's *dera*. A bulky man with jet-black comb-over, Mohammad is an influential dairy farmer in Chak 34, who worked on a Greek cargo ship for eighteen years before returning to his village in the late 1980s. He used to be a fixture in Sattar's inner circle, but now he has little good to say about Sattar. Younus brought me to Chak 34 to hear firsthand from Mohammad about how Sattar was abusing his leadership position to promote his own personal and political ambitions, hobnobbing with the Okara City elite for the nomination for a seat in the upcoming Provincial Assembly elections. This awkward encounter exemplifies how political subjectivity in the AMP is navigated through shifting bonds of solidarity, through alliances and conflicts among dissident groups of tenant farmers from diverse castes, class positions, and religious affiliations. Frictions characterize social movements like the AMP's mobilization over time and space as people make alliances with different NGOs, political parties, and civil society activists.[1]

Irfan, a caseworker with Action Aid in Lahore, argued that the AMP was the first social movement to emerge after the rights-based framework came to dominate politics in Pakistan (after 1989). He went on to give me an example of his own involvement in politics. Irfan started out as a student activist in Saraiki nationalist parties that were sympathetic to the Movement for the Restoration of Democracy that was launched in the early 1980s to protest Zia-ul-Haq's martial law regime. These movements were ideologically driven and worked on the ideals of radical transformation, and people paid out of their own pockets or raised their own funds to take part in something they believed in. Ideally, he said, people should give donations to run their own movements, but "we can't afford to do that kind of voluntarism now that we have more responsibilities." Later, when I tried to get him to clarify what he meant by this statement, he said, "Things move fast these days, and today movements take much less time to get ahead. We have to be more efficient; NGOs have had to become more specialized like the market in many cases" (interview by the author, September 23, 2007, Lahore).

Irfan replied to my questions regarding funds to AMP leaders by placing the blame on former Action Aid staff members and AMP leaders. He started by countering the AMP's and left parties' broad allegation against Action Aid for derailing the movement through funds. "There was always some funding coming from outside sources, whether the Soviets or communist parties, and things weren't as transparent as now." He went on to admit that certain staff members (without naming names), who lacked "professionalism" and "human development," made big mistakes by giving out funds without proper transparency. However, he suggested, it was hard to be open under the repression at the time, because things were moving so fast. After I pressed him further with questions regarding the *mazarins'* distrust of the organization and some leaders, Irfan explained:

> The movement had become so huge in a short span of time that they [Younus and George] weren't able to handle it. They alienated the common people in the chaks by staying away for too long or taking a car back to the villages. In contrast, we also worked with another large movement of fisher communities in coastal and interior Sindh who are fighting against very similar paramilitary [Rangers] enforcement of cash contracts that were being imposed on them by the paramilitary Ranger forces, but the Pakistan Fisherfolk Forum worked slowly to build itself against the contract system. We worked closely with them, and they didn't encounter any such divisions. In Okara, the AMP was in the spotlight, and the Rangers decapitated the movement when they picked up the leaders. (Interview by the author, September 23, 2007, Lahore)

To get another perspective on the question of the influence of NGOs, I turned to Saqib, who has worked with the movement as an activist for the Labour Party and later as a project manager for the Applied Social Research Resource Centre, an NGO that takes on special research projects on social inequity and human rights in Pakistan. Its director, Nighat Saeed, has taken a strong stance against Action Aid and political parties in derailing the AMP. I had met Saqib at various protests and different gatherings, but it was only after many meetings that he revealed to me that he was one of three employees who worked in the short-lived AMP office and that he was also arrested with Younus and George and spent eight months in jail (interview by the author, September 26, 2007, Lahore). He confirmed that Younus and George had been severely beaten. Saqib opted out of the *mazarin* struggle after his release from prison. To him it was clear that the movement was cracking from its own divisions, in contrast to the early days, when it had felt like the AMP could grow to challenge the broader landlord system and uneven land distribution in Pakistan. Saqib attributed the dramatic rise of the movement to the commitment of the tenant sharecroppers but also pointed to another contributing factor: the role of new technologies like mobile phones, which were just coming into common use in the village and gave the tenants a level of connection and coordination that had not been possible before. The rise of cable news channels was also a factor, though the media was still too scared to cover the tenants' issues at the risk of offending the all-powerful army. However, the tenants had the capability of challenging and embarrassing the media into covering the issue by circulating reports on the Internet.

According to Saqib, the movement never lived up to its larger potential because of the short-term decisions made by the leadership. Here he also blamed Younus's and George's use of funds from Action Aid without making a strong case to AMP members. He thought that the movement would have been able to come up with the money to set up the office. He did not believe that Younus and George sought out the funds for personal gain. More than the leaders of the AMP, Saqib found much to blame among various NGOs (such as Action Aid, Shirkat Gah, and the South Asia Partnership) and political parties, including his own former party, Labour Party Pakistan, for being more interested in seeking out partners in the movement (or "clients," as he put it) than working to reconcile the differences between the tenants. He blamed these groups for siding with rival factions in the conflict and working with only one group after the split. Instead of reconciling the rift, the parties and NGOs were much more eager to shape the movement as patrons.[2]

Saqib's comments rang true in the sense that following the rift in the movement, the CMKP supported Younus's faction and the PRM supported the AMP Muslims led by Abdul Sattar. The Labour Party went back and forth in their support after the split, but at the time of my fieldwork, the chairperson of the Labour Party made it clear to me that he was with the AMP Muslim camp. In fact, he sent a message to Sattar to come and see me urgently when I shared my observation that Sattar was much keener on working on his election candidacy seat than discussing the movement.

Of all three political parties, it is widely agreed that the PRM played the most crucial role in terms of getting the news about the movement into the cities. The small team of PRM coordinators spent weeks locked down in curfew-like situations in solidarity, and they helped other activists find shelter during the brutal crackdown on the villages in 2003. My own contacts in the AMP were made with the PRM's help. And now, after months of fieldwork, I had the opportunity to interview Aasim about what he thought about the movement in terms of what it had achieved, whether it had lived up to its potential as he had envisioned it, or whether it was in the end a disappointment.

Aasim replied to my question using a structural framework, wherein he argued that because this movement was based on a basic single issue about maintaining subsistence farming, it would lose steam as soon as the tenant farmers got in charge of their farmland, which is what happened. He argued that activists would need to do far more political training or create counterdiscourses to promote a more radical result. However, Aasim also decried the fact that so many civil society members promoted the movement's diversity—its large number of Christian minorities—because this came to overshadow the movement and enabled someone like Younus to play politics and work for self-interest (interview by the author, May 10, 2007, Lahore). For their part, both Younus and George claimed that PRM activists like Aasim and Bashir Buttar (who left the party) were the first to raise doubts about their leadership in the village, even before their arrests, by spreading rumors about their opulent and decadent lives in the city at a time when the tenants were facing deadly force (interviews by the author, December 20, 2014). The CMKP, conversely, takes a very critical line against the AMP's new leadership under Sattar. It sees this group as the more conservative and alleges that Younus was only kicked out of the movement at the behest of leaders who sought to make their name and also to reassert their religious and class position. Younus himself put much of the blame on the PRM for raising someone like Sattar to a position of great importance (interview by the author, December 20, 2014).

Things came to a head in 2008 as the rivalry between the different AMP camps intensified in the run-up to the elections. Abdul Sattar failed to get on the ticket with the PPP and decided to run as an independent candidate for the Provincial Assembly. Younus supported Sattar's opponent, who was allied with Rao Sikander, the defense minister, and with General Musharraf's Pakistan Muslim League, whose hold on power was slipping fast. When I asked Younus how he justified campaigning for Musharraf and Sikander, he replied that since Musharraf was desperate to hold power and keep his party going, he would resolve the tenants' land issue. Younus went on, "These lands will only be given to the *mazarin* by an army general. No politician will have the backbone to confront the army" (interview by the author, December 20, 2014, Okara Military Farms). By this time, both Sattar and Younus had moved far away from the initial vision of the peasant mobilization based on mass action, civil disobedience, and seeking recognition of other claims to land. Instead, the political vision of the leadership became constricted to electoral politics revolving around the leader persona of Sattar instead of the AMP as a political organization or movement. The symbol for Sattar's Provincial Assembly candidacy was a football, not a sickle, the symbol of the AMP.

The case of the AMP shows the multiple ways in which NGOs and urban activists helped network and legitimize the AMP, but they also altered the dynamics of the movement. Similarly, the leftist parties' and activists' crucial support of the movement also had far-reaching impact in the ways tenant farmers understood their struggle and their own differences. The activists' strong criticism of NGOs enabled the rise of a conservative political leadership that is less democratic. The interaction of a local movement with urban activists and international NGOs slowly transformed the movement's dynamic in a way that no longer reflected the hopes and aspirations of the struggle.

The rise of the AMP demonstrates the pitfalls and possibilities of political collaboration between NGOs, urban activists, and local movements. It calls for a revision of theories of state sovereignty by showcasing the limits of the Pakistani state's monopoly of violence and the ability of civil society organizations to mitigate the relations between the tenant farmers and the military by invoking human rights discourse and the moral economy of land rights (Steinmetz 1999). The case of AMP illustrates the distributed nature of state sovereignty, or what Timothy Mitchell (1991) and Michel-Rolph Trouillot (2003, 81) call state-effects, whereby the state's claims to physical and symbolic monopoly over violence are challenged. As Trouillot has argued, NGO governmentality has far-reaching effects in postcolonial states where the limited programs of social development, public health, education, and infrastructure have been sourced out to NGOs.

Trouillot argues that certain fundamental effects of sovereign power, as in cultivating national identity or identification, are no longer monopolized by nation-states, but by private civil society groups. Hence, the isolating effect of sovereign power, as in the "production of atomized individualized subjects molded and modeled for governance as part of an undifferentiated yet specific 'public,'" becomes more elusive (Trouillot 2003, 81). The nexus between the AMP and international NGOs like Action Aid creates a new understanding of politics by which the domain of rights associated with notions of civil society becomes increasingly significant in shaping the trajectory of movements, subjectivities, and social relations. Younus's sharp perception of the effectiveness of international human rights groups' pressure on the Pakistani regime is coupled with an understanding that the military is not able to crush a social movement as long as the AMP can reach out on moral grounds and evoke sympathy. The location of the Okara tenants' movement in the Punjabi heartland also evokes majoritarian sentiments (as opposed to differently located ethnic groups) that limit the military's ability to cast the tenant farmers movement as one consisting of terrorists, bandits, and other criminal types. The military administration was unable to physically destroy the tenant farmers' movement with sheer force as long as the tenant farmers could define their own narrative and project their story through advocacy networks connected with the normative regimes of multinational NGOs and foreign governments central to the Pakistani state's larger goal of attaining acceptance for military-controlled state liberalization.

In the concluding chapter, I describe the current scenario wherein the Pakistani state has used the deteriorating security conditions in the country to clamp down on the tenant movement. The war in Afghanistan and the global war on terror has proliferated into every aspect of life in Pakistan. Suicide attacks, bomb blasts—with shocking attacks on school kids in Peshawar, and at the international airport in Karachi—along with the targeting of political figures, minority communities, and even former Prime Minister Benazir Bhutto, have wreaked havoc in the country.

Since 2012, the Pakistani state has adopted stricter counterterror policies to extend its extrajudicial powers. The deteriorating security condition has created a climate of emergency and insecurity that has allowed the state to further clamp down on speech and dissent. These developments threaten to upend the gains made by the AMP in making visible the overlooked deprivation of landlessness and dispossession.

CODA

The Ethics of Staying

POSTCOLONIAL SCHOLARS have noted that concepts like *crises,* *emergency*, and *exception* lose their explanatory meaning in contexts where they become routine (Mbembe and Roitman 1995; Simone 2008). Naveeda Khan (2012) has argued that terms like *emergency* and *crises* become obstacles to understanding the pattern of political coups, the persistence of social movements, the myriad types of indirect rule, and the periodic demands for democratization that are constant sources of friction in Pakistan. Walter Benjamin's eight theses on history deal with this dilemma in midcentury Europe. He writes, "The tradition of the oppressed teaches us that the 'state of exception' in which we live is the rule. We must arrive at a concept of history which reflects this" (Benjamin 1969, 253). Benjamin's theses were directed toward the North Atlantic world, where the conceit of progress and modernity produced a body politic that refused to confront the crises, the everyday forms of fascism and racism that were fueled by colonial and corporate rule that was coming back to haunt Europe in the interwar period. Benjamin's connection between the everyday militarism and the privileges of race and class that preserve inequality through corporate rule remains pertinent in post–Cold War America, but it becomes most visible in postcolonial states like Pakistan, where security and counterterrorism become the justification for authoritarian rule (Masco 2014).

In this book, I trace the rise of the AMP mobilization, which coincided with the fateful events of 9/11 and its aftermath. General Musharraf's government was facing economic isolation for carrying out a military coup in 1999, but the geopolitics of the post-9/11 era brought the military government in from the cold as the Pakistani state joined the international coalition against Al-Qaeda and the Taliban.[1] Like the Afghanistan war in the 1980s, the global war on terror has had a major impact on the political machinations inside Pakistan, which left the major political parties out in the political wilderness as General Musharraf picked apart politicians and notables like Rao Sikander, who were willing to change their allegiances in favor of government ministries. The Pakistani military promoted General Musharraf's image as the firewall between Muslim militants/extremists and the West, whereas domestically the military leader was portrayed as the defender of Pakistan's national and economic interests. This dichotomy was best personified in Musharraf's autobiography, which was titled *In the Line of Fire* (2006a) in English but altered for the Urdu reading audience to roughly *Pakistan First and Foremost* (2006b).

At this crucial juncture, the AMP challenged the neoliberal militarism of the Musharraf era with a stubborn "land ethic" to challenge the Pakistan military's national development policy (Leopold 1949). The land rights dispute in the military farms was marginal in scale when compared to the military's ambitious projects of creating ports in Balochistan, developing affluent suburbs in the outskirts of major metropolitan cities, and promoting corporate agriculture under the pretext of national development. However, this obscure issue grew in significance as it raised important questions about the uneven land distribution, the military's policy of acquiring land to redistribute to its retiring officers, and real estate companies that are linked to officers. The military farms became a metaphor of resistance to dispossession, and a populist challenge to Pakistan's most powerful institution. The Punjab Tenants' Association (AMP) came to embody the contradiction between the idea of nation and state in Pakistan, where the state was seen as denying the basic subsistence rights of Punjabi peasants. The Pakistan military struggled to justify its wholesale change in land tenure laws in a region where the Punjabi peasant farmers were subject to prior histories of recognition.

As Rob Nixon (2011) has argued, the politics of development are tied to a spectral politics of imagining utopian futures, while evicting the existence of the poor from public imagination. The monetizing of public lands, the eviction of a "slum," or privatization of peasant farmland requires the state to erase the history of the communities, the use value of the land, in order to speculate on the potential exchange value of a utopian future city. This type of imaginative eviction is built on what Michel Foucault (2003) calls biopolitical racism, which sanctions dispossession for certain forms of life while enhancing the lot of others through social investments, such as the canal colonization policies in the Indus Plain that facilitated the settlement of a select population of peasants while banishing the existence of nomadic pastoral communities.

The Pakistan military's moves to monetize the state farmland was yet another attempt to free up the land from sharecropping. The AMP disrupted this logic by making a moral claim on the land. Central Punjab generates a kind of visibility and agricultural significance that is tied to a web of obligation and reciprocity forged between the state and peasant farmers through colonial infrastructure, which makes it difficult to evict the peasants from the national imagination or portraying them as outsiders.[2] The AMP's rhetoric against the military's land and real estate interests was picked up by other movements, such as the Pakistan lawyers' mobilization against the unconstitutional firing of the chief justice, and college students who mobilized against the declaration of martial law after November 3, 2007. These protests against General Musharraf's dictatorial rule dramatically weakened the military government by the end of 2007, when the major political parties who had been exiled were able to return to Pakistan. Benazir Bhutto returned to Pakistan after a decade-long exile. She initially agreed to an informal agreement with General Musharraf to work with his government, and Nawaz Sharif was able to regain his foothold in Punjab by championing the democratic opposition to the government in Punjab. Several AMP leaders in Okara tried to channel the success of their mobilization to enter formal politics.

Democracy was restored in Pakistan in 2008, but it came at a heavy price. Benazir Bhutto, the chairperson of the Pakistan Peoples Party (PPP) and former Prime Minister of Pakistan, was assassinated while leaving a rousing public rally in Rawalpindi.[3] The PPP rode the sympathy wave to win the parliamentary election in 2008 and formed a government at the center. The Muslim League–Nawaz won the majority of seats from Punjab. However, both the PPP and the Pakistan Muslim League reneged on their promises to the tenant farmers after initiating some lukewarm dialogue with them. The restoration of democracy brought back the topsy-turvy political climate of reneged promises, changing allegiances, and uncertainty for tenant farmers. As Hanif explained to me in 2012, "We were expecting them [Pakistani Muslim League-Nawaz, the party in power in Punjab] to give us our promised rights for resisting Musharraf's dictatorship and supporting them in polls, but they proved worse than the military dictator by using fierce force against women and children."

Sattar ran as an independent candidate for the Provincial Assembly in 2008 and a candidate for the National Assembly in 2013. He lost both times, but he significantly extended his voter base throughout the district.[4] The PPP and Muslim League-Nawaz both refused to nominate Sattar, because both parties wanted to use the tenants' issue but they did not want endanger their chances with the military once they came to power. This was the explanation given to me by Farid, the AMP's elder statesman, who wanted Sattar to focus on strengthening the movement and not running elections. Sattar became a major dignitary in the district, and he was routinely invited to important gatherings in the Okara district. Several major contractors, developers, and businessmen in Okara City patronized Sattar's candidacy and saw him as an emerging power broker in the district. Inside the military farms villages, the election cycle started to divide tenants as they aligned with different candidates according to political party affiliation (especially for the PPP), *biradari* loyalties, and not necessarily Sattar's independent candidacy.

Each election cycle exacerbated tensions within the movement and opened new cracks and mutual suspicions about split loyalties to the movement, to Sattar, to the *biradari* candidate, and other variables. Younus's faction criticized Sattar for using the movement for his own personal political ambition and not the common welfare of the tenant farmers. Younus made an all-out effort to disrupt Sattar's political ambitions and his legitimacy as an AMP leader, further polarizing the relationship between Christian tenants, who were seen as supporting Younus, and Muslim majority peasants. Younus's efforts to sabotage Sattar's election went too far when he allied with Rao Sikander and candidates aligned with Pervez Musharraf's party, thus discrediting his own case for AMP leadership. The conflicts between AMP leaders further demoralized tenants who were holding out hopes for a change in government to gain their land rights.

The mass mobilization in Okara Military Farms seemed to be dormant after the restoration of democracy, with much of the focus going to Sattar's candidacy. However, the AMP faction in the southern district of Khanewal initiated a long week-long march in 2011 from southern districts of Khanewal to Lahore to bring attention to the tenants' issues and force the politicians to honor their promises. The long march was forcibly stopped as it made its way out of Khanewal. The police seized motorcycles, tractor trollies, and buses. Hundreds of tenants were injured and dozens arrested. The attack against the AMP's long march was a major setback for the movement's hopes for working with the civilian government. Younus maintained his base among Christian tenants in Okara and Muslim-Christian tenants in Khanewal. He also maintained close contacts with nongovernmental organizations and certain elected officials. Sattar retained his mass following in the Okara district and support from the People's Rights Movement, Labour Party Pakistan, and the Communist Party of Pakistan who came together to form the Awami Workers Party (Working People's Party), a left-of-center party.

Pakistan's transition to democracy was taking place against the backdrop of increasing violence, terrorist attacks, and militancy as fallout from the wars in Afghanistan and Iraq.[5] According to the Institute for Economics and Peace's 2015 Global Terrorism Index, Pakistan endured a 940 percent rise in terror-related deaths between 1998 and 2015, with the bulk of the attacks taking place between 2007 and 2015 (Institute for Economics and Peace 2015). The news was full of stories of suicide attacks, bomb blasts, attacks on shrines, the targeting of political figures, and minority communities. This climate of fear renewed the calls for militarized responses, which was promulgated in military operations in Swat (2010) and North Waziristan (2014–present). The violence pervaded everyday life, with shocking events like the assassination of Benazir Bhutto in the streets of Rawalpindi in December 2007, the Taliban insurgency threatening to take over the Swat valley from 2007 to 2011, the devastating bombings in Quetta and Karachi in 2013, the brazen attack by Uzbek militants on the tarmac of Karachi airport in 2014, and the awful militant attack on the Army Public School in Peshawar, when Taliban-affiliated militants targeted and killed 149 schoolchildren and staff in the Peshawar cantonment area (7 Taliban attackers were also killed). These horrific events transformed Pakistan into a garrison state where every major city, thoroughfare, and cantonment was encircled with security checkpoints, traffic barriers, and severe restrictions on basic civil liberties.

The Pakistani parliament expanded counterterror legislation by adopting the Pakistan Protection Act, which expands the anti-terrorism clause to speech, action, or online postings that could be deemed threatening or hostile to the security of the Pakistani state. Thus, a Facebook entry, a Twitter posting, or a retweet could technically be used as grounds for arrest. These stringent new laws were further tightened in the aftermath of traumatic events like the carnage at the Army Public School. The attack forged a rare civil-military consensus for the passing of a constitutional amendment, the National Action Plan, that gives the military full authority to persons held on the suspicion of terrorism for military trials. These trials take place outside the ambit of the judicial review. The National Action Plan also brought back the death penalty.

The prevailing sense of insecurity emboldened the state to criminalize all dissent, thus halting the democratic process. The Pakistani state started using counterterror measures to suppress grassroots movements like the AMP and political parties that oppose the state's uneven dispensation of resources and development. In Okara, the military started installing barbed wire and gated check posts in the farmland bordering the cantonment area. All tenants whose fields lie behind the barbed wire are required to obtain a special ID from the army authority to enter and exit the cantonment to access their fields. The tenants whose fields fell behind the barbed wire had to get a special pass costing 1,000 rupees

(10 US dollars) to access their fields. It took countless trips to the local councilor's office and a signature from a Grade 18 officer for identity verification to make the security pass. The cantonment ID is mandatory for anyone to enter their own fields. There are separate IDs for tenants, land workers, and tractor operators, and each member of a household has to carry their own ID card in order to gain access to their fields.

In addition to the check posts, members of the Military Intelligence started random checking of IDs in the field. As one elder noted, "These officers find so many ways to humiliate us. Is this not Pakistan? Are we not Pakistanis? If so, why can't we use our national ID card? Why do we need to get a special cantonment pass?" (interview by the author, December 27, 2014). Crossing through check posts became an ordeal for tenant farmers, especially when some dignitaries toured the area or if the guards felt like harassing the tenants over some banal details. The tenants also complained that the soldiers routinely demanded that women uncover their faces for identification. One farmer described the questioning process as "frustrating and humiliating" (interview by the author, December 27, 2014, Okara Military Farms). Moreover, the cantonment authorities also place apparently random restrictions on what tenant farmers are permitted to grow on their land.[6] The counterterrorism policies were used to arrest and detain peasant farmers in Okara who have no links to militancy or organized violence.

The state banned all public gatherings, protests, and conventions and arrested the main AMP leaders in the case of any public protests. The main AMP leadership in Okara and its neighboring districts were arrested between 2014 and 2016. Sattar, who was accorded great respect and protocol by district officials (like the senior police officers and district commissioner), was again branded as a criminal and arrested. Sattar, like all AMP leaders, had been charged with dozens of criminal cases since the beginning of the tenants' mobilization in 2000. However, these charges were either dropped or unenforced, which is reflected in the fact that his candidacy for provincial and national assembly election was approved by the state in 2008 and 2013. However, since 2014, the leading figures of the AMP have been arrested whenever they hold public rallies or protests.

Sattar was arrested in a predawn raid at his house on April 16, 2016, when he refused to cancel the annual Peasant Solidarity Convention in Okara. The District Police Officer had warned the tenants to cancel the convention under the pretext of securing the area. The local District Commissioner Officer and Police Commissioner banned the tenants from carrying out the rally by citing the suicide attack on a Christian community that was celebrating Easter in Lahore Park. However, the tenants persisted with their plans to hold the convention by citing the decade-old precedence of peaceful gathering. The district administration called in the military and police to besiege the fields around Chak 33, based on the district-authorities-imposed Section 144 of the Criminal Procedure Code, a colonial-era law to restrict gatherings. The tenants refused to back down and proceeded to hold a rally to protest Sattar's arrest.

On April 18, 2016, a police force numbering between fifty and sixty officers raided AMP villages in the dead of night to arrest tenant farmers for participating in an "unlawful assembly." The police went door to door looking for leaders and active AMP members in the village who had taken part in a protest to ban the AMP's annual International Peasant Solidarity Day. Human Rights Watch (2016) wrote a small report on the crackdown, and in it they included testimony by Sakina, a seventy-year-old woman whose two sons were abducted by the authorities without any charges or any information about their whereabouts. According to Sakina, the police broke down the door of her house at 2:00 A.M. on April 18. They dragged her elder son, who is a schoolteacher, from his bed and started beating him with rifle butts. They grabbed her younger son and beat him with batons. Both men were taken away. Sakina was kicked on the head when she tried to prevent the police from taking her sons away. The Okara police also arrested a local reporter, Husnain Raza, for reporting on the tenants' struggle for the Urdu daily, *Nawai Waqt*. Raza's father was also arrested and beaten for covering the AMP mobilization for the same Urdu daily. Izhar (pseudonym), who is a lawyer and resident of military farms, reported that he could not leave his village to go to court to register his appeal. He was arrested when tried to go to the court in Okara City. He was quoted by Human Rights Watch shortly before he was arrested, describing the tenants' conditions this way:

They are detaining people without registering arrests. I am a lawyer who has been working for the rights of other villagers. However, now even I can't go out of the village. For the past one year, I have stopped practicing law because I am afraid of being arrested. There are check posts outside the village and they arrest anyone going in and out. Sometimes they ask for National Identification Card and if the address on the N.I.C. is of our village, the police detain the individuals without any legal cause. The government has used the National Action Plan, which is meant to counter terrorists, to use military force on us. Anti-terrorism cases have been registered against women and children. (Human Rights Watch 2016)

Sattar has been in jail since April 17, 2016. He was transferred to a maximum-security prison, where he is kept in isolation and shackled, even when brought into courts for his hearings. He has been charged with over forty-six criminal cases that range from murder and extortion to the promotion of public disorder. Sattar's house had been raided by the police and military personnel, who claimed to have found Indian currency at his house. The state has also made several attempts to connect the AMP with Jihadi militants by reporting encounters with two wanted Jihadi militants from the farm sheds of AMP leaders in Kulyana state farms. These attempts to tar the AMP as an Indian espionage conspiracy and/or Jihadi militant insurgency contradict the publicly recorded facts about the movement. However, the assertions are a sign of the renewed efforts of the state authorities to use the counterterror campaign to rein in the gains made by social movements that made great inroads in the previous eighteen years. The AMP broke the hegemony of the military narrative of national defense and development by raising the question of the military's corporate and private interests, which has led to new political developments in Punjab.

In this book, I offer ethnographic description and analysis about the dialectical relationship between law and violence, development and dispossession, rights and reciprocity, memory and history, citizenship and subalternity. Pakistan's shifting political landscape between authoritarian rule (whether in guise of military or bureaucratic technocrats) and democratic dispensations continues to offer new possibilities for the construction of an inclusive, redistributive political narrative. However, the state continues preserve order through managing social, cultural, and sectarian differences, or what Mbembe has called "private indirect governance," whereby the state lets go of its monopoly on violence in specific contexts, its monopoly on planning and even rent seeking, to local actors who work in compliance within certain limits (Mbembe 2001, 67).

A radical illustration of this point can be read in Walter Benjamin's essay, "Critique of Violence" (1978), in which Benjamin makes a distinction between law and violence, while at the same time showing their mutual dependency. Here I paraphrase a complex argument in which Benjamin reasons that the state comes to constitute its authority (its sovereignty) only by guaranteeing security. This distinction between law ("constituted violence") and violence ("constituting law") is what gives the state its surplus capital to be at once a sovereign institution and a spectral presence in everyday life of society. Thus "all violence as a means is either lawmaking or law-preserving" (Benjamin 1978, 287). According to Benjamin, "When the consciousness of the latent presence of violence in a legal institution disappears, the institution falls into decay" (1978, 288). He notes, "The law sees violence in the hands of individuals as a danger undermining the legal system" (280). The state must have a monopoly on violence because, as Benjamin puts it, violence, "when not in the hands of the law, threatens it not by the ends that it may pursue but by its mere existence outside the law" (281). Law, in other words, has its origins in violence, which is why the threat of violence against the sovereign's law is the threat of a new law.

Benjamin's critique of violence can be modified for the postcolonial context of Pakistan where the state does not aspire to fully monopolize violence as much as it seeks to regulate it, and channel it through parastate actors to preserve its hold over different populations, regions, and classes. The colonial state architecture rule was designed to serve the nondemocratic executive branch of government (military and bureaucracy) that repeatedly thwarts and suspends the constitution. This form of indirect rule has been extended in Pakistan through various experiments with basic democracy and local governance for devolution of power. Pakistan's previous experiments with democracy in the 1970s, 1980s through 1990s, and since 2008 follow a similar pattern of democratization with the rise of violence and lawlessness on the basis of sectarian and ethnic strife.

The AMP mobilization can be analyzed to look at how the distinction between law and violence, order and crime, are arbitrated by the state during the first few years after the return to democracy. The military farms were strictly policed by the farm managers for much of the postcolonial history, with farm managers enforcing strict rules for farming and village life. The tenants described life under sharecropping as one of constant surveillance, leaping fines, and everyday commands. This situation radically changed with the advent of AMP protests, when the tenants rose up against the cash contract system. Police and the military authorities ceded control over the military farm revenues, and they even ignored the presence of certain criminal gangs who took advantage of the semiautonomous nature of the military farms by setting up small bootleg operations in the military farm villages, as well as local gangs that hid out in the villages, between 2008 and 2014. Ordinary tenants complained that the police refused to maintain law and order in the military farms. As the villages in Okara went through a wave of livestock thefts, the AMP leaders had to take up the role of governing and maintaining order in their own respective villages.

The future of the AMP may seem uncertain right now, but the tenants' movement has already transformed the terms of debate about the Pakistani military, the political idea of grassroots politics in Punjab, and the wider possibilities of social movements. The AMP singlehandedly brought attention to the vast land, business, and real estate interests of the Pakistani military into the public debate (Siddiqa 2007). The AMP's approach to the land question was different from how it has been approached by economists, leftists, and state planners. The AMP brought up the history of labor, the memory of suffering, and settlement to make a moral claim against cash contracts to demand permanent rights for basic survival, to secure land for basic subsistence. The tenants narrated the history of settlement, suffering, and survival to foreground a moral political idea that links the contemporary struggle to the history of irrigation and sharecropping over the past hundred years. This experiential sense of place gives unique insights into how the AMP articulates a politics of land rights based on a wider set of moral claims that might not have legal precedents but carry other truths.

In this book, I argue that the AMP mobilization breaks down the formalist notions about the colonial or postcolonial state citizenship. My study offers concrete and expanded understanding of political agency, where tenants' claims to land rights are not exclusively tied to land ownership or secured by ethnic identity, but rather are based on prior histories of claim making, the politics of infrastructure, and political activism that inform tenants' understanding of rights. To understand rights politics, then, we need to go beyond the notion of agency at the individual level, as formal citizen or subject, and instead examine the broader conditions of possibility based on specific notions of sovereign power (the ideal king, a good ruler, a sacred example), governmentality (politics of recognition, discourse of development), and subjection, by which the state constituted itself as it constituted its population.

I see the tenants' struggle in state-owned farms in Punjab as a complex model of political agency. I argue that the AMP mobilization allows us to have a broader understanding of rights and political subjectivity in Pakistan and the possibility of democracy as a striated relationship between the state and the population, depending on the region and place. For instance, the AMP invokes its claim to land rights by referencing the history of canal colonization, recognition of customary law, and resistance to dispossession. The tenants' struggle is not a finished project but rather an ongoing negotiation with the transnational logic of capitalism, as it works through regimes of military government, prior histories of labor, claim making, and ethical practice that together produced the conditions of possibility for a group of landless farmers to hold back a powerful institution like the Pakistan army to demand land rights.

NOTES

PREFACE

1. *Chak* denotes "village" in the vernacular Punjabi. Most chaks in Okara have a numerical name. I have changed the names for all the villages where I did fieldwork. While I have given the villages arbitrary names, I follow the naming convention that designates a village number name in accordance with its direction to the canal (#/# L or R designated if the village is left of canal or right). The village naming convention in central Punjab is itself a testimony to the vast engineered nature of this landscape, which continues to distinguish the political economy and cultural politics of Okara.

2. Some interview locations are omitted for safety concerns.

3. Under the contract system, the tenants would no longer be entitled to the protection of the Punjab Tenancy Act 1887, which gives tenants (and their direct descendants) the first right to ownership if they have occupied the land for more than twenty years, whenever the land is sold or leased. They would also forfeit their right of occupancy and be vulnerable to arbitrary eviction at little or no notice. In addition to the general change in status, the tenants' fears are based on two specific clauses of the contract: "Clause 11: If the land is required for defense purposes, the land is to be evacuated at six months' notice. In this case, the contractor will be refunded for the rent already paid by him in advance" and "Clause 25: The contractor cannot claim occupancy tenancy rights. Under no circumstances does the contractor possess ownership rights." See Akhtar and Karriaper 2009.

4. The disputed state-owned farms are located in central and southern Punjabi districts: Multan, Khanewal (Pirowal), Jhang, Sargodha, Pakpattan, Sahiwal, Vihari, Faisalabad, and Lahore.

5. See Goldstein 2010 for a discussion on the shift from neoliberal developmental logic to the post-9/11 security paradigm for governance in the developing world. I follow works on postcolonial states in African anthropology and the Middle East (Comaroff, Comaroff, and Weller 2001; Mbembe 2001; Mitchell 2002; and Ali 2002) that argues that the postcolonial state has maintained emergency powers in order to preserve "order," and the neoliberal policies were attenuated and articulated with the military-led elite as it expanded its footprint in the national and even transnational market sphere.

INTRODUCTION

1. The AMP protests challenged the conservative image of central Punjab, the folkloric heartland of Pakistani nationalism, by foregrounding the history of canal irrigation and the role of infrastructure in shaping the economic and political sociality in rural Punjab. See Khan 2005; Glover 2008; and Gilmartin 2015.

2. The Subaltern Studies Collective initially came together in the 1970s to critique Indian nationalist historians and policy makers who rejected British imperialism while adopting modernist and Eurocentric understandings of capitalist development. The collective was influenced by the surge of political activism in India during the 1970s, and it set out to document the mostly unrecorded history of ordinary people's resistance against colonial rule. The Subaltern Studies Collective has had a global impact on academics and activists who followed the collective's innovative scholarship to challenge condescension of rural livelihoods in the global South and underscore the contemporaneousness of other systems of beliefs and notions of justice. The early writings of the collective emphasized the "autonomous, un-dominated" nature of subaltern consciousness that could be ascertained by studying peasant rebellions from below (Guha 1999; Chaturvedi 2000). Feminist historians like Rosalind O'Hanlon and literary critics like Gayatri Spivak who were sympathetic to the project challenged its ideational view of subalternity based entirely around the negation of the dominant colonial power and the missing account of internal hierarchies, differences of belief system, and internal power relations. O'Hanlon (1988) argues that such characterization of subalternity as a fundamentally reactive response does not hold, even in the historical accounts of the subaltern peasant rebellion where religion, caste, and tribal identities play a contributing factor to subalternity. Consequently, subalternity has come to be identified for its radical difference from Western subjectivity, even when it is the living condition of the vast majority of this world's poor population whose lives have been intimately shaped and linked to the Western hegemony for centuries (Spivak 2010; Chaturvedi 2000; Chakrabarty 2002).

3. Recent ethnographic and historical research by Mathew Hull (2012), Markus Daechsel (2015), and Tahir Naqvi (2013) on Pakistani state planning and bureaucracy has refocused attention on the Cold War modernizing era of Ayub Khan's regime, which set in motion many of the governmental processes ranging from executive rule, mass public works projects, Pakistan alliance with American foreign policy objectives, and the use of Islam or Muslim identity to craft a modern national identity, architecture, and style that break away from inherited vernacular traditions but perhaps harken back to the mythic Indus or ancient past.

4. Faisal Devji's 2013 book, *Muslim Zion*, is a prime example. Devji's "idea of Pakistan" seeks to correlate the intellectual history of Muslim nationalism with Zionism without pausing to examine the historical difference between European settler colonialism and anticolonial nationalism. Venkat Dhulipala's 2015 book, *Creating a New Medina*, offers an insight into the millennialism of the Pakistan movement in UP, but in making a strong case for the utopian intentionality of the Muslim League, he fails to address the fact that the Muslim League was not the only player among Muslims and certainly not a hegemonic party in Muslim majority areas; thus, the more variable factors in the call for Pakistan that ranged from a call for land reforms in Bengal to regional autonomy in Sindh and the fear of minoritization in UP. See Bose 2014.

5. In "Underestimating Urbanization" (2003), Reza Ali shows that Pakistan is the fastest-urbanizing country in South Asia. He argues that the driving force of urbanization is the rapid industrialization of Punjab cities along the Grand Trunk Road corridor. However, there are also other factors driving urbanization in Pakistan that range from

intensifying climate change, which became most visible through frequent flooding like the 2010 Indus floods, along with rural drought, to earthquakes. Haris Gazdar (Gazdar, Khan, and Khan 2002; Gazdar 2009) has argued that the growing disparity of landholdings in Pakistan might be single largest factor in rural dislocation. Also see Hasan 2002.

6. This is certainly a broad generalization with notable exception of Punjabi writers, intellectuals, and political activists. However, the official version of Pakistani state narrative has had a hegemonic hold in this region in a way that contrasts with alternative movements for regional autonomy, linguistic nationalism in Sindh, Balochistan, and Khyber Pakhtunkhwa (formerly NWFP).

7. This essentialist reading of the ethnic question that takes regional identities as a given is common in Pakistan studies (Ahmed 1998). However, the changing landscape of ethnic politics in Pakistan can be seen by the Muhajir (Indian migrant) community as rejection of Muslim universalism in favor of ethnic identity politics in the 1980s, based on their shared experience of exile, sacrifice, and migration from India (Verkaaik 2004).

8. A recent example of an otherwise sophisticated study of the state question in Pakistan is *Politics of Identity: Ethnic Nationalism and the State in Pakistan* by Adeel Khan (2005).

9. There is an echo of this schema present in Partha Chatterjee's (2004) reformulation of political society, in which the urban subaltern population is composed of subjects who are governed but not necessarily disciplined by institutions, schools, and factory work.

10. For a discussion of the links between global exchange and postcolonial state formation, see Radcliffe 2001.

11. For instance, the austerity policies and structural adjustment programs imposed by international financial institutions like the World Bank, International Monetary Fund, and Asian Development Bank have profoundly weakened the ability of postcolonial states to offer minimal services like public education and basic health care and guarantee job security to establish a monthly salaried middle class. See Mbembe and Roitman 1995; Ali 2002; and Gazdar and Mallah 2013.

12. Henri Lefebvre's *The Production of Space* has been helpful for me to understand the historical and geographical dimensions of state formation and political subjectivity in South Asia, especially in Central Punjab. I read Lefebvre's theory of "production of space" as not simply the physical construction of roads, canals, cities, and the infrastructure of urbanity but also the realignment of the preexisting land relations, environmental resources, and labor into new channels of circulation and spatial abstractions. Lefebvre characterizes this process of state formation as a strategy to map territory and people from the viewpoint of revenue extraction and establishment of private property (1991, 233). This process faces a series of interruptions by local customs, environments that prevent the installment of a perfectly alienable, equivalent property regime based on individual ownership. As I describe below, the revenue system in British India varied greatly in different regions and at different times under colonial rule because of political calculations and environmental constraints.

The second major element of Lefebvre's theory of "production of space' is the perception of space, which is tied to administrative, representational, and logistical breakdowns of space through land surveys, census, and administrative technologies that give rise to the state. The third element of spatial production is the imagined space as the realm of production that is the creation of the ideological truth or the construction of nationalisms and ethnic nationalism within. Local livelihood practices, moral economies, traditional identities, and even modes of resistance are constantly being made and unmade in the contentious process of social (and spatial) change. Lefebvre's spatial analysis looks at land as a set of relations (rather than an object of possession) that are tied to social reproduction. See Lefebvre 1991 and Brenner and Elden 2009.

13. A materialist reading of Pakistani nationalism is important because the idea of Pakistan has been understood through an ideological lens (as in the history of the idea of a Muslim nation), even though the movement for Pakistan gained ascendancy because of concrete, material, and regional demands for greater provincial autonomy in Sindh; competition between urban and rural elites in Punjab; and the demand of mostly Muslim peasants for swift land reforms in Bengal (Talbot 1998).

14. The idea of a sovereign right to unused land did not exist in Mughal India or under Islamic rule. Land cannot by owned exclusively but managed. It is ironic that the East India Company invoked successor sovereign rights, even after decrying the unjust Oriental despotism.

15. The East India Company presented itself as the bearer of legal rights and rational jurisprudence combined with the Orientalist spirit of restoration of an ancient civilization that had been perverted by Mughal despotism (read: Muslim rule). However, as Uday Mehta (1999) has elaborated in detail, the liberal principles of democracy and rights that were at the heart of colonial self-image were denied to Indians, who were deemed unfit for self-rule because of Oriental exception. James Mill, the East India Company company's administrator, historian, and utilitarian philosopher, justified the restriction of liberty to Indians and non-Europeans whom he deemed unfit for freedom. Colonial sovereignty was built on a generalized state of exception, where political, economic, and social rights were not extended to rival sovereigns like Tipu Sultan of Mysore state, who were treated as despots, or the itinerant nomadic populations, who were designated as criminal tribes. Achille Mbembe has called this selective granting of rights as a form of bad faith he calls *commandement*: "On the one hand, it combined weakness of, and inflation of, the notion of right: weakness of right in that, in the relation of power and authority, the colonial model was, in both theory and practice, the exact opposite of the liberal model of debate and discussion; inflation of right in that, except when deployed in the form of arbitrariness and the right of conquest, the very concept of right often stood revealed as a void" (2001, 25).

16. See Baden-Powell 1978 for a summary of land settlement policies and debates about the nature of property and land tenure in colonial India.

17. The colonial administrators sought to emancipate the Indian peasantry from rigid customs with the promulgation of new land relations that were open to monetization and cash crops. The colonial bureaucrats made claims on the authentic nature of the Indian peasantry, whom they selected for specific tasks, land allotment, and administrative and military service. As Mathew Hull (2012, 80) has illustrated, the creation and circulation of files and authoritative documents gave rise to official stamped papers that aim to secure impersonal bureaucratic order; but in practice, political administration was (and is) deeply entwined within a connected sociality in which the civil service officers, bureaucrats, and

state authority figures, down to the local revenue officer (the patwaris), exercised the power of the state over society through paper and documentation. The documentation and paper bureaucracy that was supposed to bring a greater level of transparency and order to the complex revenue arrangements in South Asia was remediated, repurposed, and recoded into bureaucratic procedures through litigation, using access to files and documentation to consolidate power and claims over land.

18. Company officials like Thomas Munro blamed the problem of settlement on absentee landowners as an exploitive class who maximized their rental incomes at the expense of the cultivators and the colonial state (Gilmartin 2015). The various administrative reports and cartographic surveys were seen as the best way to overcome the obstacles to better understand Indian society.

19. The Bengali countryside and poorer urban classes responded to the Krishak Praja Party (KPP), the farmer-tenant party, which was rallying around major land reforms and disbanding the big zamindari system dominated by absentee landlords. Neilesh Bose (2014) has argued that a rural- and land-reform-oriented Muslim nationalism came out of this nonelite population of rural, and newly urbanizing, Bengali Muslims. They saw the congress as the perpetuation of the regional elite culture that marginalized their literary and economic interests, which could be secured with the promise of regional autonomy and land reforms as offered by the nascent Muslim nationalism (enshrined in the 1940 Lahore Resolution for the creation of separate Muslim states, introduced by Bengali KPP leader, Fazlul Haq).

20. By 1820, the British India Company had revised its land settlement system in South India by transferring land titles directly to the middle peasants, or *ryots*, who were regarded as the true proprietors of the land. The state would survey the land and assign revenue liability to the actual cultivators without going through the zamindars. It was argued that these assessments would generate greater revenue while lowering the burden on the peasantry. This new revenue system required far greater administration and knowledge of local landholdings, recording existing plots for fixing and collecting revenue rates. The process required many surveys and familiarity with rural districts and expansion of administrative rule. However, this form of assessment gave greater protection to peasant farmers and it brought them into a closer relationship with the administration.

21. The Muslim community emerges out of the colonial period in a precarious position, as both minoritized outsider and insiders. However, the degree of this displacement varied greatly according to region and status. In a suggestive article, Faisal Devji demonstrates how the "politics of space" underwent significant change in the North Indian Muslim discourse in the second half of the nineteenth century with the onset of the British Raj. He shows how premodern notions of sovereignty tied to a particular idea of the moral city (or certain understanding of the public, defined as the community of *zaif*, or moral guardians) withered after the defeat of the Indian Rebellion of 1857. Like the elite Hindu nationalists, the Muslim reformers created new distinctions between the home and the outside world. The private sphere, which was previously seen as a place of moral exception and weakness (the inner domain being associated with feminine-gendered notions of *fitna*, or social chaos) became the domain of virtue, tradition, and moral sovereignty. The Islamic reformist institutions in colonial India were founded outside the major cities

in rural locales such as Aligarh and Deoband to better impart this notion of reform (see Devji 1994).

22. Similarly, there were other trends in the issue of nativism in South India that emerged in the form of Dravidian politics in South India and social reformer Bhimrao Ambedkar's politics that sought to portray the Aryan theory of invasions as a colonial conquest to advocate for the subjugated population of the Tamil non-Brahmins, or Dalits, in Ambedkar's case (Ambedkar 2014).

CHAPTER 1

1. See Shahid Amin's (1995) point about the significance of the Chauri Chaura incident in the Indian nationalist struggle in *Event, Metaphor, Memory: Chauri Chaura, 1922–1992*.

2. The PRM has since merged with Labour Party Pakistan to establish a left-of-center democratic socialist political party, the Awami Workers Party (Working People's Party).

3. Since 9/11, most scholarship on Pakistan is inflected with the discourse of security and counterterrorism that is more comfortable with classifying the alphabet soup of militant organizations and charity organizations, then asking tougher questions about the long-term effects of waging proxy wars in distant lands. The current wars in Afghanistan and Pakistan have their origins in the arming of nonstate actors by CIA factions. This is not to dismiss the extraordinary challenges faced by Pakistan, or to dispute the Pakistani military's and bureaucracy's extraordinary powers in the workings of the state. For a different social history of political ideas and debates in Pakistan, see Ali 2015 and Toor 2011.

4. The police and Rangers presence was heavy in 2004, when I started my fieldwork. The Rangers are a federal border paramilitary police force that recruits personnel from all over the country; thus, it is not closely embedded in the community or associated with the locale. Although the Rangers are the border enforcement police force, they were deployed in Karachi during the 1980s to tackle internal unrest and the breakdown in law and order after ethnic riots that overwhelmed the municipal police force. The deployment of Rangers forces in Okara Military Farms was an unprecedented move in Punjab.

5. Farid went on to discuss his thoughts about the parallels between Bangladesh and the state of Pakistan today by rephrasing the controversial quotation by General Tikka Khan regarding the military operation in East Pakistan—"I want the land and not the people" (Haqqani 2005, 74)—to make a point that military officers are interested only in the land and not people's welfare.

6. The army cantonment is another vestige of the British rule that has grown in proportion and role in postcolonial times. In colonial times the cantonment served as a reserved area of land to separately house and train British Indian troops from the native city population. It was made up of military residential houses, officers' clubs, storehouses, offices, shooting ranges, farmland, and parade grounds. Many of these cantonments grew into major towns and urban centers with large markets consuming much of the produce of the nearby countryside. The cantonments were built along the lines of colonial city planning, infrastructure, and military rules. Cantonments played a major role in intensifying the shift to commercial agriculture in many rural regions, as they absorbed the surplus produce or helped bring railways and roads by which cotton, wheat, and sugarcane could

be exported. In contemporary times, the older cantonment areas have been absorbed into large cities as posh localities or suburbs that offer reliable municipal services and security. Property and land prices in cantonments are the most expensive and most profitable for military officers who were awarded these plots at subsidized rates. See Mazumder 2003.

7. I discuss the cantonment issue in greater detail in Chapter 4.

8. Ayesha Siddiqa breaks down the land allotment of various different military institutions and private allotments to senior military officers in chapter 5 of her important book *Military Inc.*

9. Liaqat Ali was steering Pakistan toward a less-aligned position shortly before his assassination. His assassin, Said Akbar, was an Afghan national who had received asylum in Pakistan because of his antinational activities in Afghanistan. He was sitting in the front row of the audience when he killed Ali and was subsequently killed himself by the police on the ground, thus leaving the case unresolved. The army officer in charge of investigating Ali Khan's murder died in a plane crash in 1951. Liaqat Ali Khan was assassinated on the very grounds where Benazir Bhutto would be assassinated some fifty-five years later, as she left the rally at this park. See Jalal 2014, 2.

10. During his clerical training, Younus established contacts with several NGOs and human rights organizations. Later he dropped out of clerical training to work with several NGOs and human rights groups. Through this experience he made many contacts with different NGO and human rights organizations.

11. For an ethnographic case study of perceptions of the postcolonial state from an urbanizing countryside in Guatemala, see Stepputat 2001.

CHAPTER 2

1. A limited amount of documentation on the disputed farmland in Okara Military Farms can be found in " Government of India Proceeding 23-5" (1913), which states:

> Proposal of the Government of India to make a recurring assignment of Rs 15,000 rupees per annum to the Punjab Government in consideration of the loss that will be occasioned to Provincial revenues in consequence of the remission of land revenue and malikana charges in respect of the land which it is proposed to allot for an oat-hay farm in the Lower Bari Doab Colony.

2. For a discussion of the interplay between colonial history and memory in the politics of natural resources, see Sivaramakrishnan 1998.

3. The paternalist Punjab school of governance was built around the creation of a collaborative relationship. See van den Dungen 1972; Michel 1967; and Gilmartin 2015.

4. This point has been made by economic anthropologists like David Graeber, who show the hybrid nature of markets as they become embedded in the cultural and political milieus where they take shape in context. Similarly, political anthropologists like Ajanta Subramanian and Partha Chatterjee show how reciprocities and patronage politics of obligation, akin to gift relationships, survive and flourish in the contemporary market and political domains in South Asia. See Graeber 2001; Subramanian 2010; and Chatterjee 2004.

5. Veena Talwar Oldenburg (2002) has documented how the meaning of dowry gift exchange, *dahej*, changed during canal colonization period from a social custom that was

traditionally controlled by women to a transaction among property-owning families. Oldenburg argues that changes in land relations in canal colonies transformed the customary gift exchange into a more contentious, competitive, and even murderous custom.

6. The colonial administrators from Sindh province were initially skeptical of the idea that Indus Basin peasants could ever be truly transformed into modern farmers. These officers were deeply impressed and "found themselves convinced, after a visit to the colony, simply by the unimaginable geometric regularity of the new fields of the Chenab canal colony" (Talbot and Thandi 2004, 6).

7. I see the cartographic description of the canal colony landscape in much the same way as environmental and art historians describe changes in landscape in terms of a stage symbolizing space and time (Craib 2004). Raymond Craib's (2004) book on Mexican cartography describes the spatio-temporal conceit of the landscape aesthetic that transforms land into a stage to produce a teleological history that gives precedence to certain ways of living: "In other words, as space becomes a stage, history becomes teleology. The ambiguities of (and struggles in) history are reconciled and suppressed through spatial order as the open-ended yields to the inevitable" (2004, 5).

8. For a discussion of the ambiguities of praise ballads celebrating Popham Young and L. J. H Grey, see Gilmartin 2015, 2–5.

9. Manu Goswami observes that "within official discourse, railways were conceived as a magical agency that would promote and secure the material welfare of the people, tame entrenched prejudices, and enable the production of an industrious and disciplined social body" (2004, 105).

10. In the article, Kaushik Ghosh proposes a new framework to understand governmentality as a differential politics of recognition forged out of specific colonial encounters ranging from the collaborative to violent occupations. The contingent nature of the state, produced out of the processes through which it constitutes its populations, is quite unlike the all-encompassing unity that citizen-subjects often assign to it in imagining what the state is. "In this sense, the figure of the adivasi repeatedly acts as a deconstructive case in Indian modernity in particular and the metaphysics of the state in general" (Ghosh 2006, 507).

11. This information comes from multiple interviews I conducted in the field. Also see Darling 1925.

12. To understand the criminalization and eviction of the pastoral and nomadic communities who were called "Janglis" in colonial state and settler discourse, see Major 1999.

13. A passage from the report details the rehabilitation of a criminal tribe on a penal settlement where the residents were forced to work on a canal diversion project:

> This settlement, which is under Government control, was started in March 1918 at the request of the Canal Department, to supply labour for the excavation of a new head and diversion for the Mailsi Canal, just about the time when the Industrial Settlement that had been established at Montgomery in connection with Military Works had to be closed. The entire population of that settlement, therefore, moved to Luddan. There was some delay in building the settlement, and meanwhile the inmates had to live in reed huts. But in a month's time huts were completed and all the inmates accommodated. Additional accommodation was provided as fresh gangs arrived. In November last the settlement was suddenly attacked by an influenza epidemic of a

virulent type. Out of 487 inmates, 467 caught the disease and no less than 67 succumbed to it. One of the Supervisors died and the Superintendent lost his wife. The epidemic created a panic among the inmates and practically the whole staff being laid up, as many as 30 men, 38 women and 50 children, some of them in a convalescent state, managed to escape from the settlement. The staff was unable to even send a telegram to the nearest telegraph office, but as soon as the news of the situation reached headquarters another superintendent was dispatched to take charge of the settlement and measures were adopted on one hand to relieve distress and, on the other, to catch the absconders of whom 8 were arrested in Bahawalpur and brought back with their families, five were arrested in January 1919 and 13 registered members have been recently arrested from Peshawar and brought in with their women and children. One of the absconders has died and only three remain unaccounted for . . . The number of deaths due to causes other than the epidemic was 15 and the number of births was 10. . . . The settlement was originally intended to last till the end of May 1919, but as the work on the new diversion still remains unfinished, the canal authorities have proposed to keep on the settlement till the end of September next.

The number of inmates on 31st December 1918 was 292 and the number of workers was 176, the average earning per head being about 6 annas . . . The settlement is quite inaccessible owing to the dismantling of the Sutlej valley Railway. But nevertheless, the inmates have remained well in hand, except for the incident mentioned above and the school attached to the settlement in a flourishing state. (Government of Punjab 1919, v–vi)

14. Over time, the Pakistan Army has used land relations to carve out a position in the public and private sectors, industry, business, agriculture, education, scientific development, health care, travel, communication, and transportation (Rizvi 2000, 233).

CHAPTER 3

1. From another theoretical tradition, I also see this as an example of deterritorialization and reterritorialization; see Deleuze and Guattari 1987.

2. The tenants have invested heavily in the installation of tube wells on their farms since 2001, when they stopped sharecropping and took over the farmland. The AMP farms can offer an interesting case study for the benefits and tensions of land redistribution to small farmers.

CHAPTER 4

1. I haven't been able to track down this reference to an actual event. But George's larger point was about the silence around severe repression faced by the Movement for the Restoration of Democracy activists in rural Sindh.

2. Younus also told me that when AMP representatives went to meet an American diplomat in Islamabad, the representative knew all about the tenants' protests, including the Rangers' positions, the land topography, among other things. According to Younus, the embassy officer told the AMP representatives that she knew that the main priest in Chak 10 L was cooperating with the army, and that was unfortunate, and that Americans also had agents in the Rangers (interview by the author, August 10, 2004).

3. The descriptions in this section are based on my interviews with Mujahid in 2004 and 2007 in the AMP office in Okara Military Farms and at his house in Okara City.

4. See Aasim Sajjad Akhtar's (2006) reading of the AMP. Akhtar's account provides a distant and detached reading of the AMP, in which the tenants' struggle is evaluated from its conformity and deviation from classic theories about rural class formation. Akhtar was a key figure in the AMP mobilization and thus played an important role as an activist, especially in navigating the movement through the challenging work of coalition building.

CHAPTER 5

1. There is a rich and growing body of literature in anthropology on ethnographic refusal. Sherry Ortner's (1995) article "Resistance and the Problem of Ethnographic Refusal," on the anthropological literature of resistance, was critiqued for its neat formulation of domination and resistance in complex political situations that involve a great degree of complexity and gray areas. The discussion of ethnographic refusal has taken a different turn in anthropological literature. Indigenous scholars like Audra Simpson (2014, 95) use the term "ethnographic refusal" to describe a strategy by native peoples of noncooperation with anthropologists and other researchers whose research agenda does not contribute to the well-being of native communities. Simpson has argued that ethnographic refusal is an important strategy of self-writing and self-definition for native communities who have been badly misrepresented in the past or whose knowledge and social practice has been exploited. I come to this debate from the perspective of an anthropologist allied to this social movement, but I am also critical of some of the moves made by the movement's leaders and allies. In this regard, I find myself working closer to the view of ethnographic refusal as formulated by Ortner, who argues for a nuanced and more complex understanding of social movement.

2. Saqib's discussion illustrates the problem analyzed by anthropologist William Fisher in his article "Doing Good? The Politics and Antipolitics of NGO Practices" (1997). Fisher argues that the growing involvement of NGOs in grassroots mobilization in the global South has narrowed the deliberation process and forced social movements to fit into the narrow reformist framework of development or rights that are not congruent with local aspirations.

CODA

1. The redemption of General Musharraf worked in much the same way as it did for Pakistan's previous dictator, General Zia-ul-Haq (1978–1988), whose international pariah status ended when he became an American ally after the Soviet Union invaded Afghanistan and the CIA decided to use Pakistan as a proxy against the Soviet Union in Afghanistan. The bitter historical lessons of using war to solve geopolitical disputes were not learned, as the global war on terror spread from Afghanistan and Iraq to Pakistan.

2. The question of legibility, surveillance, and rendering visible has been a major object of modern forms of power. Foucault's writing on surveillance, knowledge/power, discipline, and later government and biopolitics represents some of the most systematic renderings of this process in contemporary times (Foucault 1977, 2003, 2007). The anthro-

pological focus on specific indigenous populations has shown how modern liberalism, starting from settler colonialism to contemporary multiculturalism, has evolved around the "politics of recognition" (Povinelli 2002, 10; Ghosh 2006, 503). James Scott (1998) has brought together histories of legibility to discuss the failures of state projects' high modernity to control indigenous and other fugitive populations.

3. Benazir Bhutto was assassinated by a gunman who was followed by a suicide bomber. The evidence from the crime scene was washed away by the police, and to this day her murder case remains unsolved. For more details, see United Nations 2010 and Munoz 2013.

4. I accompanied Sattar in his campaign in 2008, when he visited many constituencies outside his base in the military farms. He presented himself as the ideal candidate for lower-caste Moghul artisans of costume jewelry, who face discrimination from merchants in Okara City. This campaign outreach was followed by a trip to notable members of Arain *biradari* (Sattar's descent group) made up of Okara City bureaucrats and influential merchants (the ones keeping Moghul artisans out of the main market trade). This group voiced their support for Sattar but regretted their communities' lack of political power in the 2008 elections when Arains split their support between the pro–Nawaz Sharif group and pro–Musharraf Muslim League. These discussions seemed far removed from the politics of land rights in the military farms. Sattar's candidacy showed how the AMP had become a major entity in the political configurations of the Okara district beyond the military farms. The AMP mobilization was pivoting toward electoral politics with Sattar's candidacy, whereas other branches of the AMP were expanding the occupation campaigns in neighboring towns like the Kulyana state farms and Depalpur military farms.

5. The 2008–2013 PPP government was the first elected administration in Pakistan's history to finish its full term without being dismissed or overthrown by an unelected state body. Nawaz Sharif, the opposition leader, whose party had renewed his promises when he held a massive rally in Okara on April 29, 2013. Sattar launched another independent bid, this time for the National Assembly seat (NA-120), but came in third, this time defeated by Riaz Ul Haq Juj another independent candidate, who spent his family fortune for the election bid and channeled the popular dissatisfaction against the major political parties for being unresponsive to the poor (Hanif 2015).

6. For instance, the cantonment authorities banned tenant farmers from growing rice in 2013 from the fear that wet rice fields would attract dengue-carrying mosquitoes. The tenants are not allowed to grow cotton for fear of attracting certain bugs that have blighted crops throughout Punjab. However, the military's sponsored contractors have been growing these crops in the adjoining fields.

REFERENCES

Abrams, P. 1988. "Notes on the Difficulty of Studying the State." *Journal of Historical Sociology* 1:58–89.

Agamben, G. 1998. *Homo Sacer: Sovereign Power and Bare Life.* Stanford, CA: Stanford University Press.

———. 2005. *State of Exception.* Chicago: University of Chicago Press.

Ahmed, F. 1998. *Ethnicity and Politics in Pakistan.* Oxford: Oxford University Press.

Akhtar, A. S. 2006. "The State as Landlord in Pakistan Punjab: Peasant Struggles in Okara Military Farms." *Journal of Peasant Studies* 33 (3): 479–501.

Akhtar, A. S., and A. S. Karriaper. 2009. "Devolution and the Okara Military Farms Conflict." In *Devolution and Governance: Reforms in Pakistan*, edited by S. Ali and M. Saqib, 201–220. Oxford: Oxford University Press.

Akhter, M., 2015. "Infrastructure Nation: State Space, Hegemony, and Hydraulic Regionalism in Pakistan." *Antipode* 47 (4): 849–870.

Alavi, H. 1998. "Pakistan and Islam: Ethnicity and Ideology." In *State and Ideology in the Middle East and Pakistan*, edited by F. Halliday and H. Alavi, 64–111. London: Macmillan.

Ali, I. 1988. *The Punjab Under Imperialism, 1885–1947.* Princeton, NJ: Princeton University Press.

Ali, K. A. 2002. *Planning the Family in Egypt: New Bodies, New Selves.* Austin: University of Texas Press.

———. 2015. *Communism in Pakistan: Politics and Class Activism, 1947–1982.* London: I. B. Tauris.

Ali, R. 2003. "Underestimating Urbanization." *Economic and Political Weekly* 37 (45): 4554–4555.

———. 2013. "Estimating Urbanization." Harvard South Asia Institute Working Paper. https://mittalsouthasiainstitute.harvard.edu/wp-content/uploads/2013/10/Estimating-Urbanization.pdf.

Aloys, M. 1967. *The Indus Rivers.* New Haven, CT: Yale University Press.

Ambedkar, B. R. 2014. *Annihilation of Caste: The Annotated Critical Edition.* London: Verso Books.

Amin, S. 1995. *Event, Metaphor, Memory: Chauri Chaura, 1922–1992.* Berkeley: University of California Press.

Amirali, A. 2002. "Rebellion in Pakistan" *ZNet*, July 5. https://zcomm.org/znetarticle/rebellion-in-pakistan-by-asha-amirali.

Anderson, B. 1991. *Imagined Communities: Reflections on the Origin and Spread of Nationalism*. Rev. and extended ed. New York: Verso.

Aretxaga, B. 1997. *Shattering Silence: Women, Nationalism, and Political Subjectivity in Northern Ireland*. Princeton, NJ: Princeton University Press.

Asad, T. 2003. *Formations of the Secular*. Stanford, CA: Stanford University Press.

Arnold, D. 1986. *Police Power and Colonial Rule: Madras, 1859–1947*. Delhi: Oxford.

Baden-Powell, B. H. 1978. *Administration of Land Revenue and Tenure in British India*. Oxford: Clarendon Press.

Bagchi, A. K. 1992. "Land, Tax, Property Rights and Peasant Insecurity in Colonial India." *Journal of Peasant Studies* 20:1–49.

Bano, M. 2012. *Breakdown in Pakistan: How Aid Is Eroding Institutions for Collective Action*. Stanford, CA: Stanford University Press.

Basharat, M., A. Umair, and H. Azhar. 2014. "Spatial Variation in Irrigation Demand and Supply Across Canal Commands in Punjab: A Real Integrated Water Resources Management Challenge." *Water Policy* 16 (2): 397–421.

Bellenoit, H. J. 2017. *The Formation of the Colonial State in India: Scribes, Paper and Taxes, 1760–1860*. Abingdon, UK: Routledge.

Benjamin, W. 1969. "Theses on the Philosophy of History." In *Illuminations: Essays and Reflections*, edited by Hannah Arendt, translated by Harry Zohn, 253–264. New York: Schocken Books.

———. 1978. "Critique of Violence." In *Reflections: Essays, Aphorisms, Autobiographical Writings*, edited by Peter Demetz, translated by Edmund Jephcott, 277–300. New York: Schocken Books.

Bhattacharya, N. 2006. "Predicaments of Mobility: Peddlers and Itinerants in Nineteenth-Century Northwestern India." In *Society and Circulation: Mobile People and Itinerant Cultures in South Asia, 1750–1950*, edited by C. Markovits, J. Pouchepadass, and S. Subrahmanyam, 163–214. London: Anthem.

Bjorkman, L. 2015. *Pipe Politics, Contested Waters: Embedded Infrastructures of Millennial Mumbai*. Durham, NC: Duke University Press.

Blomley, N. 2002. "Mud for the Land." *Public Culture* 14:557–584.

Bose, N. 2014. "Purba Pakistan Zindabad: Bengali Visions of Pakistan, 1940–1947." *Modern Asian Studies* 48 (1): 1–36.

Bose, S., and A. Jalal. 1998. *Modern South Asia: History, Culture, Political Economy*. Lahore: Sang-e-Meel.

Brenner, N., and S. Elden. 2009. "Henri Lefebvre on State, Space, Territory." *International Political Sociology* 3 (4): 353–377.

Chakrabarty, D. 2002. *Habitations of Modernity: Essays in the Wake of Subaltern Studies*. Chicago: University of Chicago Press.

Chatterjee, P. 1993. *The Nation and Its Fragments: Colonial and Postcolonial Histories*. Princeton, NJ: Princeton University Press.

———. 2004. *The Politics of the Governed*. New York: Columbia University Press.

Chatterji, J. 2018. "Why Ramachandra Guha Is Wrong to Compare Jinnah with Amit Shah." *Scroll*, September 30. https://scroll.in/article/895084/why-ramachandra-guha-is-wrong-to-compare-muhammad-ali-jinnah-with-amit-shah.

Chaturvedi, V. 2000. *Mapping Subaltern Studies and the Postcolonial.* London: Verso.

Cheema, A. 2003. "Local Devolution and Okara Farmers Movement." Unpublished paper. Lahore University of Management Sciences.

Cohn, B. S. 1961. "The Pasts of an Indian Village." *Comparative Studies in Society and History* 3 (3): 241–249.

———. 1996. *Colonialism and Its Forms of Knowledge: The British in India.* Princeton, NJ: Princeton University Press.

Comaroff, J., and J. L. Comaroff. 1991. *Of Revelation and Revolution.* Chicago: University of Chicago Press.

Comaroff, J. L., J. Comaroff, and R. P. Weller. 2001. *Millennial Capitalism and the Culture of Neoliberalism.* Durham, NC: Duke University Press.

Corrigan, P., and D. Sayer. 1985. *The Great Arch: English State Formation as Cultural Revolution.* New York: Blackwell.

Craib, R. B. 2004. *Cartographic Mexico: A History of State Fixations and Fugitive Landscapes.* Durham, NC: Duke University Press.

Crehan, K. A., 2002. *Gramsci, Culture and Anthropology.* Berkeley: University of California Press.

Daechsel, M. 2015. *Islamabad and the Politics of International Development in Pakistan.* Cambridge: Cambridge University Press.

Darling, M. 1925. *The Punjab Peasant in Prosperity and Debt.* New York: Oxford University Press.

Das, V. 1995. *Critical Events: An Anthropological Perspective on Contemporary India.* New York: Oxford University Press.

Das, V., A. Kleinman, M. Ramphele, and P. Reynolds, eds. 2000. *Violence and Subjectivity.* Berkeley: University of California Press.

Deleuze, G., and F. Guattari. 1987. *A Thousand Plateaus: Capitalism and Schizophrenia.* Translated by Brian Massumi. Minneapolis: University of Minnesota Press.

Devji, F. 1993. "Muslim Nationalism: Founding Identity in Colonial India." PhD diss., University of Chicago.

———. 1994. "Gender and the Politics of Space: The Movement for Women's Reform, 1857–1900." In *Forging Identities: Gender, Communities, and the State in India,* edited by Zoya Hasan, 22–37. Boulder, CO: Westview Press.

———. 2013. *Muslim Zion: Pakistan as a Political Idea.* Cambridge, MA: Harvard University Press.

Dhulipala, V. 2015. *Creating a New Medina: State Power, Islam, and the Quest for Pakistan in Late Colonial North India.* Delhi: Cambridge University Press.

"District (Okara): Foreign NGOs Blamed for Military Farm Deadlock." 2003. *Pakistan Newswire,* July 4.

Executive District Officer Revenue. 2003. "Issue of Military Farms Land—Okara." September 9. No.45/DOR/TSC, District Commissioner's Office, Okara.

Fazl, A. (1591) 1894. *The Ain i Akbari.* Translated by H. S. Jarrett. Calcutta: Asiatic Society of Bengal.

Fisher, W. F. 1997. "Doing Good? The Politics and Antipolitics of NGO Practices." *Annual Review of Anthropology* 26:439–464.

Foucault, M. 1977. *Discipline and Punish: The Birth of the Prison*. New York: Vintage.

———. 2003. *Society Must Be Defended: Lectures at the Collège de France, 1975–76*. New York: Picador.

———. 2007. *Security, Territory, Population: Lectures at the Collège de France, 1977–78*. New York: Picador.

Fox, R. G. 1985. *Lions of the Punjab: Culture in the Making*. Berkeley: University of California Press.

Gardezi, H. N., and J. Rashid. 1983. *Pakistan, the Roots of Dictatorship: The Political Economy of a Praetorian State*. London: Zed Press.

Gazdar, H. 2009. "The Fourth Round, and Why They Fight On: An Essay on the History of Land and Reform in Pakistan." PANOS South Asia working paper. http://researchcollective.org/Documents/The_Fourth_Round.pdf.

Gazdar, H., A. Khan, and T. Khan. 2002. "Land Tenure, Rural Livelihoods and Institutional Innovation." http://www.researchcollective.org/Documents/paper2_land_tenure.pdf.

Gazdar, H., and H. Mallah. 2013. "Inflation and Food Security in Pakistan: Impact and Coping Strategies." *IDS Bulletin* 44 (3): 31–37.

Ghosh, K. 2006. "Between Global Flows and Local Dams: Indigenousness, Locality and the Transnational Sphere in Jharkhand, India." *Cultural Anthropology* 21 (4): 501–534.

Gidwani, V. K. 2004. "The Limits to Capital: Questions of Provenance and Politics." *Antipode* 36:527–543.

———. 2008. *Capital, Interrupted: Agrarian Development and the Politics of Work in India*. Minneapolis: University of Minnesota Press.

Gilmartin, D. 1988. *Empire and Islam: Punjab and the Making of Pakistan*. Berkeley: University of California Press.

———. 1994. "Scientific Empire and Imperial Science: Colonialism and Irrigation Technology in the Indus Basin." *Journal of Asian Studies* 53:1127–1149.

———. 2004. "Migration and Modernity: The State, the Punjabi Village, and the Settling of the Canal Colonies." In *People on the Move: Punjabi Colonial, and Post-Colonial Migration*, edited by I. Talbot and S. Thandi, 3–20. Karachi: Oxford University Press.

———. 2015. *Blood and Water: The Indus River Basin in Modern History*. Oakland: University of California Press.

Glover, W. J., 2008. *Making Lahore Modern: Constructing and Imagining a Colonial City*. Minneapolis: University of Minnesota Press.

Godelier, M. 1999. *The Enigma of the Gift*. Chicago: University of Chicago Press.

Goldstein, D. M. 2010. "Toward a Critical Anthropology of Security." *Current Anthropology* 51 (4): 487–517.

Gordon, C., ed. 1994. *Power*. Vol. 3 of *The Essential Works of Foucault*. New York: New Press.

Goswami, M. 2004. *Producing India: From Colonial Economy to National Space*. Chicago: University of Chicago Press.

Gould, D. 2009. *Moving Politics: Emotion and ACT UP's Fight Against AIDS*. Chicago: University of Chicago Press.

"Government of India Proceeding 23-5." 1913. August. File 208, India Office Library, British Library, London.

Government of Punjab. 1853. *General Report upon the Administration of the Punjab Proper, for the Years 1849–50 and 1850–51, Being the First Two Years After Annexation, with a Supplementary Notice of the Cis and Trans-Sutlej Territories*. Calcutta: T. Jones.

Government of Punjab. 1919. *Report on the Administration of Criminal Tribes in Punjab, for the Year Ending December 1918*. Lahore: Government Printing.

————. 1920. *Youngest Punjab Canal Colony*. Lahore: Government of Punjab.

Graeber, D. 2001. *Toward an Anthropological Theory of Value: The False Coin of Our Own Dreams*. New York: Palgrave.

Gramsci, A. 1971. *Selections from the Prison Notebooks of Antonio Gramsci*. Edited by G. Nowell-Smith and Q. Hoare. New York: International.

————. 2005. *The Southern Question*. Translated by P. Verdicchio. Toronto: Guernica Editions.

Gregory, C. A. 2015. *Gifts and Commodities*. 2nd ed. Chicago: Hau Books.

Guha, R. 1999. *Elementary Aspects of Peasant Insurgency in Colonial India*. Durham, NC: Duke University Press.

Hanif, M. 2015. "Analysis: Okara—Punjab's Political Nowhere." *Dawn*, October 14. http://www.dawn.com/news/1212952.

Hansen, T. B. 2002. *Wages of Violence: Naming and Identity in Postcolonial Bombay*. Princeton, NJ: Princeton University Press.

Hansen, T. B., and F. Stepputat, eds. 2001. *States of Imagination: Ethnographic Explorations of the Postcolonial State*. Durham, NC: Duke University Press.

Haqqani, H. 2005. *Pakistan: Between Mosque and Military*. Washington, DC: Carnegie Endowment for International Peace.

Harding, C. 2008. *Religious Transformation in South Asia*. Oxford: Oxford University Press.

Hardt, M., and A. Negri. 1999. *Empire*. Cambridge, MA: Harvard University Press.

Hares, W. 1920. *Gojra Jangal Vichch Mangal*. Mysore, India: Wesley Press.

Harvey, D. 1995. "Militant Particularism and Global Ambition: The Conceptual Politics of Place, Space, and Environment in the Work of Raymond Williams." *Social Text*, no. 42: 69–98.

Hasan, A. 2002. "The Changing Nature of the Informal Sector in Karachi as a Result of Global Restructuring and Liberalization." *Environment and Urbanization* 14 (1): 69–78.

Hashim, A. 2017. "Disappeared: Silencing Pakistan's Activists." *Al Jazeera*, January 21. https://www.aljazeera.com/indepth/features/2017/01/disappeared-silencing-pakistan-activists-170121074139848.html.

Hoodbhoy, P. 2003. "Terror in Okara." *Outlook*, June 3. https://www.outlookindia.com/website/story/terror-in-okara/220339.

Hull, M. S. 2012. *Government of Paper: The Materiality of Bureaucracy in Urban Pakistan*. Berkeley: University of California Press.

Human Rights Watch. 2004. "Soiled Hands: The Pakistan Army's Repression of the Punjab Farmers' Movement." https://www.hrw.org/reports/2004/pakistan0704/.

———. 2016. "Pakistan: Crackdown on Farmers' Protest." https://www.hrw.org/news/2016/05/04/pakistan-crackdown-farmers-protest.

Institute for Economics and Peace. 2015. "Global Terrorism Index, 2015." http://economicsandpeace.org/wp-content/uploads/2015/11/Global-Terrorism-Index-2015.pdf.

Iqbal, N. 2009. "This Land Is . . . for Institutional Use." *News on Sunday*, April 19. https://jang.com.pk/thenews/apr2009-weekly/nos-19-04-2009/spr.htm#7.

IRIN (Integrated Regional Information Networks). 2002. "Focus on Peasant Protest." August 29. http://www.irinnews.org/report/18567/pakistan-focus-peasant-protest.

———. 2003. "Special Report on the Struggle for Land Ownership in Punjab." July 7. http://www.irinnews.org/fr/node/189588.

Jaffrelot, C. 2015. *The Pakistan Paradox: Instability and Resilience*. Translated by Cynthia Schoch. Oxford: Oxford University Press.

Jalal, A. 1995. *Democracy and Authoritarianism in South Asia: A Comparative and Historical Perspective*. Cambridge: Cambridge University Press.

———. 2014. *The Struggle for Pakistan: A Muslim Homeland and Global Politics*. Cambridge, MA: Harvard University Press.

Khan, A. 2005. *Politics of Identity: Ethnic Nationalism and the State in Pakistan*. New Delhi: Sage.

Khan, M. A. 1967. *Friends Not Masters: A Political Autobiography*. Oxford: Oxford University Press.

Khan, N. 2012. *Muslim Becoming*. Durham NC: Duke University Press.

Khan, S. 2007. "Pakistani Lawyers, Police Clash over Judge." *Reuters*, March 17. https://www.reuters.com/article/idUSISL28691.

Klingensmith, D. 2007. *"One Valley and a Thousand": Dams, Nationalism, and Development*. Delhi: Oxford University Press.

Lancaster, J. 2003. "Fighting an Army's Empire." *Washington Post*, June 29. https://www.washingtonpost.com/archive/politics/2003/06/29/fighting-an-armys-empire/6666a2c1-3548-4d7d-9677-cabf0ebd5d36.

Larkin, B. 2008. *Signal and Noise: Media, Infrastructure and Urban Culture in Nigeria*. Durham, NC: Duke University Press.

Lefebvre, H. 1991. *The Production of Space*. Translated by D. Nicholson-Smith. Oxford: Blackwell.

Leopold, A. 1949. *A Sand County Almanac*. Oxford: Oxford University Press.

Li, T. M. 2014. *Land's End: Capitalist Relations on an Indigenous Frontier*. Durham, NC: Duke University Press.

Locke, J. 2003. *Two Treatises of Government and a Letter Concerning Toleration*. New Haven, CT: Yale University Press.

Ludden, D. 2003. "Presidential Address: Maps in the Mind and the Mobility of Asia." *Journal of Asian Studies* 62 (4): 1057–1078.

Maine, H. S. 1861. *Ancient Law: Its Connection with the Early History of Society, and Its Relation to Modern Ideas*. London: John Murray.

Major, A. J. 1999. "State and Criminal Tribes in Colonial Punjab: Surveillance, Control and Reclamation of the 'Dangerous Classes.'" *Modern Asian Studies* 33:657–688.

Mantena, K. 2010. *Alibis of Empire: Henry Maine and the Ends of Liberal Imperialism.* Princeton, NJ: Princeton University Press.

Markovits, C., J. Pouchepadass, and S. Subrahmanyam. 2006. *Society and Circulation: Mobile People and Itinerant Cultures in South Asia, 1750–1950.* London: Anthem Press.

Marx, K., and F. Engels. 1967. *Capital.* Vol. 1. New York: International.

Masco, J. 2014. *Theater of Operations.* Durham, NC: Duke University Press.

Mauss, M. 2016. *The Gift: The Form and Reason for Exchange in Archaic Societies.* Translated by Jane Guyer. Chicago: University of Chicago.

Mazumder, R. K. 2003. *The Indian Army and the Making of Punjab.* Delhi: Orient Blackswan.

Mbembe, A., and J. Roitman. 1995. "Figures of the Subject in Times of Crisis." *Public Culture* 7 (2): 323–352.

Mbembe, J. A. 2001. *On the Postcolony.* Berkeley: University of California Press.

Mehta, U. 1999. *Liberalism and Empire.* Chicago: University of Chicago Press.

Michel, A. A. 1967. *Indus Rivers: A Study of the Effects of Partition.* New Haven, CT: Yale University Press.

Mishra, A. 2007. "Nations out of Fantasy." *Himal Southasian,* August. http://old.himalmag .com/himal-feed/56/1425-nations-out-of-fantasy.html.

Mitchell, T. 1991. "The Limits of the State: Beyond Statist Approaches and Their Critics." *American Political Science Review* 85 (1): 77–96.

———. 2002. *Rule of Experts: Egypt, Techno-Politics, Modernity.* Berkeley: University of California Press.

Moin, A. A. 2012. *The Millennial Sovereign: Sacred Kingship and Sainthood in Islam.* New York: Columbia University Press.

Moore, D. 1998. "Subaltern Struggles and the Politics of Place: Remapping Resistance in Zimbabwe's Eastern Highlands." *Current Anthropology* 13:654–689.

———. 2005. *Suffering for Territory: Race, Place, and Power in Zimbabwe.* Durham, NC: Duke University Press.

Munoz, H. 2013. *Getting Away with Murder.* New York: W. W. Norton.

Musharraf, P. 2006a. *In the Line of Fire: A Memoir.* New York: Free Press.

———. 2006b. *Sab Se Pehle Pakistan* [Pakistan First and Foremost]. Lahore: Feroz Sons.

Naqvi, T. H. 2013. "Nation, Space, and Exception Pakistan's Basic Democracies Experiment." *Comparative Studies of South Asia, Africa and the Middle East* 33 (3): 279–294.

Nixon, R. 2011. *Slow Violence and the Environmentalism of the Poor.* Cambridge, MA: Harvard University Press.

O'Hanlon, R. 1988. "Recovering the Subject Subaltern Studies and Histories of Resistance in Colonial South Asia-Subaltern Studies." In *Mapping Subaltern Studies,* edited by V. Chaturvedi, 72–115. New York: Verso.

Oldenburg, V. T. 2002. *Dowry Murder: The Imperial Origins of a Cultural Crime.* New York: Oxford University Press.

Ortner, S. B. 1995. "Resistance and the Problem of Ethnographic Refusal." *Comparative Studies in Society and History* 37 (1): 173–193.

Oxfam. 2005. "A Round for Free: How Rich Countries Are Getting a Free Ride on Agricultural Subsidies at the WTO." Oxfam Briefing Paper 76. https://oxfamilibrary

.openrepository.com/bitstream/handle/10546/114123/bp76-round-free-150605-en
.pdf.

Pandey, G. 2001. *Remembering Partition: Violence, Nationalism, and History in India.* Cambridge: Cambridge University Press.

"Pakistan Military Rejects Rights Body's Report on Mistreatment of Farmers." 2004. *BBC Monitoring South Asia,* July 23, p. 1.

Paustian, P. W. 1930. *Canal Irrigation in the Punjab: An Economic Inquiry Relating to Certain Aspects of the Development of Canal Irrigation by the British in the Punjab.* New York: Columbia University Press.

Pels, P. 1997. "The Anthropology of Colonialism: Culture, History, and the Emergence of Western Governmentality." *Annual Review of Anthropology* 26:163–183.

Polanyi, K. 1957. *The Great Transformation.* Boston: Beacon Press.

Povinelli, E. A. 2002. *The Cunning of Recognition: Indigenous Alterities and the Making of Australian Multiculturalism.* Durham, NC: Duke University Press.

Qasmi, A. 1973. "Thal." In *Pakistani Kahania'n,* edited by I. Hussain and A. Farrukhi, 10–24. Lahore: Sang-e-Meel.

Radcliffe, S. 2001. "Imagining the State as a Space: Territoriality and the Formation of the State in Ecuador." In *States of Imagination: Ethnographic Explorations of the Postcolonial State,* edited by T. B. Hansen and F. Stepputat, 123–146. Durham, NC: Duke University Press.

Rashid, A. 2008. *Descent into Chaos: The United States and the Failure of Nation Building in Pakistan, Afghanistan, and Central Asia.* New York: Penguin.

Rizvi, H. A. 2000. *Military, State, and Society in Pakistan.* New York: St. Martin's Press.

Rizvi, M. 2018. "From Terrorism to Dispossession: Pakistan's Anti-terrorism Act as a Means of Eviction." *Anthropology Today* 34 (3): 15–18.

Rooney, J. 1986. *Into Deserts: A History of the Catholic Diocese of Lahore, 1886–1986.* Rawalpindi, Pakistan: Christian Study Centre.

Said, E. 1995. "Secular Interpretation, the Geographical Element and the Methodology of Imperialism." In *After Colonialism: Imperial Histories and Postcolonial Displacements,* edited by G. Prakash, 21–39. Princeton, NJ: Princeton University Press.

Scott, J. C. 1998. *Seeing Like a State: How Certain Schemes to Improve the Human Condition Have Failed.* New Haven, CT: Yale University Press.

Seremetakis, N. 1994. *The Senses Still: Perception and Memory as Material Culture in Modernity.* Boulder, CO: Westview Press.

Shaikh, F. 2009. *Making Sense of Pakistan.* New York: Columbia University Press.

Shipton, P. 1994. "Land Culture in Tropical Africa: Soils, Symbols and the Metaphysics of the Mundane." *Annual Review of Anthropology* 23:347–377.

Siddiqa, A. 2007. *Military Inc.: Inside Pakistan's Military Economy.* London: Pluto Press.

Simone, A. 2008. "Emergency Democracy and the 'Governing Composite.'" *Social Text* 26 (2): 13–33.

Simpson, A. 2014. *Mohawk Interruptus: Political Life Across the Borders of Settler States.* Durham, NC: Duke University Press.

Sivaramakrishnan, K. 1998. "Imaging the Past in Present Politics: Colonialism and Forestry in India." *Comparative Studies in Society and History* 37:3–40.

Smith, R. S. 1985. "Rule-by-Records and Rule-by-Reports: Complementary Aspects of the British Imperial Rule of Law." *Contributions to Indian Sociology* 19 (1): 153–176.

Sparke, M. 2005. *In the Space of Theory: Postfoundational Geographies of the Nation-State.* Minneapolis: University of Minnesota Press.

Spivak, G. C. 2010. "Can the Subaltern Speak?" In *Can the Subaltern Speak? Reflections on the History of an Idea*, edited by R. Morris, 21–78. New York: Columbia University Press.

Star, S. L. 1999. "The Ethnography of Infrastructure." *American Behavioral Scientist* 43 (3):377–391.

Steinmetz, G. 1999. *State/Culture: State-Formation After the Cultural Turn.* Ithaca, NY: Cornell University Press.

Stepputat, F. 2001. "Urbanizing the Countryside: Armed Conflict, State Formation, and the Politics of Place in Contemporary Guatemala." In *States of Imagination: Ethnographic Explorations of the Postcolonial State*, edited by T. B. Hansen and F. Stepputat, 284–312. Durham, NC: Duke University Press.

Stewart, K. 1996. *A Space on the Side of the Road: Cultural Poetics in an "Other" America.* Princeton, NJ: Princeton University Press.

"Strict Inspection for Governor Visit to Okara City and Okara Cantonment." 2004. *Nawaiwaqt,* June 18, p. 3.

Subramanian, A. 2010. *Shorelines: Space and Rights in South India.* Stanford, CA: Stanford University Press.

Talbot, I. 1998. *Pakistan: A Modern History.* New York: St. Martin's Press.

Talbot, I., and S. S. Thandi, eds. 2004. *People on the Move: Punjabi Colonial, and Postcolonial Migration.* Karachi: Oxford University Press.

Tarlo, E. 2001. *Unsettling Memories: Narratives of the Emergency in Delhi.* Berkeley: University of California Press.

Taussig, M. T. 1986. *Shamanism, Colonialism, and the Wild Man: A Study in Terror and Healing.* Chicago: University of Chicago Press.

Thorburn, S. S. (1886) 1983. *Musalmans and Money-Lenders in the Punjab.* Delhi: Mittal.

Toor, S. 2011. *The State of Islam: Culture and Cold War Politics in Pakistan.* London: Pluto Press.

Traub, J. 2008. "The Lawyers' Crusade." *New York Times*, June 1. https://www.nytimes.com/2008/06/01/magazine/01PAKISTAN-t.html.

Travers, R. 2007. *Ideology and Empire in Eighteenth-Century India: The British in Bengal.* Cambridge: Cambridge University Press.

Trouillot, M-R. 2003. *Global Transformations: Anthropology and the Modern World.* New York: Palgrave Macmillan.

United Nations. 2010. "UN Report on Bhutto Murder Finds Pakistani Officials 'Failed Profoundly.'" *UN News*, April 15. http://www.un.org/apps/news/story.asp?NewsID=34384#.WdqvFdOGOi4.

van den Dungen, P. H. M. 1972. *Punjab Tradition: Influence and Authority in Nineteenth-Century India.* London: Allen and Unwin.

van der Veer, P., and H. Lehmann. 1999. *Nation and Religion: Perspectives on Europe and Asia.* Princeton, NJ: Princeton University Press.

Verkaaik, O. 2004. *Migrants and Militants: Fun and Urban Violence in Pakistan*. Princeton, NJ: Princeton University Press.

Williams, R. 1977. "Structure of Feeling." In *Marxism and Literature*, 127–135. Oxford: Oxford University Press.

Winichakul, T. 1994. *Siam Mapped: A History of the Geo-Body of a Nation*. Honolulu: University of Hawaii Press.

Wolf, E. R. 1982. *Europe and the People Without History*. Berkeley: University of California Press.

Wolford, W. 2010. *This Land Is Ours Now: Social Mobilization and the Meanings of Land in Brazil*. Durham, NC: Duke University Press.

Zaidi, S. A. 1999. *Issues in Pakistan's Economy*. Oxford: Oxford University Press.

INDEX